WRITER'S TOOLBOX

A Sentence-Combining Workshop

William Strong
Utah State University

McGraw-Hill, Inc.

New York St. Louis San Francisco Auckland Bogotá
Caracas Lisbon London Madrid Mexico City
Milan Montreal New Delhi San Juan Singapore
Sydney Tokyo Toronto

Writer's Toolbox

A Sentence-Combining Workshop

This book is printed on acid-free paper.

1 2 3 4 5 6 7 8 9 0 DOC DOC 9 0 9 8 7 6 5

ISBN 0-07-062561-1

This book was set in Goudy Old Style by Ruttle, Shaw & Wetherill, Inc.
The editors were Tim Julet and Susan Gamer;
the designer and illustrator was Armen Kojoyian;
the production supervisor was Annette Mayeski.
R. R. Donnelley & Sons Company was the printer and binder.

Library of Congress Cataloging-in-Publication Data

Strong, William, (date).
Writer's toolbox: a sentence-combining workshop / William Strong.
p. cm.
Includes index.
ISBN 0-07-062561-1
1. English language—Sentences. 2. English language—Rhetoric.
3. English language—Grammar. I. Title.
IN PROCESS
428.2—dc20 95-8524

ABOUT THE AUTHOR

William Strong directs the Utah Writing Project at Utah State University in Logan, where he teaches reading/writing courses and chairs the Department of Secondary Education. In addition to *Writer's Toolbox*, his McGraw-Hill texts include *Sentence Combining and Paragraph Building* (1981), *Practicing Sentence Options* (1984), *Crafting Cumulative Sentences* (1984), *Writing Incisively: Do-It-Yourself Prose Surgery* (1991), and *Sentence Combining: A Composing Book*, Third Edition (1994). He is also the consulting author in composition for Writer's Choice (1993), the Glencoe/McGraw-Hill textbook series for grades 9 to 12. In 1988, he received an award for teaching excellence at Utah State University, and in 1990 he was honored by the Utah Council of Teachers of English for service to the state. In addition to his work with teachers of writing at all levels, he enjoys downhill skiing and motorcycle touring.

For Carol
and
Hawaii suppers together

CONTENTS

PART TWO TOOLBOX

PREFACE

Writer's Toolbox: A Sentence-Combining Workshop is designed to help students build sentence and paragraph skills collaboratively by working together in groups. Instructors may use this book as a stand-alone text or as a supplement to other materials—among them, its third-generation companion, *Sentence Combining: A Composing Book*, Third Edition (McGraw-Hill, 1993).

The utility of sentence combining (SC) has been documented in many research studies. What this book offers is an extension and refinement of the approach. Organized to reflect a recursive model of the writing process, it provides student writers with workshop contexts for SC practice. In addition, students learn from minilessons that demonstrate skills of grammar, usage, and punctuation.

Unit 1, Introduction, provides an overview of the book's approach. Then, Part One—Writing Processes—presents a variety of formats for sentence combining. Unit 2 focuses on generating and planning through six strategies, with single-cluster exercises for combining and imitation serving as springboards for prewriting. Unit 3, centered on drafting and freewriting, provides SC closure exercises for oral or choral practice, in small or large groups, to develop fluency. Unit 4 promotes shaping and revising; its "open" exercises emphasize stylistic choice as well as sentence additions and expansions. Unit 5, with emphasis on editing and proofreading, helps writers tighten loose, flabby sentences and spot errors.

Part Two, Toolbox, includes 26 minilessons in Units 6 through 9, which cover basic grammar, advanced grammar, usage, and punctuation. Each minilesson has follow-up SC exercises for practice. These compact lessons help students get their questions answered quickly and directly, with terms defined in context. Of course, minilessons can also serve as a point of departure for discussions and workshops. As a fingertip reference, the back cover of this book offers a quick reference guide to the minilessons. The final unit of Part Two—Unit 10, Using the Toolbox—contextualizes the skills and alerts writers to advanced strategies for SC. This unit of independent practice invites individual writers to move from SC prompts to minilessons of particular interest.

To keep SC workshops lively and varied in Parts One and Two, you should consider drawing on different SC formats rather than working through each unit from beginning to end. Note that the skills of grammar, usage, and mechanics in Part Two are always connected to a specific SC problem, and that students are in charge of deciding what they need to study, either on their own or in workshop groups. For motivation, it seems essential to contextualize language skills and put writers in control of their own learning.

SC practice works because it engages students and stimulates them. Each whole-discourse exercise has a follow-up "Invitation" to writing; students collect their responses to these invitations in personal portfolios. This textual array provides a writer-centered context for response groups and portfolio writing options. In selecting pieces to revise and develop, students revisit the skills of the writing process as well as the grammar and punctuation minilessons. The rationale for this approach (which also includes options proposed by students) is described in Unit 1, Introduction.

You may want to organize your course so that student writers receive points or credit for each SC exercise and follow-up "Invitation." The portfolio writing options, as graded assignments in each unit, will then enable you to assess the extent to which students are applying what they have practiced. Two writing tasks are found in the "Portfolio" section for each unit. However, you may want to design your own portfolio-related assignments.

Because developing writers need immediate feedback as they take risks and acquire skills, the text provides a built-in Answer Key for half of the exercises (the odd-numbered ones) in both Part One and Part Two. An Instructor's Manual (IM), available on request from the McGraw-Hill College Division, provides an Answer Key for the remaining exercises; these answers appear on transparency (or photocopy) masters for easy use in class. Besides the transparency masters, the IM offers a "Framework for Writing" as well as advice on response groups and in-class workshops.

In closing, I salute my fellow directors in the National Writing Project network for their friendship and advice. With our aim of empowering instructors and students in mind, I have tried to write a resource for informed instruction—a research-based (and student-friendly) way to teach skills in context.

I also want to acknowledge here the reviewers who helped shape *Writer's Toolbox* into its present form:

Michael Berberich, *Galveston College*

Honora Berninger, *Hillsborough Comunity College*

Gertrude Coleman, *Middlesex County College*

Sandra Comerford, *College of San Mateo*

Vanessa Jackson, *Del Mar College*

Kathleen Krager, *Walsh University*

Maureen O'Brien, *Springfield Technical Community College*

Jerry Olson, *Middlesex County College*

Sybil Patterson, *Hillsborough Community College*

Margaret Pigott, *Oakland University*

Richard Prystowsky, *Irvine Valley College*

Sid Smith, *Yakima Valley College*

William Smith, *Western Washington University*

Allison Wilson, *Jackson State University*

Edith Wollin, *North Seattle Community College*

Finally, let me extend my appreciation to Tim Julet, Elizabeth Fogarty, and Susan Gamer, my editors at McGraw-Hill, for their encouragement and support of this project, not to mention their exquisite attention to the details of production. To Armen Kojoyian, I offer special thanks for artwork and design.

William Strong

UNIT 1

Introduction

Many times I feel empty, without ideas—and then suddenly the first sentence appears.

—Octavio Paz

WRITER TO READER

I don't know you, and you don't know me, but we already have a relationship. You can hear me speaking through the words you read, and I can imagine you wherever you might be—in a dormitory room, on a bus, or at a thousand other locations.

Let's start there, with you and me and the voice of this book.

The voice you hear right now is a *made* thing, set left to right in space, one word after another. It's a voice I hear as well; but for me, the hearing takes time, like trying to tune in a distant radio station. With you in mind, I try to get a static-free signal by adding, deleting, and rearranging words.

We call this process ***writing,*** and I'm assuming that it's one you want to learn. I won't pretend that learning this process is easy, because you know better. Instead, I'll tell the truth—that learning to write takes commitment on your part. For our purposes, *commitment* means paying attention and applying what you learn.

Are you willing to pay attention and apply what you learn?

Note that I didn't ask, "Are you *able* to do that?" The fact that you're able to speak—and that you're now reading my words—is abundant proof of your basic ability. Because you've spoken and read countless sentences over the years, there's no question about your mental equipment for writing. The only real question concerns commitment, and you are the one who must answer it.

Your instructor and I believe that you *can* make breakthroughs in the weeks to come, even if writing is now a struggle for you. What we want is your commitment. Why? Because, as Shakespeare once put it, "the readiness is all." To get ready, read on.

HOW THIS BOOK WORKS

A Learning Strategy: Sentence Combining

Sentence combining—SC for short—is a basic learning strategy we'll use in this book. According to research on writing, SC is a method that improves writing skills.

As its name implies, ***sentence combining*** involves putting sentences together, using what you already know about language from your own experience of speaking and reading. The SC approach mirrors what happens when you put meanings together in everyday life.

Because SC is a putting-together approach, you won't be taking sentences apart. Instead, you'll learn new ways of constructing sentences by building on patterns you already know and use.

Here's a typical group of sentences, called a ***cluster,*** that offers a combining problem for you to consider. The "question" posed by a cluster is how to combine the sentences. Notice that this cluster, like most clusters, has several possible "answers," all correct and grammatical.

Example

I don't know you.

You don't know me.

We already have a relationship.

Possible answers

Although I don't know you and you don't know me, we already have a relationship.

or

I don't know you, and you don't know me; however, we already have a relationship.

or

In spite of the fact that you and I don't know each other, we already have relationship.

or

You and I already have a relationship—even though we don't know each other.

or

A relationship already exists between you and me, despite our lack of knowledge about each other.

In addition to these five possible answers, there's the one I chose to open this Introduction. Why did I choose that sentence rather than any of the ones above? My choice relates to the writer-to-reader voice I wanted. None of the sentences above *felt* completely right to me, so I tried another one.

To me, writing is like fishing. When it's going well, sentences circle beneath the surface of my thoughts, like trout swimming in circles below the surface of a stream. My task is to hook sentences and haul them flapping onto the page. I keep only the ones I want and let the others go, knowing I can hook them again later. As I write, I'm always eager to see what I'll pull in. Each sentence has its own special appeal, of course, but I'm fussy about keepers.

This process of fishing—pulling in possible sentences and then making choices—lies at the heart of SC. No one can tell you how to do it. It's something you have to experience. However, you can admire sentences that other students hook, and you can learn from their techniques. In fact, teaming up with others teaches you more than you'd ever learn by fishing (or writing) alone. Not only that, but teamwork speeds up your learning and makes it fun.

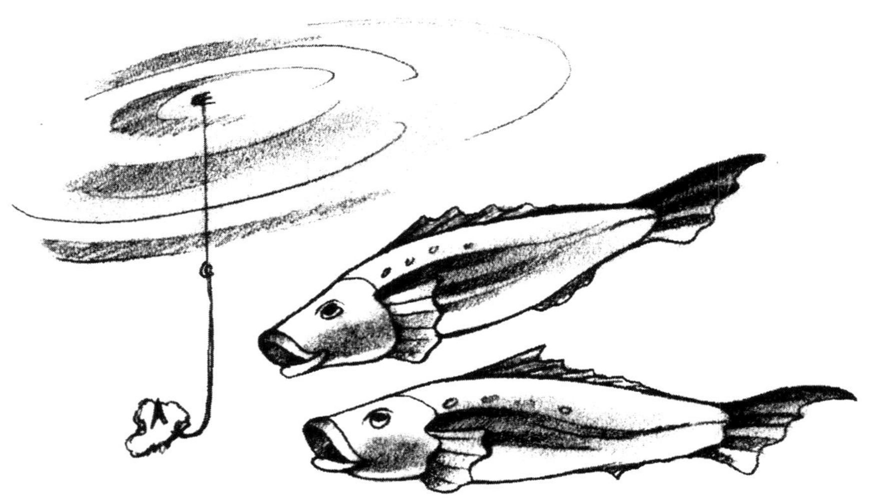

A Basic Model: The Writing Process

Gene Fowler once remarked, "Writing is easy; all you do is sit staring at a blank sheet of paper until drops of blood form on your forehead." Simple.

Perhaps there's comfort in knowing that others struggle with writing, just as you do. However, real comfort comes from *using* the writing process to "work smart"—to work efficiently and intelligently. Basically, "*working smart*" means thinking about writing as a series of stages and then using that knowledge to focus on one stage at a time. This is quite different from the typical approach used by too many students (and one you may have practiced): "Get it over with and hope for the best."

The diagram on page 6 shows what many skilled writers do. It outlines a process, or model, that involves several stages: planning, drafting, shaping, correcting, and finally "publishing." As you examine the elements of this model, notice that *revising* is at the heart of the writing process. Notice, too, that even though writers move "forward" in time, they may move "backward" to earlier stages.

This diagram also provides the framework of Part One, Writing Processes. Each unit in Part One helps you learn strategies associated with a particular phase of the writing process:

Unit 2 Generating and Planning
Unit 3 Freewriting and Drafting
Unit 4 Shaping and Revising
Unit 5 Editing and Proofreading

The aim of Part One is to help you learn a variety of strategies through SC activities. Your own aim, of course, is to internalize these strategies so that you can transfer them to other writing tasks. As you work on such tasks, it's important to keep in mind the model of the writing process. The diagram is like a map that will help you see where you are in relation to your destination.

As you'll learn in Unit 2, you can ***generate*** ideas in at least six ways. These range from listing to questioning and outlining.

In Unit 3, you'll learn that after the generating stage, you can use newly generated ideas to ***draft*** an early version of your paper, sometimes through "freewriting."

A preliminary draft gives you something to ***revise***—a text to shape; this is discussed in Unit 4. Working on the content and organization of a

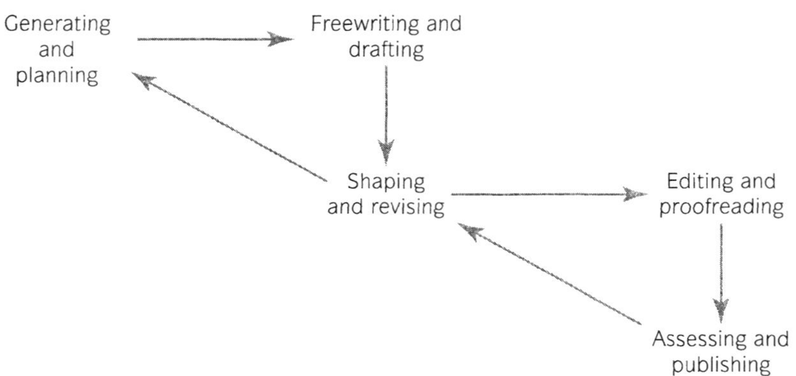

draft, perhaps in collaboration with others, can often send you back to earlier stages of the writing process (see the first backward-pointing arrow). In fact, repeated loops through the early stages are not unusual.

Sooner or later, however, you'll shift attention from issues of content, sequencing, and development to matters of form. As you'll see in Unit 5, a revised draft provides you with a text to ***edit*** (or change) at the sentence level. Editing, in turn, challenges you to ***proofread*** your text for errors, perhaps after a "cooling-off" period.

To ***publish*** your writing means to share it with others. You might share your ideas with a broad audience, for instance, by writing a letter to the editor of the campus newspaper. Submitting your résumé to a prospective employer and sending a memo to your colleagues are further examples of publishing. Still another example is submitting a paper to your instructor. In each of these contexts, published writing must speak for itself. Therefore, as the diagram indicates, it's important to ***assess*** your writing for publication. This self-assessment may return you to earlier stages of the writing process, as the second backward-pointing arrow implies.

Throughout *Writer's Toolbox*, as you work with the SC exercises, the writing "Invitations," and the "Portfolio" options, you'll practice this recursive model of the writing process. You'll see that the process will encourage you to focus first on ideas, organization, and development; only later will you deal with correctness and conventions. Remember that it takes time to write well. In order for the process to work, you have to budget time for it. Remember, too, that knowing *where* you are in the process enables you to take control—to "work smart"—by tackling one task at a time.

A Workshop Approach to Writing

The term ***writing workshop*** has two meanings. First, it can refer to collaboration with others—working to improve your writing within a group or as part of a team. Second, and more generally, the term also refers to an approach that gives you a choice of topics for writing practice (and sometimes graded assignments as well). Both meanings apply in *Writer's Toolbox*: you'll be working in response groups, responding to writing "Invitations," and developing a personal writing portfolio.

Working in a response group Whenever you team up with partners to share and compare sentences, you're part of an informal writing workshop, designed to improve your sentences—to make them more fluent and more mature. The experience of hearing and seeing various possibilities, and *then* making choices, improves both your knowledge of writing and your self-confidence.

In a rèsponse group, you share your writing, usually aloud, with one or more partners. Such a group provides an audience whose purpose is to help you understand what's effective (and perhaps not so effective) in written work. Armed with constructive ideas from your writing partners, you can look critically at your own writing and perhaps make changes.

A response group may be as small as two people or as large as an entire class. Most of the time, however, your group will involve three to five students.

Regardless of size, a successful group requires mutual respect and hard work from all participants. The aim of the group is to help each student develop his or her own writing.

By listening to ideas from your peers and asking questions, you can learn much about how to develop, revise, and edit your writing. Sometimes, you'll find that feedback from others confirms your hunches about strengths or weaknesses in your writing. At other times, feedback will challenge you to rethink your content, organization, or writing style. In either case, though, after listening to the comments of others, *you* will decide what's best for your paper. No one else can make decisions for you.

Following are guidelines on getting and giving feedback in response groups:

Getting feedback on your writing

- Never apologize for a piece you're going to read.
- Unless your work is quite long, read it aloud twice.
- Listen carefully to what others tell you, and take notes.
- As you get feedback, don't "defend" or explain your work.
- Ask questions to clarify what others say or suggest.
- Thank your partners for their comments.

Giving feedback on your partners' writing

- During the first reading, listen for the overall effect.
- During the second reading, make notes or comments.
- First, tell what you liked *best* about the writing.
- Later, identify a place in the text that may need work.
- Comment on content and organization first, mechanics later.
- Ask questions; point to places on the page as you comment.

In a response group, it is helpful to have a "common code"—shared written symbols for commenting on each other's papers. Shown below are four symbols that many students find useful. You can use these symbols to mark words, sentences, or paragraphs; afterward, of course, you can explain your responses more fully.

Symbol	Meaning
+	I like this.
*	Say more here.
?	This puzzled me.
✓	Check for an error.

You can put these symbols above specific words or sentences, of course. But you can also highlight words or sentences and write the symbols in the margin. After you're comfortable with these symbols, you and your partners may decide to invent others.

Another way of "pointing" to features of writing (your own or someone else's) is to use this simple marking system:

A marking system

- Underline striking images, strong verbs, vivid details, or memorable phrases.
- Draw a wavy line under pompous language, including stale, empty, or repeated phrases.

- Put brackets [ ] around short, choppy sentences—sentences that might better be combined.
- Use parentheses ( ) to mark any sentences that seem overloaded or garbled.

If you have questions about this approach, ask your instructor for a workshop demonstration. With a few minutes of practice, you'll learn a system for helping others as well as yourself.

Invitations for writing As noted above, the term *writing workshop* also refers to an approach that gives you a choice of topics for writing practice (and sometimes graded assignments as well). That's why this book offers ***invitations*** to extend the writing you've begun in SC exercises. Certain topics in the writing invitations will interest you; other won't. But the more invitations you accept—and the more fully you write in response to them—the more progress you'll make. Such follow-up writing will help you develop ease of expression. The point is to accept the invitations that interest or challenge you.

When you respond to an invitation, you'll *apply* strategies and skills you've learned during SC practice. Revisiting topics you've already learned will help you *use* what you've studied and practiced.

Your writing portfolio You should plan to keep your drafts of SC exercises, and your responses to writing invitations, in a ***workshop portfolio.*** Make sure to date each piece of writing, so that you will have a chronological record and can review your progress at the end of the term or semester.

Your portfolio can serve many purposes, depending on how your writing course is organized. First, you may be asked to evaluate your own learning on the basis of your portfolio. Second, pieces from your portfolio will probably be used in response groups. Third, you may be asked periodically to search your portfolio for writing you'd like to develop more fully and then revise and edit. Fourth, your instructor may design assignments using portfolio selections. Therefore, the more pieces you put into your portfolio, the better prepared you'll be.

You'll discover another function of your portfolio when you work on editing and proofreading in Unit 5. In the editing exercises, you'll tighten loose, flabby sentences and improve the flow of your writing; in the proofreading exercises, you'll spot errors in spelling, punctuation, and usage. Both

editing and proofreading will lead you back to your portfolio for application of skills.

At the end of each unit in Part One, you'll find a "Workshop Portfolio" section. This section offers options for writing—ideas for developing or using material that you've already begun. In each "Workshop Portfolio" section, two writing options are suggested.

In addition, you can always develop your own portfolio options and propose them to your instructor. Searching your folder for a piece to extend, and then proposing your own assignment, can help put you in charge of your writing. Suppose, for example, you've combined sentences and responded to invitations in Unit 3. Perhaps the SC exercise "School Dance" reminds you of years gone by. Could this lead to an essay about social cliques in your high school? Or perhaps you're interested in the issues in "White Christmas" or "Greenhouse Effect." If so, you might research the causes of homelessness or describe effects of global warming.

The idea is to propose to your instructor (in writing, of course) the kind of writing assignment you'd prefer—an assignment *linked to the work in your portfolio*. Explain *what* you'd like to do, *why* you'd like to do it, and *how* you'll proceed. Indicate the approximate length of your paper and the approach you plan to take. Put your proposal in the form of a memorandum addressed to your instructor. A typical memo begins in the form shown below, with your signature accompanying your name:

MEMORANDUM
To: Professor Shirley M. Wright
From: Andy Mann (English 100, Section 4)
Date: 20 October 1995
Re: Writing Assignment Proposal (Unit 3)

Unless your instructor specifies otherwise, use single spacing and a "block" style of paragraphing in your memorandum. That is, each paragraph is a block of text. No paragraph indention is required; instead, leave an extra line of space between paragraphs.

A Toolbox for Writing

Besides learning from writing practice, you can also develop skills by paying attention to demonstration lessons in grammar, usage, and punctuation—and then applying what you have learned. This book provides tools for such learning.

The tools you need Perhaps you break into a cold sweat at the very mention of "grammar, usage, and punctuation." You may have been marched lockstep through grammar units without any chance to control the pace of learning. Or your textbooks and teachers may have used confusing terms without providing examples you could understand. Under such circumstances, it's natural to get discouraged. On the other hand, you'd probably like to learn such skills if you could find a good way to learn them, a clear and helpful presentation. After all, knowing is better than not knowing.

Part Two, Toolbox, includes 26 minilessons arranged in four units:

Unit 6 Tools of Basic Grammar
Unit 7 Tools of Advanced Grammar
Unit 8 Tools of Usage
Unit 9 Tools of Punctuation

Each minilesson teaches a specific topic, and each is followed by practice exercises.

Here is a quick reference guide to the minilessons; for your convenience, the guide is also shown on the back cover:

Toolbox minilessons

If you feel shaky about the "basics," take some time to read the minilessons. Don't do them all at once, of course. Try one or two at a time, and make sure you understand the concepts. Moving back and forth between the "Writing Tips" in Part One and the minilessons in Part Two will help you learn what you need to know.

Think of Units 6 to 9 as a fingertip resource to answer your questions. For example, if you're not sure how to use a semicolon in your sentence combining, refer to "Semicolons" in Unit 9. If a "Writing Tip" calls for a relative clause, glance at Unit 7 for a quick reminder. If you're curious about the difference between adverbs and adjectives, read these two minilessons in Unit 6 back to back.

With the Toolbox, you're in charge of your learning. If you already understand a concept of grammar, usage, or punctuation, you probably won't review that minilesson. However, when you encounter new concepts, or concepts you're unsure about, or concepts you remember only vaguely, you'll pause to learn. In other words, as you combine sentences and notice the "Writing Tips," you'll make your *own* learning assignments and refer to the minilessons as necessary.

Give this approach a try. If what you've experienced before was aimless study of grammar, usage, and punctuation, you'll find the Toolbox very different. By studying the minilessons you need—and then applying the skills you learn from these demos—you'll improve your prose.

You can check your skills by referring to the Answer Key, which gives answers to odd-numbered exercises.

Practice in using the tools After the Toolbox minilessons, Unit 10—Using the Toolbox—offers independent practice: a dozen SC exercises designed to help you *apply* the Toolbox principles. This practice material not only will broaden your ability to create sentences but will also increase your awareness of what you're doing as a writer.

In Unit 10, you won't work on grammar, usage, or punctuation in the abstract. Instead, the "Writing Tips" will suggest ***target sentences*** in which you'll use Toolbox concepts to solve problems in sentence combining. A tip might lead you to a target sentence that has a participle phrase, an appositive, or an absolute. Such structures are easy to make once you understand how. After you've hit the target in two or three exercises, you'll begin to catch on, and soon these structures will show up in your own writing. It's a good feeling to open your portfolio and see sentences much like the ones you've been practicing.

Remember: *you* decide whether to try for a target sentence; *you* use principles of grammar, usage, and punctuation to construct new sentences; and *you* check your work in the Answer Key. Because you set up your own targets, you're in charge of your learning.

As you practice the Toolbox concepts, you'll acquire a new vocabulary for talking about writing. Your eyes won't glaze over when someone uses these terms in discussing your prose. Finally, these concepts may increase your *awareness* of what you're doing as you write, so that you notice new options for creating sentences.

In Unit 10—unlike traditional approaches—you won't memorize or underline parts of speech, take sentences apart, or diagram their inner workings. Instead, you'll do what writers do: *put sentences together.* You'll *use* tools of grammar, usage, and punctuation to get a job done, not to pass a test. In short, you'll learn what you need as you need it.

BEFORE YOU BEGIN: A FEW TIPS

When you work on SC exercises, on your own or with others, remember that your goal is not long sentences but *good* ones—the best you can muster. Leaving a sentence uncombined is always an option. Why? Brevity is often best.

It's also worth remembering that you learn nothing by putting words together in random or haphazard ways. Take your time. The idea, after all, is to take control—and to improve your skills by *paying attention* to the choices you make.

Here are some more tips for SC exercises:

- Always *read the directions* first. There are different kinds of SC exercises, so the explanatory directions are very important.
- As you combine sentences, *listen* to them. Say them aloud to a partner or whisper them to yourself. Take risks by experimenting with new patterns. Imitate sentences that appeal to you.
- To improve your decision making, jot a sentence down. Then read it in the context of previous choices. Make revisions as necessary. When you decide which version you prefer, try to figure out why.
- Compare your sentences with those of other students. Watch for stylistic patterns—habits of writing—in your sentences. Consciously *vary* your patterns, to flex your language muscles in new ways.
- Use the "Writing Tips" and the Toolbox minilessons. As you finish each SC exercise, double-check your punctuation and spelling. Make proofreading a regular habit, a matter of personal pride.
- Accept the "Invitations" for follow-up writing. Share your responses with your workshop partners, and enjoy what they have written.
- As you look over your portfolio, find opportunities to *apply* SC skills.

Finally, if you'd like to make comments about this book or offer suggestions for its next edition, McGraw-Hill and I would very much like to hear from you. We value your opinions and advice. To communicate with us, please direct your letter to the following address:

English Editor, College Division
McGraw-Hill, Inc.
1221 Avenue of the Americas
New York, NY 10020

PART ONE

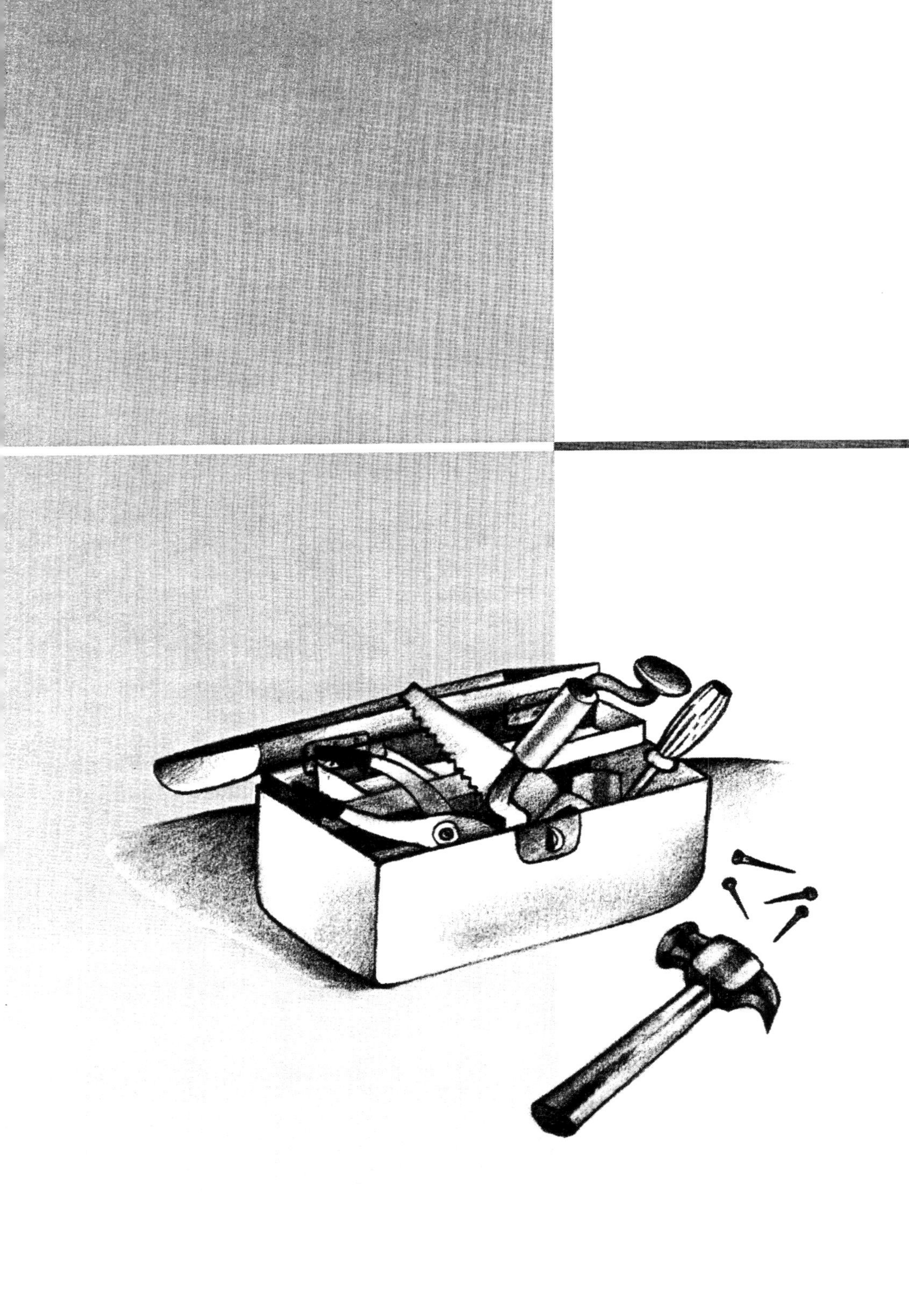

PART ONE

Writing Processes

STRATEGIES AND PRACTICE

UNIT 2

Generating and Planning

I write because I don't know what I think until I read what I say.

—Flannery O' Connor

As you saw in Unit 1, writing is a recursive process. Here, in Unit 2, you'll focus on generating and planning. You'll learn six prewriting strategies for getting pieces of writing started.

You also saw in Unit 1 that sentence combining (SC) helps develop writing skills. The first section of Unit 2 will offer some "warmup" exercises in SC, as well as opportunities to imitate combined sentences, using your own content. Imitating sentences is a good way to apply your sentence-combining skills, develop your creativity, and have fun with writing. After this warmup, you'll go on to the six prewriting strategies.

One more point about Unit 2: all of the SC exercises here are derived from well-crafted sentences by famous people. When you compare your own combined sentences with the original versions, you'll quickly see similarities and differences. Decide for yourself which sentences you prefer—which ones "sound right" to you.

WARMUP

Combining Sentences

Your first aim in this warmup is to work orally—with a partner in class, or on your own at home—to *combine sentences* in different ways. (Teaming up with a partner will let you hear some good possibilities for combining.) These warmup SC exercises will develop your fluency at the sentence level and will also be interesting springboards for independent writing practice. Remember, you can check the Answer Key afterward for answers to odd-numbered exercises; your instructor has answers for even-numbered exercises.

A ***cluster,*** as defined in Unit 1, is a group of sentences to be combined. A sentence-combining (SC) exercise can involve a single cluster or several related clusters. Let's begin here by considering some single-cluster exercises in sentence combining.

SC examples 1 and 2 (on the following page) deal with two humorous viewpoints—one male, the other female.

Example 1

I hate women.
Women always know where things are.

↓

___

___

Example 2

Marriage is a great institution.
I'm not ready for an institution.

↓

___

___

As you work on these and other clusters, keep in mind that one of your options, always, is to leave one or more sentences *un*combined. When you check the answers, you'll find that some professional sentences are actually shorter than ones you've composed. Also, keep punctuation in mind. For instance, you'll find that the semicolon can be an important tool for combining ideas. By paying attention to punctuation, you can learn more about options for sentences.

Here are the original versions of examples 1 and 2—but you may prefer your own constructions to these:

I hate women because they always know where things are. (James Thurber)

Marriage is a great institution, but I'm not ready for an institution. (Mae West)

Here's another SC warmup example:

Example 3

Life is like playing a violin.
The playing is in public.
It is learning the instrument as one goes on.

And here is the original version of example 3:

> Life is like playing a violin in public and learning the instrument as one goes on. (Samuel Butler)

Imitating Sentences

Your second aim in this warmup is to *imitate sentences* like the examples you've just been considering. For instance, you might imitate examples 1 and 2—the sentences by James Thurber and Mae West—as follows:

> I hate work because it interferes with my coffee breaks.
>
> Sentence combining is interesting, but I'm not ready for a life sentence.

When you imitate sentences, give your mind plenty of freedom; in other words, choose whatever you want as topic material. You'll find that you have lots of ideas waiting to be verbalized. Current events, personal matters, ideas from other courses—all of these can be topics for imitation (or for follow-up writing). Perhaps you've just seen a TV special about the history of the civil rights movement. Or perhaps you've just returned to school after an absence. You can use thoughts and feelings from these experiences.

Following are three successful (but quite different) imitations of Samuel Butler's sentence.

Divorce is like flushing the toilet and then watching it overflow.

or

Writing is like feeling your way through a darkened apartment and finally finding the light switch.

or

Returning to college is like driving in rush-hour traffic and noticing the gas gauge on empty.

Imitating sentences is something like computer programming—with your brain as the computer. The method actually goes back 2,500 years, to the ancient Greeks. Used faithfully, it will help you internalize sentence patterns and stimulate your creativity. In addition, each imitated sentence can be a springboard for writing—as you'll see next.

Developing Topic Sentences

Your third aim in this warmup is to *develop topic sentences*. Practice in developing topic sentences is basic to effective writing.

A ***topic sentence*** is an idea that organizes one or more paragraphs. To put this another way, it's an organizing idea for a collection of several sentences. A topic sentence is "what the writing is about," from the reader's point of view.

Although a topic sentence may occur anywhere in a paragraph, you'll see it most often as a paragraph opener. In your textbooks, for instance, typical paragraphs open with a topic sentence, which is then developed through examples, facts, illustrations, comparisons, or details. On occasion, though, a topic sentence will serve as a paragraph summary; less frequently, you'll find a topic sentence in the middle of a paragraph.

Both sentences you combine and sentences you construct through imitation can become topic sentences for your follow-up writing. For example, let's consider how one student, a young father, used Samuel Butler's sentence (example 3 above) as the opener for a mini-essay that went into his portfolio for later revision and development.

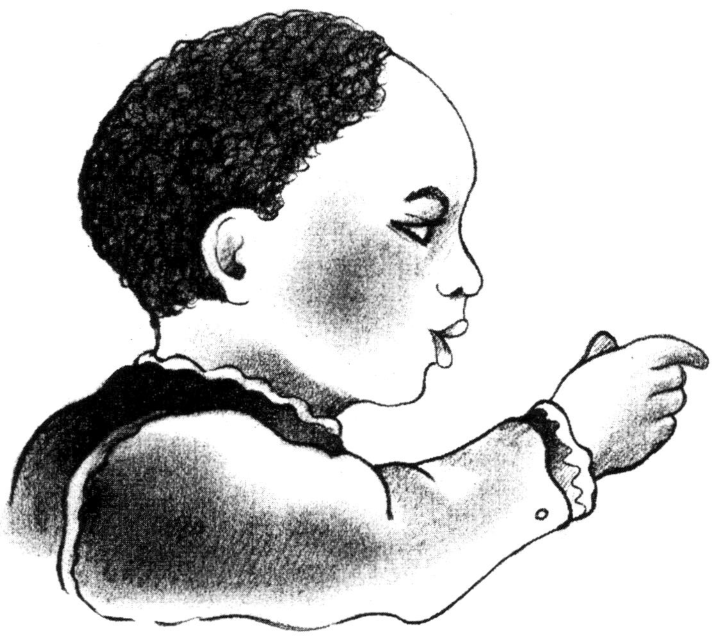

> Life is like playing a violin in public and learning the instrument as one goes on. When children are born, they can't really do anything but cry, which they do a lot. However, over a period of weeks and months, they learn other ways of communicating. The terrible squawks are replaced by pointing and cooing. Children begin to smile and babble to get what they want. Soon, words like "wah" (water) are there, and these are music to a parent's ears, compared with the crying. As children learn more words, they start making simple sentences like "wah-ha" (water is hot). Each day that passes, they learn something new about the "instrument" of speech. Yes, there are mistakes, but the squawks are fewer!

As you can see, this student developed a topic sentence by beginning with an existing sentence (Butler's) and using observations from his own experience to expand on it. Basically, he drew an analogy between learning to play a violin in public and acquiring language as an infant.

PREWRITING: SIX STRATEGIES

Where did the student who developed Butler's sentence into a mini-essay get his idea? He probably got it from one or more prewriting activities. ***Prewriting*** activities are strategies for generating and planning. In the following sections you'll learn six prewriting strategies:

- 1—Listing
- 2—Webbing
- 3—Sketching
- 4—Collaborating
- 5—Questioning
- 6—Outlining

You'll see how to use these planning techniques early in the writing process and return to them later if necessary. You may find that one method for generating and planning works better than others for you. If so, use it. And don't hesitate to switch to a different prewriting activity if you get stuck. Remember that the goal is to learn strategies you can use.

Strategy 1: Listing

Most of us make lists to plan future events—Saturday's errands, Monday's shopping, or Wednesday's study sessions for midterms. Lists are quick, efficient, and flexible. Having a list at hand frees your mind to attend to other important matters.

Listing is our first important freewriting strategy. To develop a prewriting list, follow two steps. *First,* simply jot down ideas as they occur to you. Write quickly, using words or phrases. Reject nothing. The aim of this first step is simply to write down as much as possible. *Second,* go back to your list for a second look.

A prewriting list serves as a memory bank, of course, but it also enables you to select and organize. Making such a list can help you find an approach to a topic.

To see how listing works as a prewriting strategy, let's consider one of the sentence imitations we looked at above:

> Divorce is like flushing the toilet and then watching it overflow.

This sentence focuses on divorce—that is, *divorce* is its topic. Here's a sample list related to that topic:

DIVORCE

anger	clean up the mess
helplessness	problem remains
panic	tears
unexpected event	frustration
must be dealt with	no one to turn to
awful consequences	alone

This list, composed in just two minutes, provided one writer with the direction she needed to write an interesting piece for her portfolio.

> Divorce is like flushing the toilet and then watching it overflow. You don't expect to see water and waste spreading over your freshly scrubbed bathroom floor. When it does, you don't know what to do. Your feelings are panic, anger, and helplessness. After all, you're on your own, and there is no one to turn to. You have a mess on your hands, and you must deal with cleaning up the smelly, awful consequences. And not only that. You must figure out why the damn thing doesn't work and get it fixed. You cry because you are frustrated and alone. Crying doesn't fix anything, but it's what you do when you get divorced or when the toilet overflows.

This writing reveals the writer's interest in her topic. While she could probably have written a safe but boring essay, she chose a topic that motivated her. (Later in the term, she went back to her draft and developed it into a major essay for her final grade.)

You can follow this writer's example when you use listing as a prewriting strategy—and when you combine and imitate sentences. Be alert for whatever sparks your interest. Take risks as you learn.

➔ SC: Happiness

Directions (1) Work with a partner to *combine* the following sentences. Then check your sentences in the Answer Key or against answers provided by your instructor. (2) Using your own ideas, choose at least three sentences to *imitate*; share these with a partner. (3) Try the listing strategy to *generate* ideas for one sentence you have combined or composed. Then write a brief follow-up essay, using ideas from your list.

1.1 Happiness is a mystery like religion.
1.2 It should never be rationalized.

2.1 We can't be happy.
2.2 We must always be cheerful.

3.1 Remember that happiness is a way of travel.
3.2 It is not a destination.

4.1 It is not easy to find happiness in ourselves.
4.2 It is not possible to find it elsewhere.

5.1 There is an indispensable part of happiness.
5.2 This is to be without some of the things you want.

6.1 The secret of happiness is not in doing what one likes.
6.2 The secret of happiness is in liking what one has to do.

7.1 There is only one way to happiness.
7.2 That is to cease worrying about things.
7.3 The things are beyond the power of our will.

8.1 Happiness is the light on the water.
8.2 The water is cold.
8.3 The water is dark.
8.4 The water is deep.

9.1 One door of happiness closes.
9.2 Another opens.
9.3 Often we look so long at the closed door.
9.4 We do not see the one which has been opened for us.

10.1 Happiness is essentially a state of going somewhere.
10.2 The going is wholehearted.
10.3 The going is one-directional.
10.4 The going is without regret.
10.5 The going is without reservation.

Strategy 2: Webbing

Webbing is sometimes called *clustering* or *mapping*. Whatever its name, it works well for many student and professional writers. Webbing is our second prewriting strategy. Like listing, it taps your creative powers of memory and association.

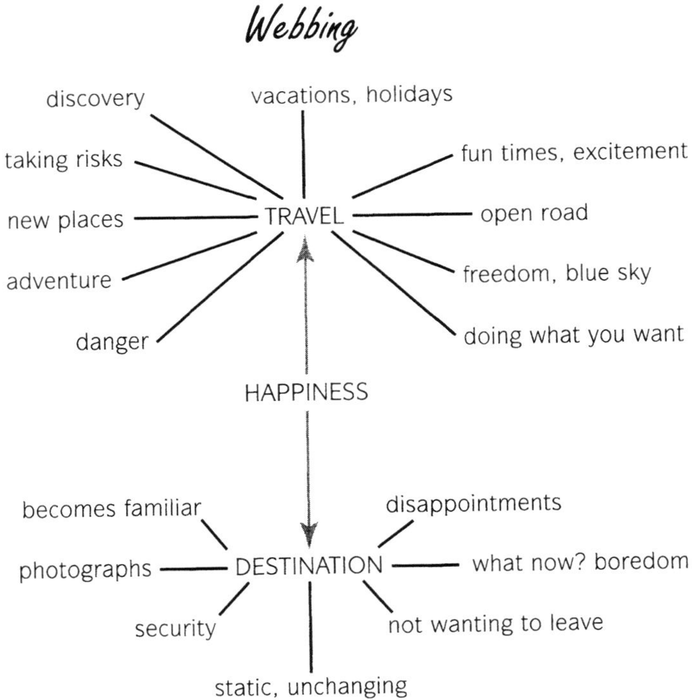

To demonstrate how webbing is used in prewriting, let's consider the topic of the previous set of SC exercises, *happiness*. Suppose you find yourself thinking about cluster 3 above: the idea that "happiness is a way of travel, not a destination." You can develop this idea by writing the word *happiness* in the center of a sheet of paper and arranging around it a web of your associations with the two related ideas, *travel* and *destination:*

The idea is to work fast, jotting down whatever words or phrases come to mind. Some of these words and phrases may be unexpected; but remember that unexpected words or memories actually help you find a way into your topic—in fact, your mind thrives on surprises. When you connect your memories and associations, you'll often feel a "click" of recognition as a pattern begins to emerge.

Because webbing is fast and easy, you can use it regularly. You'll find that the more webbing you do, the easier it becomes. This strategy seems especially effective when you get stuck while drafting a piece.

SC: Work

Directions (1) Work with a partner to *combine* the following sentences. Then check your sentences in the Answer Key or against answers provided by your instructor. (2) Using your own ideas, choose at least three sentences to *imitate*; share these with a partner. (3) Try the webbing strategy to *generate* ideas for one sentence you have combined or composed; then write a brief follow-up essay, using ideas from your web.

1.1 Miracles sometimes occur.
1.2 One has to work terribly hard for them.

2.1 Most people like hard work.
2.2 This is particularly when they're paying for it.

3.1 Work and love are the basics.
3.2 Without them there is neurosis.

4.1 Work expands.
4.2 It fills the time available for its completion.

5.1 Leisure time is less structured than work.
5.2 Leisure time leaves workaholics at a loss for what to do.

6.1 Work faithfully eight hours a day.
6.2 You may eventually get to be a boss.
6.3 A boss works 12 hours a day.

7.1 Work is the condition of human life.
7.2 The condition is inevitable.
7.3 It is the true source of human welfare.

8.1 Work banishes those three great evils.
8.2 One evil is boredom.
8.3 One evil is vice.
8.4 One evil is poverty.

9.1 No fine work can be done without concentration.
9.2 No fine work can be done without self-sacrifice.
9.3 No fine work can be done without toil.
9.4 No fine work can be done without doubt.

10.1 White-collar people get jobs.
10.2 They sell their time.
10.3 They sell their energy.
10.4 They sell their personalities.

Strategy 3: Sketching

Sketching—our third prewriting strategy—is a process of trying to visualize abstract ideas. A sketch can be an actual drawing, but it can also be a chart, a diagram, a floor plan, a street plan, and so on. The diagram of the writing process in Unit 1 is an example: it sketches a complex process. You can use a sketch to "think on paper," and this is a good way to generate ideas for writing.

Floor plans and stick figures may seem crude, or even silly, but in fact they can be powerful prewriting strategies. Suppose, for instance, that you're trying to remember the details of a house from your childhood, which will

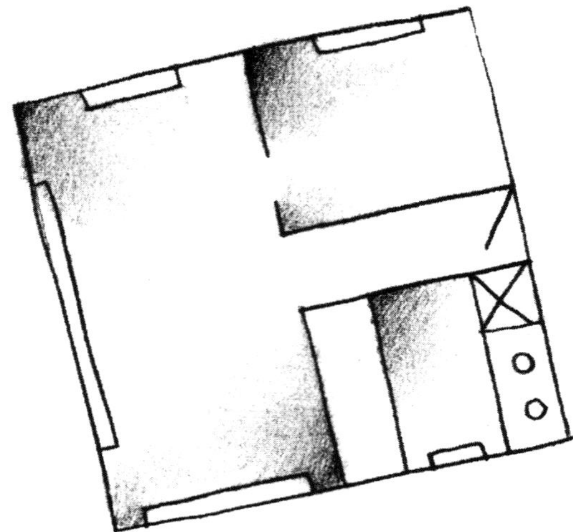

be the setting for a personal narrative. As you begin to draw a rough floor plan, you'll probably experience a flood of memories. You can then use listing or webbing to put these memories into words and phrases.

Suppose, further, that in this narrative you want to describe and explain a relationship—say, between you and your mother. You could approach this by sketching some scenes with stick figures. Perhaps you remember holding your mother's hand as a child, on a walk through a park. Perhaps you remember her hand pointed at you in anger, scolding you for

some misdeed. Perhaps you remember her uplifted hand waving good-bye at an airport gate. You can capture such gestures—and the stories they reveal—with a quick sketch or two. The act of sketching brings out words and memories.

Diagrams provide another way to visualize ideas and information. You can use circles, arrows, and other simple shapes to sketch complex relationships. Do you and your mother share certain personality traits? Try sketching this concept as overlapping circles, labeling areas of similarity and difference. Does your mother dominate others, including you? Make one shape larger than another and label that "Mother." Does your mother have unique or outstanding individual qualities? Draw a star and label the points, one for each quality.

Don't forget that sketching can be used with other prewriting strategies. Also, don't worry about the quality of your artwork. A sketch is simply a means to an end.

➔ SC: Money

Directions (1) Work with a partner to *combine* the following sentences. Then check your sentences in the Answer Key or against answers provided by your instructor. (2) Using your own ideas, choose at least three sentences to *imitate*; share these with a partner. (3) Try the sketching strategy to *generate* ideas for one sentence you have combined or composed; then write a brief follow-up essay, using ideas from your sketch or sketches.

1.1 Money isn't everything.
1.2 It's a long way ahead of what comes next.

2.1 Money is like a queen.
2.2 It gives rank and beauty.

3.1 Money is like muck.
3.2 It is not good unless it be spread.

4.1 Money can't buy friends.
4.2 It gives you a better class of enemy.

5.1 It is a question of money.
5.2 Everybody is of the same religion.

6.1 The rich could hire other people to die for them.
6.2 The poor would make a wonderful living.

7.1 Making money is fun.
7.2 It's pointless if you don't use the power it brings.

8.1 Bankruptcy is a legal proceeding.
8.2 You put your money in your pants pocket.
8.3 You give your coat to your creditors.

9.1 The conspicuously wealthy turn up.
9.2 They urge the character-building value of privation.
9.3 Privation is for the poor.

10.1 There is only one thing for a man to do.
10.2 The man is married to a woman.
10.3 The woman enjoys spending money.
10.4 That is to enjoy earning it.

Strategy 4: Collaborating

"Understanding," according to the philosopher Thomas Hobbes, "is nothing else than conception caused by speech." The idea that talking can *cause* understanding, that speaking actually *leads* to understanding, is both profound and surprising. Most of us think of it the other way around.

Collaborating—talking with others—is our fourth prewriting strategy. This is a powerful tool when you are preparing to write. When you sit down with friends to discuss writing ideas, the give-and-take of conversation stimulates your mind. At first, you may have only vague thoughts, but questions from your writing partners will help focus and sharpen your thinking. If you stick with the process of collaborating, you will find yourself verbalizing ideas that you didn't know you had.

It's helpful to establish some ground rules for collaborating. One of the most basic rules is that no one criticizes any one else's ideas as "dumb."

Why? Criticism like this destroys the spirit on which successful groups depend. A second ground rule is that each member feels responsible for the group's success. While one person may lead the group or make more comments than other group members, no one should dominate.

When you're collaborating with others on a writing project, begin by explaining the *problem* you face. Describe what you've been thinking about and where you are stuck. Then—and only then—should you ask for the group's help. Tell the group, as clearly as you can, what kind of help you need: background ideas? organization? overall purpose? something else? In order to get to work, the group will need direction from you. Therefore, tell the others how they can help you. By specifying what you need, you focus the efforts of the group.

As the discussion proceeds, take notes, perhaps in the form of lists, webs, or sketches. You'll use these later, when you are writing. The point, of course, is not for others to do your thinking; the point is for others to think *with* you.

Finally, be sure to thank the others for their collaboration.

➔ SC: Politics

Directions (1) Work with a partner to *combine* the following sentences. Then check your sentences in the Answer Key or against answers provided by your instructor. (2) Using your own ideas, choose at least three sentences to *imitate*; share these with a partner. (3) Try the collaborating strategy to *generate* ideas for one sentence you have combined or composed; then write a brief follow-up essay, using ideas from your collaboration.

1.1 Politics is war without bloodshed.
1.2 War is politics with blood.

2.1 Three people would soon reinvent politics.
2.2 The people were marooned on a desert island.

3.1 Politics is the gizzard of society.
3.2 It is full of gut and gravel.

4.1 The politician poses as the servant.
4.2 This is in order to become the master.

5.1 The great nations have always acted like gangsters.
5.2 The small nations have always acted like prostitutes.

6.1 The sad duty of politics is to establish justice.
6.2 The justice is in a world.
6.3 The world is sinful.

7.1 Politics is shaped by men.
7.2 The fate of mankind is shaped by men.
7.3 The men are without ideals.
7.4 The men are without greatness.

8.1 Power is a drug.
8.2 Politicians are hooked on it.
8.3 They buy it from the voters.
8.4 The use the voters' own money.

9.1 The world is a dangerous place to live.
9.2 This is not because of the people who are evil.
9.3 It is because of other people.
9.4 They don't do anything about it.

10.1 We are strong.
10.2 Our strength will speak for itself.
10.3 We are weak.
10.4 Our words will be no help.

Strategy 5: Questioning

Questioning is our fifth prewriting strategy. Questions are the most powerful intellectual tools that human beings possess. Without questions, our libraries would be empty and modern technology would not exist. In fact, what we call "civilization" is the product of people's discovering or inventing answers to questions.

Good writing always answers basic questions. For example, a description of a sunlit meadow may answer the question, "What was the place like?" An essay about racism may answer the question, "Why do people think like this?" A job application may answer the question, "How can this person contribute to our organization?"

Journalists use specific questions as they write news stories and articles; these questions can also work for you:

- Who?
- What?
- When?
- Where?
- Why?
- How?

In journalism, these questions are called the *five W's and H*—a good way to remember them.

To see how questioning works in prewriting, suppose you're interested in cluster 10 above: John F. Kennedy's idea that "if we are strong, our strength will speak for itself." You might focus your questions on politics, asking about the role of the United States as a superpower after the collapse of communism in eastern Europe and Asia. Or you might focus your questions on your own personal experience, to see if your experiences support or contradict Kennedy's assertion. Here's a brief example of a personal approach. The questions come first; then come words and phrases that provide direction for writing:

STRENGTH SPEAKS

WHO? My grandfather, strongest man in the shipyards. Polio at 39, unable to move. Down for two years—silent and determined. Inner strength.

WHAT? His own plan for physical therapy. Home-made equipment. Disdain for doctors. Refusal to give up. Unwillingness to accept help.

WHEN? September 1954. Elvis on the radio. Ozzie and Harriet on TV. Eisenhower and Nixon in the White House. United States during the cold war.

WHERE? The living room, my grandfather on the floor. Weights and pulleys. The wheelchair nearby. A clock on the mantle, the squeak of pulleys. His mouth set, according to my grandmother.

WHY? A matter of pride. Was that it?

HOW? By himself. Through guts alone.

As this example shows, the six questions can help you find a way into a topic; in this case, they helped the writer develop a personal essay about a family member. Of course, you can also use one or more of the questions in conjunction with other prewriting approaches. In brief, questioning is a way of thinking.

➔ SC: Writing

Directions Work with a partner to *combine* the following sentences. Then check your sentences in the Answer Key or against answers provided by your instructor. (2) Using your own ideas, choose at least three sentences to *imitate;* share these with a partner. (3) Try the questioning strategy to *generate* ideas for one sentence you have combined or composed; then write a brief follow-up essay, using ideas from your questions.

1.1 The limits of my language are the limits of my mind.
1.2 All I know is what I have words for.

2.1 Writing is one of the easiest things.
2.2 Erasing is one of the hardest things.

3.1 An original writer is not one who imitates nobody.
3.2 An original writer is one whom nobody can imitate.

4.1 A good writer is basically a story-teller.
4.2 A good writer is not a scholar.
4.3 A good writer is not a redeemer of mankind.

5.1 A woman must have money.
5.2 A woman must have a room of her own.
5.3 This is if she is to write fiction.

6.1 There are two kinds of writers.
6.2 The great ones can give you truths.
6.3 The lesser ones can only give you themselves.

7.1 Your manuscript is both good and original.
7.2 The parts that are good are not original.
7.3 The parts that are original are not good.

8.1 Words are subjects of revision.
8.2 Sentences are subjects of revision.
8.3 Paragraphs are subjects of prevision.
8.4 Whole compositions are subjects of prevision.

9.1 Writing is no trouble.
9.2 You jot down ideas as they occur to you.
9.3 The jotting is simplicity itself.
9.4 It is the occurring which is difficult.

10.1 A sentence should contain no unnecessary words.
10.2 A paragraph should contain no unnecessary sentences.
10.3 A drawing should have no unnecessary lines.
10.4 A machine should have no unnecessary parts.

Strategy 6: Outlining

Consider for a moment the notion of *maps*. You probably wouldn't try to drive to a new state, or walk around a new city, without some kind of map to serve as a guide. By consulting your map from time to time, you can see where you are in relation to your destination.

Like maps, various kinds of outlines provide direction for the journey of writing, and ***outlining*** is our sixth prewriting strategy. Outlines are especially important for major writing projects, the projects that stretch over weeks or months. Such projects may be quite complex in terms of ideas or organization; therefore, some kind of outline, however tentative or rough, is often a necessity. Otherwise, you'll spend most of your time trying to remember your original direction.

To develop an outline, try beginning with 3- by 5-inch note cards (or notebook paper cut to the same size). Jot down key ideas, one idea per card. If you're doing a research report, such ideas might come from background reading and interviewing.

Later, as you read through your cards, sort them into piles. Then go through the cards in each pile again; this second reading will enable you to sequence and organize them.

It's then a simple matter to construct a tentative outline. All you do is develop logical headings for the different piles of cards and arrange these headings in an order that makes sense. You can then clip the cards under each heading together and file them in order.

Finally, subsequent research will extend your existing stacks of cards or create new stacks.

The form your outline takes is a matter of personal preference. A traditional outline format is shown below.

OUTLINING

I. Analogy between maps and outlines
   A. How maps are useful
   B. Why outlines help with major projects
II. Note-card approach to outlining
   A. Write one idea per card
   B. Sort cards into piles
   C. Sequence and arrange within piles
   D. Write headings
   E. With more research, add to existing stacks or make new stacks
III. Outline form: example
IV. Usefulness of outlines

Remember that an outline is merely a map for writing, not the writing itself. Even the most conscientious and disciplined writers find that "the writing takes over" as they begin a draft. That experience is wonderful, of course, because it means that the outline may no longer be necessary; but if it happens to you, don't throw your outline away. Sooner or later, you may find yourself losing direction—and you'll be glad that you kept the outline. Maps become useful when you're off the beaten path, wandering in unfamiliar territory; the same goes for outlines.

➔ SC: Life

Directions (1) Work with a partner to *combine* the following sentences. Then check your sentences in the Answer Key or against answers provided by your instructor. (2) Using your own ideas, choose at least three sentences to *imitate*; share these with a partner. (3) Try the outlining strategy to *generate* ideas for one sentence you have combined or composed; then write a brief follow-up essay, using ideas from your outline.

1.1 Life is a handful of short stories.
1.2 The short stories pretend to be a novel.

2.1 The first half of our lives is ruined by our parents.
2.2 The second half of our lives is ruined by our children.

3.1 Life can only be understood backwards.
3.2 It must be lived forwards.

4.1 You only live once.
4.2 Work it right.
4.3 Once is enough.

5.1 The rat race has one trouble.
5.2 You win.
5.3 You're still a rat.

6.1 The true meaning of life is to plant trees.
6.2 The trees have shade.
6.3 You do not expect to sit in their shade.

7.1 A single event can awaken within us a stranger.
7.2 The stranger is totally unknown to us.
7.3 To live is to be slowly born.

8.1 Life is all memory.
8.2 This is except for the one present moment.
8.3 The moment goes by so quickly.
8.4 You hardly catch it going.

9.1 Life is made up of sobs.
9.2 Life is made up of sniffles.
9.3 Life is made up of smiles.
9.4 Sniffles predominate.

10.1 Life is a halo.
10.2 The halo is luminous.
10.3 Life is an envelope.
10.4 The envelope is semi-transparent.
10.5 The envelope surrounds us from the beginning.

A Review of the Six Strategies

The six prewriting strategies are methods for generating and planning in writing: (1) listing, (2) webbing, (3) sketching, (4) collaborating, (5) questioning, (6) outlining.

These strategies are flexible enough to be used in a variety of writing situations. Some take only five or ten minutes; others—like collaborating, questioning, and outlining—may take longer.

Now that you've experienced all six strategies, you may feel a "pull" toward one strategy or another. For example, if you're a visual learner, you may find that you prefer webbing and sketching; however, if you're a person who values clear, logical structure, you may prefer questioning or outlining. Use whatever works for you.

➔ *SC for Extra Practice*

Directions This set of SC exercises provides additional practice. After combining and imitating, choose whichever prewriting approach you prefer. Use that approach to develop a topic sentence for your follow-up writing. Share your results with a writing partner.

1.1 Education is not the filling of a pail.
1.2 Education is the lighting of a fire.

2.1 You can't make anything idiot-proof.
2.2 Idiots are so ingenious.

3.1 Entrepreneurship is the last refuge of the individual.
3.2 The individual is a trouble maker.

4.1 Courage is resistance to fear.
4.2 Courage is mastery of fear.
4.3 Courage is not absence of fear.

5.1 Hair and fingernails continue to grow.
5.2 This is for three days after death.
5.3 Phone calls taper off.

6.1 A compliment is a gift.
6.2 It is not to be thrown away carelessly.
6.3 This is unless you want to hurt the giver.

7.1 Slang is language.
7.2 The language takes off its coat.
7.3 The language spits on its hands.
7.4 The language goes to work.

8.1 Gossip is vice enjoyed vicariously.
8.2 It is satisfaction without the risk.
8.3 The satisfaction is sweet.
8.4 The satisfaction is subtle.

9.1 Science is built of facts.
9.2 A house is built of bricks.
9.3 An accumulation of facts is not science.
9.4 A pile of bricks is not a house.

10.1 Patriotism is not outbursts of emotions.
10.2 The outbursts are short.
10.3 The outbursts are frenzied.
10.4 Patriotism is the dedication of a lifetime.
10.5 The dedication is tranquil and steady.

WORKSHOP PORTFOLIO FOR UNIT 2

So far in Unit 2, you've combined and imitated sentences, focused on the concept of *topic sentences*, and practiced six prewriting strategies for generating and planning. By now you should have several paragraphs in your portfolio. Here are two possible ways you can use the writing you've completed. Choose *one* of these assignments or work with the one specified by your instructor.

Option 1: A Memory about Learning As you examine your portfolio, identify writing that has to do with *learning*, either in school or elsewhere. For example, let's say you've written a piece about the SC topic *writing* earlier in the unit. Do you have memories associated with writing? Use a prewriting strategy to bring out your memories.

Develop an essay in which you recall a situation where you learned something important, either positive or negative. To write this essay, you'll need to depict the *place* where the learning occurred and tell *what happened* in some detail. Finally, you'll need to comment on the significance of this learning—in other words, what it means to you now. This statement of significance will be the ***thesis*** of your essay: the main idea. Just as a topic sentence is an assertion for a paragraph, a thesis is an assertion for an essay.

In developing your paper, you may want to include one or more pieces from your portfolio. As you weave this writing into a larger essay, you'll probably need to make changes. The process of transforming paragraphs and integrating them into a new and different text can be quite interesting. Have fun with it.

Option 2: A Job Application Imagine that you are applying for a job with an organization that values its employees. The take-home application form asks you to compose an essay that reveals *two aspects* of your personality and character. The managers of the organization want to know who you are and how you see yourself. Such information enables them to make good hiring decisions.

Reread your portfolio, asking yourself what each piece of writing reveals about you. Decide on two pieces that clearly reflect your personality and character. Now, compose a *thesis*—a main point, an organizing statement—about yourself; remember that a thesis is an assertion for an essay, just as a topic sentence is an assertion for a paragraph. For example, you might assert, "I am a person who has strong feelings about happiness and work."

Use portfolio pieces to develop your thesis. For example, if you are new to the United States, you might illustrate this point with your paragraph on *happiness*. If you are working your way through school, you might illustrate that point with your paragraph on *work*. Think of your portfolio pieces as snapshots in a photo album. It's up to you, as a writer, to link them together into a new whole.

UNIT 3

Freewriting and Drafting

Inspiration usually comes during work, rather than before it.

—Madeleine L'Engle

In Unit 2, you warmed up by combining sentences, imitating sentences, and developing topic sentences. You saw that processes of generating and planning help you get moving as a writer, and you learned and practiced six prewriting strategies.

Now, in Unit 3, let's consider how you get sentences onto paper, one word after another. This process is called ***drafting,*** and it involves transcribing *oral meanings* into *written symbols*. One special technique, ***freewriting,*** is closely related to speaking. When you freewrite, you let your ideas—your "inner speech"—flow naturally, without extensive planning or rehearsal. You'll learn some skills to facilitate drafting, and you'll see how oral and "choral" sentence combining can further develop those skills.

Since freewriting and drafting have to do with turning speech into writing, we'll begin Unit 3 by looking at that process. Understanding the process of turning speech into writing will help you understand freewriting and drafting. Such knowledge is power.

SPEECH AND WRITING: OUTER SPEECH, INNER SPEECH

To understand how speech becomes writing, let's think about two different forms of speech in everyday life. The first form—***outer speech***—is the language you use for oral reports and conversations. The second form—called ***inner speech***—is an interior language for planning, remembering, and thinking in general.

Outer speech and inner speech are different but related activities that shape our lives. For example, sometimes we literally "talk out" a problem with a close friend as a way of thinking more clearly about it. On the other hand, sometimes we use inner speech to "plan words" before committing ourselves to important oral or written statements.

Developmentally, outer speech precedes inner speech. As any parent knows, infants and small children continually say what's on their minds. Only gradually, at about the time they enter preschool or kindergarten, do children develop inner speech. You may have heard very young children talking to themselves as they play with puzzles or games; such outer speech has not yet "gone underground"—that is, it hasn't yet become internalized.

How do outer speech and inner speech relate to writing? When we are writing, few of us have the luxury of a personal secretary to transcribe our outer speech, or dictation, into written text. Instead, we have to rely on inner speech—the voice of our own thinking. In one way or another, then, most of us *talk to ourselves* as we write. Talking to ourselves mentally is actually the way we transcribe, or *draft*, our inner speech into written text.

In Unit 2, you saw that planning strategies can get your writing started. Now, you see that unless you hear a voice within—a voice speaking your thoughts—you cannot really transcribe. This is a basic concept: *drafting involves inner speech*.

FREEWRITING: DEVELOPING INNER SPEECH

Let's consider a practical problem of composition: sitting down to write and hearing only crackling static between your ears. "This is hopeless," you think. "I'm stuck, with nothing to say."

But suppose you write *about that thought itself*—the thought that you have "nothing to say." If you do, you may surprise yourself. As you transcribe your inner speech, it becomes externalized; that is, it becomes words you can *read:*

> Nothing to say? How come? Just procrastinating? . . .

Somehow, the act of putting inner speech down in writing serves to stimulate and focus that inner speech. Writing, in turn, seems to stimulate further thinking.

The process of voicing inner speech is called ***freewriting*** because it "frees" your thoughts so that they can first be expressed and later organized. Freewriting allows the voice within to speak its mind—*your* mind—without fear of censure or criticism or interference from you. When your inner voice is treated with respect, it develops confidence and strength.

Treating your inner voice with respect may be a new idea for you. Everyone knows what it means to respect another speaker: pay attention and don't interrupt. Giving *yourself* such basic courtesy is no less important. As a writer, try to minimize internal criticism; let yourself take risks. If you make fun of freewriting or don't give it an honest try, should you really be surprised to find that you've nipped your own thinking and writing in the bud?

You can clarify your inner speech and develop fluency in transcribing by using ***timed freewriting.*** In timed freewriting, you record your inner speech word for word as it happens, without worrying about spelling, usage, or punctuation. For two minutes at first—then, later on, for stints of five or ten minutes—put down whatever comes to mind. Hear your innermost language and keep your pen moving. If you get stuck, write about being stuck!

Another useful technique is ***focused freewriting.*** After finishing a timed freewriting session, read what you have written. Circle a word or phrase that interests or surprises you. Then use this word or phrase as a starting point. Focused freewriting can lead to wonderful writing discoveries—and it's absolutely painless.

Here's what one student wrote in a brief freewriting exercise:

Example: Freewriting

Don't know why, but I'm supposed to keep the flow going for two or three minutes. So what's the point? Listen to yourself, get the words down? I thought you were supposed to know what you want to say first, make an outline, then write. Hated that in school. Always made the outline afterward. Others faked it too, like on research papers. I remember taking my notes on yellow pads, then sorting through the sheets. . . .

This student then circled the phrase *hated that in school* and began focused freewriting. Here's the text that resulted:

Example: Focused Freewriting

I always hated outlining in school, but Mr. G was a stickler for detail. He'd show us the correct outline form and make us practice on incredibly boring paragraphs. Like igneous rocks, the exports of Brazil. You listed the main ideas and details, then compared them with his answers. Then you wrote boring paragraphs of your own. Like comparing apples and oranges. How to tie your shoelaces. A favorite TV program. At some point in the spring we did research papers. What I remember is . . .

As you can see from these examples, freewriting can lead to surprising, and interesting, results. The example of focused freewriting, for instance, could evolve into a personal essay about memories of learning to write. There are seeds here that can be planted and cultivated.

Because learning involves *doing*, freewrite as often as you can. Try timing yourself and tracking your fluency in words per minute. Be sure to try focused freewriting. To make your freewriting even more productive, use the six prewriting strategies in Unit 2.

Keep in mind that the point of freewriting is to develop your *writing fluency*. Fluency involves willingness to take risks and "go with the flow." Freewriting is *practice* in writing. Of course, it's great when a freewriting piece becomes part of a larger, more public piece. But even when this doesn't happen, your writing skills are still developing—and that's what counts.

DRAFTING: TIPS AND GUIDELINES

Tools of the Drafting Trade

Do you remember using a fat yellow pencil as a child—and gripping it so tightly that it left a red welt on your finger? Do you remember the terrifying emptiness of lined paper on your desk. Do you remember the dark, sweaty smudges from your eraser?

If you have unpleasant memories of writing with a scratchy pencil on a tablet of poor-quality paper, perhaps you should invest in better ***drafting tools***—tools that are more user-friendly and more pleasant to work with. Writing is a made thing, a physical act. Therefore, search for tools that feel comfortable in your hand or at your fingertips. Your tools don't have to be expensive. What matters is that they feel right and work well for you.

Many writers like to use note cards for drafting practice. Note cards are cheap; they fit into a shirt or jacket pocket; and you can sort and rearrange them when it comes time to organize the parts of a larger composition.

Another student-friendly idea is a 6- by 9-inch wirebound notebook. This fits nicely into a backpack and folds open whenever you have a few minutes to spare in the Student Center. Also, you may like the idea of keeping all your drafting work in one place.

Perhaps you'll like felt-tip pens in rainbow colors, or a soft lead pencil, or jet-black ink from a ballpoint. Perhaps a laptop computer will help you hear the voice within.

You'll want to discover not only what tools you prefer, but where you prefer to use them. Perhaps you're a person whose drafts come to life in anonymous places like fast-food restaurants and coffee shops. Perhaps you need a quiet corner of the library or computer lab for your drafting. Know where you're likely to do your best work. Then go there on purpose, relaxed and ready. Routines and habits will help sustain your writing efforts.

In your special place, with your tools at hand, you're ready to write. Look back at your freewriting, asking yourself what you can focus on—what you're most interested in. Can you focus on an image, a word, or a quotation? Can you focus on a question, a remembered scene, or a fragment of language? Use this point of departure to launch your draft.

If you get stuck, don't panic. Simply reread your own words, listening for a voice. Often that voice will get you started again. If it doesn't, try rereading your prewriting notes. Somewhere in those notes you'll find the idea you need.

An Experiment in Drafting

It's important to understand that drafting is a *physical* process. Therefore, let's conduct a drafting experiment.

First, examine the following cluster of short sentences.

Example: Experiment

Freewriting is a drafting activity.

A writer commits words to paper.

A writer does *not* try to direct their outcome.

Second, combine this cluster—grammatically—*in your head;* but don't write your combined sentence down. The sentence you compose should summarize ideas from the three sentences above. Whisper that single sentence to yourself to make sure that it contains all the essential information.

Third, when you have your sentence clearly in mind, try the experiment. Follow these directions exactly:

- Handwrite the sentence you have mentally composed, just as you would normally.
- Now, switch your pen or pencil to your other hand and write the same sentence again. Ready? Go!

Did you write your sentence twice as directed above? If so, you undoubtedly noticed striking differences between the two experiences. Whereas the first sentence flowed effortlessly from your pen or pencil, the second sentence took much longer to write. In the second experience, you found yourself concentrating on individual letters and words. And the second attempt probably looks much like the writing of your grade-school days—clumsy, uneven, misshapen.

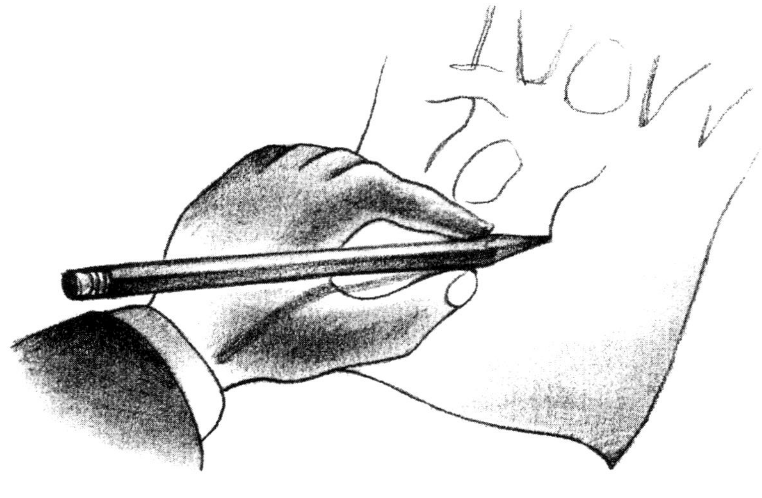

What's the point of this experiment? With your usual writing hand, you're able to transcribe speech into writing quite fluently; but with the other hand, transcription is hampered, even virtually blocked. So which hand is more likely to produce clear, interesting writing? The answer is obvious.

This simple experiment shows dramatically that *practice* plays a crucial role in drafting, and thus in your development as a writer. If your goal is to draft sentences easily and "naturally," you need to understand that physical practice is required—lots of it.

Drafting is like riding a bicycle. Once you get on, it's essential to develop forward momentum. If you're tentative or hesitant, you may find yourself headed for scrapes and bruises. So don't be shy. Write for all you're worth.

IMPROVING YOUR DRAFTING SKILLS: ORAL AND CHORAL SENTENCE COMBINING

We said at the beginning of this unit that oral and choral sentence combining can further develop your drafting skills. In ***oral sentence combining,*** you voice sentences aloud and check how they sound. Of course you're interested in improving your skills, but you may be asking, "Why get *oral* practice in combining sentences? How will this help my writing?"

To answer these questions, remember first that writing develops from speech. To put it simply, how you speak influences how you write. Think back to getting a newsy letter from a good friend and "hearing" your friend's voice echoing in the written lines. In an office, it's easy to see speech becoming writing: just watch a manager dictating correspondence to a secretary, who in turn keyboards it. Though this process may be less evident when managers keyboard their own correspondence at their own PCs, it is still at work.

It's for this reason that combining sentences orally can improve your freewriting and drafting: oral practice helps develop your inner speech.

The sentence-combining (SC) exercises in this unit begin with outer speech: you'll combine sentences orally by working in pairs or small groups. You and your workshop partners will be using "closure clues"—or hints—that will lead you to target sentences. These hints consist of key words, punctuation marks, and blank spaces. By reading each SC exercise and studying its hint, you will be able to figure out most of the sentences.

As a follow-up activity, you may be asked to participate in ***choral sentence combining*** with the entire class. Choral combining reinforces learning, because it helps "program" your brain to recognize and produce increasingly varied sentences—sentences you may not ordinarily use in everyday speaking or writing.

The idea of oral and choral combining is to help you *see* and *hear* new patterns for sentences. Later, when you work with closure clues on your own—using inner speech—you will hear "echoes" from your oral and choral activities. These inner echoes represent the "programming" of your internal computer, your brain. Because you *remember* new patterns, you will be better able to *write* them.

In fact, many skilled writers use oral methods when they revise and tinker. Professionals aren't satisfied until their text "speaks" to the reader, so they rely on outer speech as well as inner speech to guide their changes at the sentence level.

To repeat a point made earlier: *unless you hear a voice within, you cannot really engage in writing*. The aim of oral and choral combining is to develop that voice.

WORKSHOP PORTFOLIO FOR UNIT 3

As you freewrite and draft in response to the writing invitations in Unit 3, be sure to keep papers in your workshop portfolio. Each entry should be dated. Your instructor may ask you to develop one or more of these entries in greater depth. You may also be able to propose your own writing assignments. For details on how to do this, refer back to "Your Writing Portfolio" in Unit 1.

Option 1: A Remembered Place Read your portfolio to find pieces related to places. Don't overlook short passages describing places within longer writings. As you review these pieces, try to find material that sparks your interest or calls up memories. Perhaps you'll see whole paragraphs that you can use; or perhaps you'll spot a line or two that you'd like to expand and develop.

This assignment is to describe a place you know or remember well—a place that's important to you. The significance of this place will probably lie in your feelings about it. The place may be associated with a turning point in your life or with a strong emotion such as love, anger, joy, or sorrow. After reading your essay, a reader should have a sense of knowing the place and be able to understand its significance in your life.

Consider opening your piece with a specific description. Use words that will enable the reader to see, smell, hear, and touch the place you have in mind. Now consider how you can share the significance of the place. Will you show what happened there? What words will disclose your feelings toward the place—then and now? How can you close your piece thoughtfully?

Option 2: An Opinion Paper As you examine your portfolio, you're sure to find pieces in which you express opinions or make judgments. You may have strong views on topics like child abuse, race relations, the value of education, television ads, or gun control. Of course, the stronger your base of knowledge, the more informed and persuasive your views are likely to be.

One approach for an opinion paper is to construct it as a *dialogue*—a conversation between two characters. Using dialogue will let you explore tension between opposing views. If you try this approach, though, beware of making one character a genius and the other a buffoon. Your paper will probably be more intellectually exciting to readers if opposing opinions are expressed with respect and clarity.

A second approach is to think of your paper as an *editorial*. If you examine editorials, you'll find that they often begin by defining an issue, problem, or situation; then they go on to take a stand or make a judgment of some kind. To help create a reasonable tone, a good editorial will often acknowledge other opinions or points of view. Typically, the editorial then reasserts its own position.

SC FOR UNIT 3

Directions On your own or with a partner, combine the following sentence clusters *orally*, using the hints ("closure clues"). Check your sentences for odd-numbered SC exercises in the Answer Key; your instructor has answers for even-numbered exercises.

School Dance

It's the end of the week, and you feel like loosening up after a hard week of classes. Are you ready to boogie?

1.1 I stood on the sidelines.
1.2 The sidelines were shadowy.
1.3 I watched the dance scene at school.

Hint Standing ______________________________,
______________________________.

2.1 Students lounged along the walls.
2.2 They were in tight clusters.
2.3 They were separated by sex.
2.4 They were separated by social class.

Hint Students ______________________________,
separated ______________________________.

3.1 The room was sweaty.
3.2 The room was dark.
3.3 It was a drama of flesh.
3.4 The drama was intense.
3.5 The flesh was jostling.

Hint ____

—an ____.

4.1 Girls swayed with the rhythms.
4.2 The girls were glittering.
4.3 The girls were slump-shouldered.
4.4 The rhythms were insistent.

Hint Girls— ____________________ and ____________________—

swayed ____.

5.1 Boys pawed the dusty floor.
5.2 The boys were tight-lipped.
5.3 They scratched out patterns.
5.4 The patterns were mysterious.

Hint ____,

scratching ____.

6.1 The couples bobbed and dipped.
6.2 The couples circled each other.
6.3 There was little eye contact.
6.4 There was almost no touching.

Hint As ____,

there ____.

7.1 Like an echo from the distant past.
7.2 The music was pulsing.
7.3 The music was heavy.
7.4 The music was almost hypnotic.

Hint Like ____________________,

the ____________________, almost ____________________.

8.1 Its energy seemed to express impulses.
8.2 The impulses were primitive.
8.3 The impulses were tribal.

Hint Its ____________________

____________________ impulses.

Writing Tip Study how dashes are used for emphasis in the combined sentences for clusters 3 and 4. See "Dashes" in Part Two, Toolbox, Unit 9.

Invitation Suddenly you're at the center of the dance floor, with a partner. Describe what happens next in clear, rich detail.

➡ Eric's Locker

Being able to describe a place vividly is a basic writing skill. What better place to start than Eric's locker?

1.1 Eric's locker is a place.
1.2 The place is very unpleasant.
1.3 It is a kind of disaster area.

Hint ____________________—

a kind of ____________________.

2.1 It is a dumping ground.
2.2 Books are dumped there.
2.3 Papers are dumped there.
2.4 Sandwiches are dumped there.
2.5 The sandwiches are half-eaten.

Hint ______________________________ for

______________ , ______________ , and ______________.

3.1 A bike chain hangs from the coat hook.
3.2 The chain is oily.
3.3 The chain is covered with grime.

Hint ____________________, covered ______________________,

____.

4.1 Also hanging there is a pair of socks.
4.2 The socks are stained and smelly.
4.3 Also hanging there is a pair of gym shorts.
4.4 The gym shorts are unwashed.
4.5 The gym shorts are wrinkled.

Hint Also hanging there are____

and ____.

5.1 Fruit has collected on the top shelf.
5.2 The fruit has decayed.
5.3 An open can of soda has a gray culture.
5.4 The culture is growing at its rim.

Hint ____,

and ____.

6.1 Photographs are taped to the locker door.
6.2 School assignments are taped to the locker door.
6.3 Candy-wrapper coupons are taped to the locker door.

Hint Taped ____,

__________________________, and ____________________________.

7.1 At the bottom of the locker is a box.
7.2 In it lives a small green turtle.

Hint ______________________________,

where ______________________________.

8.1 And yet Eric's locker seems tidy.
8.2 It seems well organized.
8.3 This is in comparison with his bedroom.

Hint And yet, compared______________________________,

______________________________.

Writing Tip Notice in cluster 4 above how the singular verb *is* changes to the plural form, *are*. See "Verbs" in Toolbox, Unit 6; and "Subject-Verb Agreement" in Unit 8.

Invitation This exercise makes a transition from Eric's locker to his bedroom. Describe his bedroom in rich, specific, spatial detail—like a movie camera sweeping the scene.

➔ Body Defenses

Why do we automatically cry when the air is dusty or smoky? Is crying a good thing? As you'll see, there's more to tears than meets the eye.

1.1 A series of defenses safeguards our bodies.
1.2 The series is remarkable.
1.3 The defenses are efficient.

Hint A ______________________________ bodies.

2.1 These defenses are like an army.
2.2 The army is ever-alert.
2.3 These defenses form chemical lines.
2.4 The chemical lines ward off invaders.

Hint Like ________________, these ____________________

____ invaders.

3.1 Suppose an example.
3.2 Some dust gets into your eye.
3.3 The dust is germ-laden.

Hint Suppose, ________________, that ________________.

4.1 There is probably nothing to worry about.
4.2 The eye's surface is bathed in tears.
4.3 The bathing is quick.
4.4 The tears are abundant.

Hint ____

because ____.

5.1 These tears help wash away the dust.
5.2 They also serve another purpose.
5.3 The purpose is important.

Hint Not only do ________________________________

but ____.

6.1 Tears contain an antiseptic called lysozyme.
6.2 The antiseptic is very powerful.
6.3 The antiseptic destroys most bacteria.
6.4 The bacteria threaten the eye's surface.

Hint Tears ______________________________

that ______________________________.

7.1 Lysozyme dramatizes something.
7.2 The body "overprotects" itself.
7.3 Overprotection is for self-defense.
7.4 Overprotection is for survival.

Hint ______________________________,

both for ______________________________.

8.1 Teardrops are diluted in a half-gallon of water.
8.2 Lysozyme will still destroy germs.
8.3 The germs are potentially dangerous.

Hint When ______________________________,

______________________________ germs.

Writing Tip Notice how adjectives (like *remarkable* in cluster 1) come before nouns. See "Adjectives" in Toolbox, Unit 6.

Invitation Study how this exercise uses an example to support generalizations in clusters 1 and 2. Using "Body Defenses" as a model, describe how *reflexes* protect us against sudden dangers.

➔ *TV Stereotypes*

Consider what happens when children compare their real world with the world of TV. What if the two worlds are different?

1.1 TV kids come in two categories.
1.2 The categories are adorable.
1.3 Children wear glasses.
1.4 Children don't wear glasses.

Hint TV kids______________________________—

children ______________________________.

2.1 Eyewear suggests intelligence.
2.2 The intelligence is precocious.
2.3 Good vision signals cuteness.
2.4 The cuteness is all-American.

Hint ______________________________,

just as ______________________________.

3.1 But neither group has unwashed hair.
3.2 Neither group has ill-fitting jeans.
3.3 Neither group has torn sneakers.
3.4 Older children have worn out the sneakers.

Hint ______________, ______________,

or ______________________________.

4.1 And neither group goes to bed hungry.
4.2 Neither group sleeps in a room with others.
4.3 Rats or roaches prowl the darkness.

Hint And ______________________________

while______________________________.

5.1 TV kids always seem to have new toys.
5.2 TV kids always seem to have nice clothes.
5.3 Their loving parents provide them.

Hint ______________________________

that ______________________________.

6.1 Typical TV kids get hugs.
6.2 TV kids get bedtime stories.
6.3 They do not get tired shrugs.
6.4 They do not get indifference.

Hint Rather than ______________________________________,

____.

7.1 Their summers are for airplane travel.
7.2 Their summers are for long vacations.
7.3 Their summers are not for boredom.
7.4 The boredom is sweltering.

Hint ____,

not ____.

8.1 The contrast confuses many children.
8.2 The contrast is between TV and reality.
8.3 It is especially painful to poor children.
8.4 Poor children believe television's lies.

Hint Although ______________________________________,

it ____.

Writing Tip In clusters 1 and 8, use a *who* connector as you combine. See "Relative Clauses" in Toolbox, Unit 7.

Invitation "TV Stereotypes" defines a problem. In a follow-up paragraph or two, address the problem from a parent's viewpoint.

Free Ride

Life often requires us to make quick decisions based on our instincts and our values. How would you handle this situation?

1.1 Imagine a straight road.
1.2 The road is almost deserted.
1.3 The road is through a landscape.
1.4 The landscape is oppressively hot.

Hint Imagine ________________, ____________________,
____.

2.1 There's no state patrol around.
2.2 I am making good time.
2.3 I have the windows cranked down.
2.4 I have the radio turned up.

Hint ______________________, so ____________________,
with ____.

3.1 The country is mostly ranchland.
3.2 The ranchland is parched and unforgiving.
3.3 It is dotted with a few farms.
3.4 The farms are run-down.
3.5 The farms have seen better days.

Hint ____;
it ____
that ____.

4.1 I slow down for a junction.
4.2 It is 50 miles from nowhere.
4.3 I spot a teenage hitchhiker.
4.4 His desperate look pleads for a ride.
4.5 His outstretched thumb pleads for a ride.

Hint Slowing ______________________________,

I ______________________________,

whose ______________________________.

5.1 The drive is monotonous.
5.2 The drive is mind-numbing.
5.3 Picking up a stranger makes me uneasy.
5.4 The stranger's motives may be questionable.

Hint ______________________________;

however, ______________________________

______________________________.

6.1 I am like most people.
6.2 I have heard stories about hitchhikers.
6.3 The stories are chilling.
6.4 The hitchhikers attack good samaritans.
6.5 The hitchhikers take advantage of them.

Hint Like ______________, I ______________

______________________________.

7.1 The young man stands lean and wiry.
7.2 He is in blue denim.
7.3 The blue denim is sweltering.
7.4 He has a satchel at his feet.
7.5 He has a bedroll at his feet.

Hint ______________________________,

with ______________________________.

8.1 The sunlight hammers down.
8.2 I hesitate for just an instant.
8.3 I glance uneasily in his direction.
8.4 I make my decision.

Hint As ______________, ______________

before ______________________________.

Writing Tip Clusters 3 and 5 use semicolons. See "Transitions" in Toolbox, Unit 7; and "Semicolons" in Unit 9.

Invitation Do you pick up the hitchhiker? If so, describe what happens. If not, explain the reasons why you choose not to.

➔ Major Move

Looking back, you can remember certain moves you made and how they changed your life. For Sharon as well, things will be different.

1.1 The curtains were down.
1.2 Afternoon light flooded the apartment.
1.3 The light was from the tall west windows.
1.4 The windows overlooked the street.

Hint With ______________, ______________

______________________________.

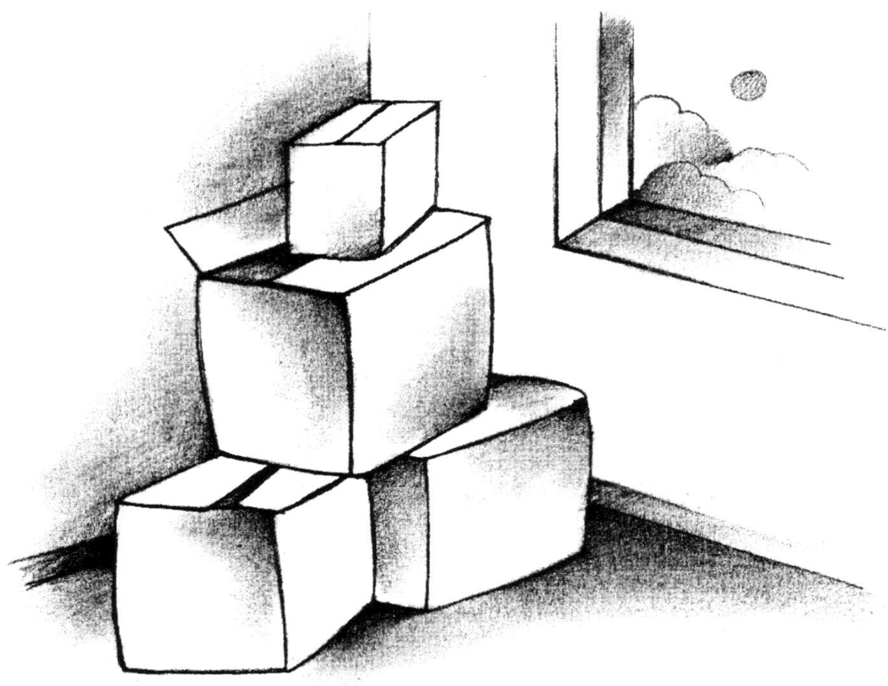

2.1 Cardboard boxes were neatly stacked.
2.2 The boxes were bulging.
2.3 They were near the door.
2.4 They were the result of two nights' work.

Hint Bulging ______________________________________,

the ______________________________________.

3.1 Inside them were personal effects.
3.2 She valued them deeply.
3.3 She wasn't sure why she still kept them.

Hint ______________________________________,

even though ______________________________________.

4.1 Sharon padded across the room.
4.2 The room was hollow-sounding.
4.3 Sharon leaned against the boxes.
4.4 Her eyes were closed.
4.5 This was to shut back the tears.

Hint ______________________________,

with ______________________________.

5.1 Then she heard a car's horn.
5.2 It honked from the curb out front.
5.3 Its sound was abrupt.
5.4 Its sound was impatient.

Hint Then ______________________________,

its sound ______________________________.

6.1 Sharon glanced out the window.
6.2 Sharon waved to the cab driver.
6.3 She took one last look at the apartment.
6.4 She would miss the apartment.

Hint Glancing ______________, Sharon ______________

______________________________.

7.1 Challenges were elsewhere.
7.2 Opportunities were elsewhere.
7.3 New friends were elsewhere.
7.4 She would make the best of her decision.

Hint ______________, ______________, ______________,

and ______________________________.

8.1 Sharon gave herself a salute.
8.2 The salute was thumbs-up.
8.3 This was in the hall mirror.
8.4 Sharon smiled bravely.
8.5 Sharon whispered, "Good luck!"

Hint As ______________________________,
______________________________!

Writing Tip To combine cluster 5, delete *was* in sentences 5.3 and 5.4. See "Absolutes" in Toolbox, Unit 7.

Invitation In a paragraph that *precedes* this exercise, give background for Sharon's move. *Or* write about a move that changed your life.

Greenhouse Effect

Today, everyone seems to be talking—and worrying—about global warming and the greenhouse effect. What do you think?

1.1 Combustion releases energy.
1.2 Energy is essential for modern life.
1.3 It also releases carbon dioxide (CO_2).

Hint ______________________________;
however, ______________________________.

2.1 Concentrations of CO_2 continue to rise.
2.2 The concentrations are in the atmosphere.
2.3 Industries burn fossil fuels.
2.4 Automobiles burn fossil fuels.
2.5 The burning is relentless.

Hint ______________________________

as ______________________________.

3.1 The effects of CO_2 buildup are still unknown.
3.2 Many scientists predict a "greenhouse effect."
3.3 It would result in global warming.

Hint Although ______________________________,

______________________________.

4.1 They think this could happen.
4.2 CO_2 could form a gas layer.
4.3 The layer would trap the earth's heat.
4.4 The layer would raise average temperatures.
4.5 The temperatures are around the world.

Hint ______________________________,

raising ______________________________.

5.1 Such warming could affect weather patterns.
5.2 Such warming could have devastating effects.
5.3 The effects would be in the polar regions.
5.4 Massive ice caps are located there.

Hint By affecting ______________, ______________

______________________________,

where ______________________________.

6.1 A 6-degree rise would melt ice sheets.
6.2 The ice sheets are in the northern hemisphere.
6.3 Rising seas would inundate Antarctica.
6.4 The ice averages 6,000 feet thick there.

Hint ______________________________,

and ______________________________,

______________________________.

7.1 This is according to some geologists.
7.2 Seas would rise 20 feet in 200 years.
7.3 This would be a disaster for many nations.
7.4 The disaster would be unprecedented.

Hint According ______________, ______________—

an ______________________________.

8.1 The world's ports would be flooded.
8.2 The world's coastal cities would be flooded.
8.3 Geography would be forever altered.
8.4 Commerce would be forever altered.

Hint Because ______________________________,

______________________________.

Writing Tip Use an appositive for emphasis in cluster 7. See "Appositives" in Toolbox, Unit 7.

Invitation Develop a follow-up paragraph using this sentence—a true one—as your opener: *Global temperatures have risen 2 degrees in the last 30 years.*

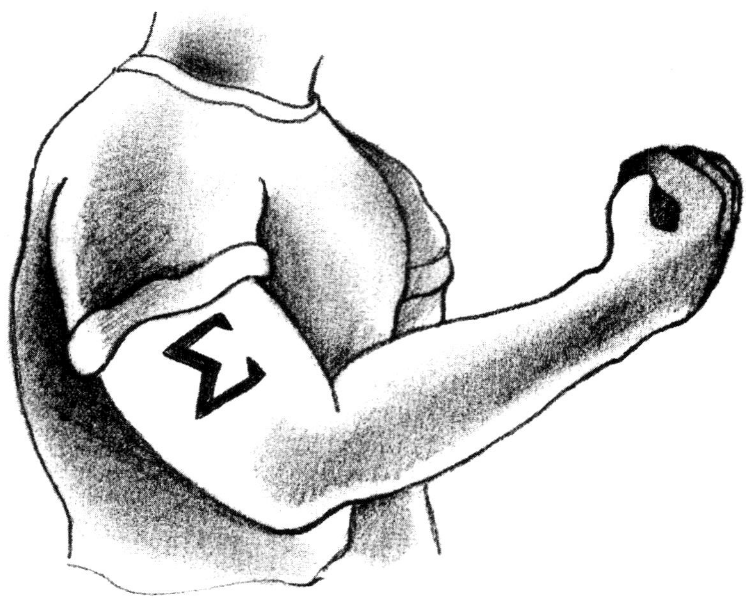

➔ *Human Branding*

Is branding a form of higher consciousness or a way of vandalizing the human body? You decide.

1.1 Fraternity brothers gather around.
1.2 One of their members takes off his shirt.
1.3 He agrees to be branded with a coat hanger.
1.4 The coat hanger is twisted into a Greek letter.

Hint ______________________________

as ______________________________.

2.1 Someone heats the branding iron over a flame.
2.2 Another holds ice on the young man's shoulder.
2.3 This is to numb the flesh.

Hint While ______________________________,

______________________________.

3.1 The coat hanger glows red-hot.
3.2 The room grows tense.
3.3 The room grows quiet.

Hint With ______________________________,
______________________________.

4.1 Branding leaves a permanent scar.
4.2 This young man feels loyalty.
4.3 The loyalty is to those around him.
4.4 The loyalty is a sense of brotherhood.

Hint Branding ______________________________,
but ______________________________ —
a sense ______________________________.

5.1 Something happens in just a few moments.
5.2 The young man's shoulder bears a stigma.
5.3 The stigma is permanent.
5.4 The stigma expresses love for his fraternity.

Hint In ______________, the ______________
______________________________.

6.1 Tears form in his eyes.
6.2 His frat brothers laugh.
6.3 His frat brothers shake his hand.
6.4 His frat brothers get ready to celebrate.

Hint Tears ______________________________,
______________, and ______________.

7.1 The young man is now part of the group.
7.2 The young man is no longer an outsider.

Hint Now ______________________________,
the ______________________________.

8.1 Yet he wonders about his decision.
8.2 He wonders whether he did the right thing.

Hint Yet ______________________________ —
______________________________.

Writing Tip Try using forms of the *appositive* in clusters 4 and 8. See "Appositives" in Toolbox, Unit 7.

Invitation Like branding, tattoos and body piercing are sometimes used to symbolize group loyalty or to express identity. What is your view of such actions?

➔ Getting Organized

Organizing from scratch is hard work. Sometimes the key to success is persistence coupled with a change of pace. And perhaps luck?

1.1 It is approaching midnight.
1.2 A young writer turns words and phrases.
1.3 The writer thinks about possibilities.
1.4 The possibilities are for organization.

Hint ______________________________,
thinking ______________________________.

2.1 Things seem confused.
2.2 Things seem muddled.
2.3 The muddle is hopeless.
2.4 Things seem without direction.

Hint ________________, ________________, ________________.

3.1 Notes litter the work table.
3.2 The notes await assembly into a structure.
3.3 The structure will be logical.
3.4 The structure will be well-built.

Hint Notes ____

____ table.

4.1 The writer stares at the notes.
4.2 The writer tries to imagine a design.
4.3 The design is coherent and interesting.
4.4 The design is a blueprint for writing.

Hint Staring ____________________, ____________________

__________________________, a blueprint ____________________.

5.1 Questions reverberate like echoes.
5.2 The questions are familiar.
5.3 The questions are unanswered.

Hint Familiar ____.

6.1 The writer paces to the window with a sigh.
6.2 The sigh is tired and frustrated.
6.3 The writer looks out into a night.
6.4 The night is cloudless.

Hint With ____________________, ____________________

____.

7.1 It feels good to relax for a moment.
7.2 It feels good not to stare at notes.
7.3 The notes represent hours of research.
7.4 The research was in the library.

Hint It ____

____.

8.1 This is a moment of relaxed attention.
8.2 The night's quiet can do its work.
8.3 The writer feels a sudden glimmer.
8.4 The glimmer is unexpected.
8.5 The glimmer is an idea for organization.

Hint In this moment ____________________,

the ____________________________________,

an ____________________________________.

Writing Tip Clusters 4 and 8 lend themselves to appositives at the end of each combined sentence. See "Appositives" in Toolbox, Unit 7.

Invitation In a follow-up paragraph, introduce your thoughts on getting organized for writing when you can't find a direction.

The Pawnbroker

The world is filled with characters—each unique and different. What details help you to see and know the following character?

1.1 The pawnbroker moves behind his counter.
1.2 The pawnbroker surveys his estate.
1.3 His survey is done with a cat's cunning.
1.4 The cunning is quiet.

Hint Moving ______________________, ______________________

____.

2.1 He keeps his gray eyes glazed.
2.2 He keeps his gray eyes bored.
2.3 He sizes up customers.
2.4 The customers wander in from the street.
2.5 The customers handle his merchandise.

Hint He ______________________________________

who ______________________________________.

3.1 His face is like a rubber mask.
3.2 The mask is loosely fitting.
3.3 His voice is a whisper.
3.4 The whisper is raspy.
3.5 The whisper is from years of smoking.

Hint ______________________________________,

and ______________________________________.

4.1 Wisps of hair hang over his ears.
4.2 The hair is limp and graying.
4.3 The ears are fleshy.

Hint Wisps ______________________________________.

5.1 His appearance and manner belie a mind.
5.2 His appearance is disheveled.
5.3 His manner is rude.
5.4 The mind is razor-quick.

Hint His ______________________________________.

6.1 He knows the value of all items.
6.2 The items are unclaimed.
6.3 The items gather dust in his window.
6.4 He knows how to work customers.

Hint He ______________________________;

moreover, ______________________________.

7.1 Years of business have honed his skills.
7.2 His skills are for negotiating.
7.3 Years of business have taught him lessons.
7.4 The lessons are hard-won.

Hint Years ______________________________.

8.1 He may act wounded by each sale.
8.2 He may act bewildered by each sale.
8.3 He makes a profit on every transaction.
8.4 The profit is substantial.

Hint While ______________________________,

he ______________________________.

Writing Tip Try a *not only . . . but also* construction in cluster 7. See "Coordinators" in Toolbox, Unit 6.

Invitation Develop a paragraph describing an unforgettable person you have seen or known. Make sure to "show" as well as "tell."

➡ *Upward Mobility*

All of us want to "fit in" and be successful. Is there still room for individuality in American business and corporate life?

1.1 Young trainees ease into the elevator.
1.2 The trainees are freshly combed.
1.3 The door closes with a hiss.
1.4 The hiss is faintly mocking.

Hint ______________________________,

and ______________________________.

2.1 Their eyes remain fixed on numbers.
2.2 The numbers are above the door.
2.3 The elevator lifts with an electric hum.

Hint ______________________________

as ______________________________.

3.1 They have physical differences.
3.2 The physical differences are minor.
3.3 Their similarities in appearance are striking.

Hint Although______________________________,

their ______________________________.

4.1 Each trainee has a face.
4.2 The face is earnest.
4.3 The face shows ambition.
4.4 The ambition is youthful.

Hint Each______________________________.

5.1 Each wears a jacket.
5.2 The jacket is fashionably conservative.
5.3 The jacket is matched to trim slacks.
5.4 The slacks are cuffless.

Hint Each ______________________________.

6.1 Each has a silk tie.
6.2 The tie has muted colors.
6.3 The tie has a bold stickpin.
6.4 Each carries a leather briefcase.
6.5 The briefcase is tastefully finished.

Hint Each ______________________________,

and ______________________________.

7.1 All have the same stamped-out look.
7.2 All have the same well-rounded appearance.
7.3 It is as if they were produced from a mold.
7.4 The mold shapes workers for corporate life.

Hint All ______________________________—

as if ______________________________.

8.1 Their lives are like the elevator they ride.
8.2 Their lives appear greased and grooved.
8.3 Their lives follow the numbers to a final "Exit."
8.4 Their own cubicle awaits there.

Hint Like ______________, ______________,

following ______________________________,

where ______________________________.

Writing Tip Clusters 2 and 3 use two very common patterns of subordination. See "Subordinators" in Toolbox, Unit 6.

Invitation What? No women? Broaden the description to include women. Use the connector *or* to introduce women's apparel and accessories. What point is being made in "Upward Mobility"?

➔ White Christmas

Bing Crosby's "White Christmas" is the largest-selling recording of all time. Does the song evoke positive memories for you?

1.1 Light glared from a globe.
1.2 The light was raw.
1.3 The light was white.
1.4 The globe was uncovered.
1.5 It was high on the ceiling.

Hint Raw ______________________________________.

2.1 The room had a mattress.
2.2 The mattress was without blankets.
2.3 The mattress was without bedframe.
2.4 The room had a wash basin.
2.5 The wash basin sagged from the wall.

Hint ______________________________________

and ______________________________________.

3.1 On the shelf was a frying pan.
3.2 The pan was soot-blackened.
3.3 The shelf held utensils.
3.4 The utensils were bent.
3.5 The utensils were stained.

Hint On ______________________________

that ______________________________.

4.1 Dark smoke swirled in the fireplace.
4.2 Flames licked at wood.
4.3 The wood was charred.
4.4 The wood was from a bedframe.
4.5 The bedframe was broken.

Hint ______________________________

as ______________________________.

5.1 The fire gave off little heat.
5.2 Two people huddled close to it.
5.3 They were bundled in winter coats.

Hint Although______________________________,

______________________________ it.

6.1 The woman had auburn hair.
6.2 Her hair was graying.
6.3 Her hair was pulled back into a bun.
6.4 Her face was etched with lines.
6.5 The etching was deep.

Hint ______________________________,

and ______________________________.

7.1 The man's face was chapped.
7.2 The man's face was scowling.
7.3 It had watery blue eyes.
7.4 It had a red-veined nose.

Hint ______________ , ______________,

had ______________________________.

8.1 Their breath was white.
8.2 Their breath was frosty.
8.3 They waited silently for food.
8.4 The food was due to arrive soon.
8.5 The food was from the Salvation Army.

Hint With ____________, ________________

that ________________________________.

9.1 The man touched his wife.
9.2 His wife sat unmoving.
9.3 Her hands were folded in her lap.
9.4 Her hands were gloved.

Hint ________________, who ______________,

with ________________________________.

10.1 She looked up at him.
10.2 She had a tired smile.
10.3 She murmured something.
10.4 "I'm dreaming of a white Christmas."

Hint Looking ________________________,

she ________________________________.

Writing Tip Try putting adjectives *after* the noun in cluster 7. See "Adjectives" in Toolbox, Unit 6.

Invitation Write a "White Christmas" scene from your own memory—either cheerful or sad.

UNIT 4

Shaping and Revising

The beautiful part of writing is that you don't have to get it right the first time—unlike, say, a brain surgeon.

—Robert Cormier

In Unit 3, you learned about two kinds of speech—words you speak aloud (outer speech) and words you hear inside your head (inner speech). You learned that inner speech is closely associated with freewriting and drafting: the more clearly you hear a voice inside, the more likely you are to draft clearly and precisely.

But generating and planning in Unit 2, and freewriting and drafting in Unit 3, are preliminaries to the main event: ***shaping and revising,*** our topic in Unit 4. Shaping and revising enable you to clarify and develop your meaning. You may add details, rearrange ideas for emphasis, qualify certain statements, or change your wording. Through shaping and revision, you improve your writing, from the reader's viewpoint.

REVISION: THE HEART OF THE WRITING PROCESS

In this unit, you'll see that revision is the heart of the writing process, and you'll consider strategies for revision. You'll also find that it takes *courage* to make changes in text.

Finding the Courage to Revise

Sometimes the first draft is the best draft. When Moses received the ten commandments and carved them in stone, for example, no revision was deemed necessary—or possible. However, for most of us whose first drafts are not divinely inspired, revision is a fact of life. Rarely are our first words perfectly crafted or our first meanings perfectly clear.

Nevertheless, we often try to avoid revision. Do any of these excuses sound familiar?

Revision takes time.
It requires hard thinking.
It makes a mess of a clean document.
It can go on and on, with no end in sight.

We may try to avoid revising because we see writing as a one-step process rather than a process with several steps. Or perhaps we see revision as a sign of deficiency and weakness rather than a sign of strength. Perhaps we're afraid to confront what we don't know about a subject. Perhaps we have self-doubts that make us reluctant to revise; after all, what if we can't think of the right words or the right examples?

When we think of revision as something to be avoided, we're assuming that if we were smarter, or better organized, or more talented, we wouldn't have to revise. But that assumption is wrong.

The fact is that all good writers revise. You may be surprised to learn that highly skilled writers generally revise *more* than writers whose skills are undeveloped: indeed, research shows that skilled writers not only make more textual changes but also make more extensive changes. Therefore, *as your writing skills increase, you're likely to revise more*, not less.

Admittedly, it takes courage to revise—to read and reread your own words with care. But it's helpful to realize that the more skillful you become, the more you'll revise. Moreover, if you're prepared to invest time in revision, you'll find it intellectually exciting. Simply *paying attention* will help you see gaps in logic, undeveloped paragraphs, and irrelevant points. The more you study your own writing, the more it will teach you.

Becoming Your Own First Reader

As a writer, you first wear a "creative hat." You take notes, freewrite, scribble on the backs of envelopes; and you draft a text, in your notebook, say, or on a word processor. One way or another, you find words and get them down. Eventually, though, you put on a second hat: a "critical hat" for self-evaluation.

Actually, your critical hat belongs to an imaginary ***first reader,*** a hypothetical person who considers the text with care. This reader is fair and generous, praising you for the parts of your draft that make good sense or hold special interest. However, this reader also squints a critical eye at the parts that need revision.

Becoming your own first reader requires you to "doubt" your text—to ask questions about it and raise objections to it. What examples support your generalizations? Why are your paragraphs organized as they are? How is each of your points relevant? What is your main idea? When you ask questions like these, you are thinking more deeply about your writing. Your comments—which can actually be written in the margin—provide you with cues for revision.

Of course, close reading takes time; it can't be rushed. To slow down your reading, you'll find it helpful to read one paragraph at a time, outlining as you go along. Reading slowly and making an outline will often reveal lapses in logic or thin development. Whispering the text aloud is another strategy for close reading. This helps you *hear* and *see* where changes may be necessary.

A first reader reads with purpose, with key questions in mind. Here are some useful questions:

- What is my main point? Does everything contribute to that main idea? What could be added or deleted?
- What is the topic of each paragraph? Are these the best points to achieve my aim?
- Does the order of paragraphs make sense? Could I add, delete, or combine points?
- Is each paragraph clearly and fully developed? Is all the material relevant?
- Do any sentences interrupt my reading? Do any words or phrases seem awkward?

In follow-up readings, you may also ask questions about your purpose, your audience, your tone; the level of interest you're achieving; your transitions; or anything else you regard as important to good writing.

As a first reader, your goal is to improve readability. To do this, you compare your aims as a writer with what you have actually said. In short, you read beyond or *through* your words. You see what *might* be there. Revision is really a process of envisioning your text again, as the term implies (*re-vision*).

Developing a new vision of your text demands all the commitment, intelligence, and verbal savvy you can muster. You may need to add or delete paragraphs. You may need to cut out or compress some sections so that the writing reads more forcefully or more smoothly. You may need to rearrange ideas for emphasis. You may need to change particular words.

Remember that revising requires a shift in role—from *producing* ideas to *evaluating* them. In becoming a first reader, you ask tough questions that lead to changes. When you revise, you're always a learner; and as we noted earlier, learning to revise takes courage.

MANAGING THE PROCESS OF REVISION

What to Focus On

Expert writers do not revise haphazardly. First, they focus on large, global issues: content, organization, development. Next, they deal with style and grammatical details. It is only when they are satisfied with the basic thrust of their message that they turn to the finer points of expression.

To put it another way, in writing—as in life—it's best to deal with first things first. After all, why sweat the details if the basic message needs attention? If you're a writer who takes the *reverse* approach—dealing first with mechanics, punctuation, and spelling instead of with content and organization—you should reconsider your strategy. Ask your partners in a response group to help you with questions of content, organization, and development first. After getting help in those areas, shift your attention to style and form.

Increasing your expertise in writing means developing *awareness* of what needs to be revised. If your essay lacks information, your revision should focus on new research, not on aimless tinkering with old material. If your essay lacks style and sizzle, you probably need to work with its language.

Tips for Revising

Here are some helpful tips for managing revisions. Adhering to these principles will save you grief.

First, as you budget time for writing, *plan to spend at least half your time revising*. If a paper is due in two weeks, for instance, at least one week should be reserved for revision.

Second, if you are working with a PC or word processor, do most of your actual revision on "hard copy," not on a monitor. This strategy ensures that your total effort will be considered, not just a narrow window of text on a screen.

Third, if you're working with handwritten text, try to use photocopies for revisions, rather than the original. Having a clean backup copy can save you hours of work, so it's particularly useful if you're up against a tight deadline.

Fourth, double-space or (preferably) triple-space your lines, and leave margins. Write, type, or print out only on the front side of each sheet of paper, and revise only on the front side. All this will give you enough room for changes; it will also let you cut and tape pieces of text if necessary.

Fifth, number your paragraphs, especially as you add, delete, or reorganize your material. Numbered paragraphs will help you prepare accurate final copy. Incidentally, there's no need to change the numbering system if you add a new section to your paper. At the point where a new section will be inserted, simply repeat the identifying number followed by letters (a, b, c, etc.).

Sixth, if you are moving paragraphs or sentences around, you may find it useful to draw lines and arrows in your text. But if these lines and arrows get confusing, try cutting and pasting, as noted above. You can chop a paper into sections—such as paragraphs—and work with those. Tape the sections onto fresh sheets of paper, leaving plenty of room for transitional sentences or new material. Don't forget to renumber your paragraphs.

Finally, remember that it's easy to introduce *new* errors as you revise. New errors may creep in, for example, if handwritten words or passages haven't been integrated into the original. To be on the safe side, *read your revisions aloud* and recopy any extensive or complex revisions. If changes are minor, though, recopying is a waste of time.

SENTENCE COMBINING AS A TOOL FOR REVISION

In this section, you'll practice three ways of revising your writing: adding details, exploring sentence options, and expanding and elaborating sentences.

Adding Details

First, let's practice ***adding details*** to sentences and paragraphs. This represents one way to revise an existing text.

For example, suppose you've combined sentences and produced a six-sentence paragraph that looks likes this:

> STUDY SESSION
> (1) It is past midnight and time for bed. (2) An all-night music station lulls me with monotonous rhythms, and a space heater pumps warm air across my feet. (3) My brain remains inert and disengaged, unwilling to function. (4) Finally, a powerful tide carries me deep into dream. (5) I am totally alone, listening to smooth waves whisper against stone-strewn sands. (6) I am thinking that being here is better than studying for midterm exams.

While this paragraph is clearly written, it could be revised by adding sentences. You might challenge yourself to produce a *twelve-sentence* paragraph by writing a new sentence *between* each two original sentences. To make these additional sentences, try to picture the scene that the six original sentences depict. After you read each original sentence, ask yourself questions. After sentence 1, for example, you might ask: "What is happening?" Your answer to that question would be an additional sentence.

The result of adding sentences will be an enriched narrative. Compare the following twelve-sentence version with the original; the added sentences are *italicized:*

> STUDY SESSION
> (1) It is past midnight and time for bed. (2) *Blinking at the words in my textbook—words that must be read before morning—my eyes burn with fatigue.* (3) An all-night music station lulls me with monotonous

rhythms, and a space heater pumps warm air across my feet. (4) *I have repeatedly read a text passage, but nothing is happening.* (5) My brain remains inert and disengaged, unwilling to function. (6) *As I put my head down and close my eyes, sleep washes in like a white, murmuring wave.* (7) Finally, a powerful tide carries me deep into dream. (8) *Lying on a sandy shore, I am far from the reality of tomorrow's exam.* (9) I am totally alone, listening to smooth waves whisper against stone-strewn sands. (10) *Soft light from a gentle sun warms my face.* (11) I am thinking that being here is better than studying for midterm exams. (12) *And then I wake up.*

As this example shows, writing and inserting additional sentences will develop both your revising skills and your imagination.

It's an interesting challenge to add your own sentences to sentences constructed in sentence-combining (SC) activities. Of course, there's no rule saying that you must make additional sentences for each SC exercise—and if you do add sentences, there's no rule saying how many new sentences you must add to each exercise. You may, for instance, choose to put three or four of your own new sentences between a pair you've combined. You're in charge of adding sentences.

Exploring Sentence Options

The SC activities for Unit 4 will help you explore many ***sentence options***—what linguists call ***syntax***. The SC activities here (they start on page 102) are "open" exercises, which have no "hints," "closure clues," or "target" answers. For each cluster, your aim is to produce various possible sentences and then choose the specific sentence you prefer. A team approach to ***open combining*** can be very helpful, since it alerts you to new patterns of sentence construction—patterns you might overlook on your own.

Practice in choosing a "best" sentence from among several right answers will help you develop as a writer. In fact, this kind of practice is absolutely essential for success in revising. Such practice *trains your ear* to notice how sentences differ in clarity, rhythm, and contextual "fit."

To understand how open combining works, let's look at an example. Imagine that you are teamed up with one or two writing partners, listening to possible sentences.

Suppose that your team has been working on the cluster shown in example 1 and has created possible sentences 1X, 1Y, and 1Z:

Example 1

Communism collapsed in the Soviet Union.
Americans breathed a sigh of relief.
The threat of nuclear war was greatly reduced.
The threat was ominous and persistent.

1x When communism collapsed in the Soviet Union, Americans breathed a sigh of relief because the ominous and persistent threat of nuclear war was greatly reduced.

or

1y The collapse of communism in the Soviet Union caused Americans to breathe a sigh of relief: the threat of nuclear war—ominous and persistent—was greatly reduced.

or

1z With the ominous, persistent threat of nuclear war reduced greatly by communism's collapse in the Soviet Union, Americans breathed a sigh of relief.

Feeling pleased with these options, your team goes on to a second cluster (example 2), which logically follows the first:

Example 2

Something is unfortunate.
Our relief has been short-lived.
Terrorist groups are trying to build atomic bombs.
The bombs could decimate civilian populations.

↓

2x Our relief has been unfortunately short-lived because terrorist groups are trying to build atomic bombs that could decimate civilian populations.

or

2y Unfortunately, with terrorist groups trying to build atomic bombs that could decimate civilian populations, our relief has been short-lived.

or

2z It is unfortunate how short-lived our relief has been: terrorist groups are trying to build atomic bombs, and these could decimate civilian populations.

Then your group goes to work on a third cluster (example 3):

Example 3

The threat of global war may be reduced.
Other threats have escalated.
These threats include nuclear terrorism.
These threats include urban guerrilla warfare.

↓

3x Global war may be a reduced threat, but others—including nuclear terrorism and urban guerrilla warfare—have escalated.

or

3y There has been a reduction in threat from global war; however, nuclear terrorism and urban guerrilla warfare now threaten to escalate.

or

3z While the threat of global war may be reduced, other threats have escalated—among them, nuclear terrorism and urban guerrilla warfare.

Your group has now produced nine sentences—raw material for 27 different paragraphs! Deciding which of the possible sentences and paragraphs are best will depend on your individual writing styles. Here's one paragraph for you to consider; it is made up of sentences 1X, 2Y, and 3X:

> (1X) When communism collapsed in the Soviet Union, Americans breathed a sigh of relief because the ominous and persistent threat of nuclear war was greatly reduced. (2Y) Unfortunately, with terrorist groups trying to build atomic bombs that could decimate civilian populations, our relief has been short-lived. (3X) Global war may be a reduced threat, but others—including nuclear terrorism and urban guerrilla warfare—have escalated.

Clearly, SC exercises like these have more than one right answer. In fact, the whole point of "open" combining is to explore stylistic options and then choose what you regard as the *best* sentences.

Exploring sentence options with your group represents an important way of revising. But you need to remember to *take your time* as you do SC exercises involving syntax. Listen to the options you produce, and choose the clearest and most direct sentences to construct effective paragraphs. Your ear will benefit from such practice.

Here's what Peter Elbow, an authority on writing and an expert teacher, has to say on this subject: "The ear, in the last analysis, is the most trustworthy and powerful organ for learning syntax; and fortunately it is the easiest to teach—as long as we give some time to it."

Expanding and Elaborating Sentences

"Open" SC exercises also give you practice in ***expanding and elaborating sentences***. As you saw earlier, paragraphs can be revised by adding complete sentences. Sentence expansion or elaboration is similar, except that details are added to existing sentences. Expanding SC patterns enables you to elaborate meanings in ways that make sense to you. This represents a third way of revising. In fact, revising by expansion and elaboration mirrors what you often do with your portfolio or in class assignments.

To see how the process of expanding and elaborating works, let's now consider some examples that continue our sample exercise on nuclear terrorism.

Here are three more clusters (examples 4, 5, and 6):

Example 4

Imagine a world.
Terrorists have access to weapons.
The weapons could inflict mass destruction.

Example 5

This prospect is horrible to consider.
To ignore a problem seems irrational.
The problem has consequences.
The consequences are potentially catastrophic.

Example 6

Civilization must rehearse scenarios.
The scenarios provide responses to terrorists.
The responses are calculated.
The terrorists may inhabit a future world.

Of course, we can produce several different options for each of these clusters. Here is one possible paragraph, made up of one possible sentence for each cluster; note that it has *47 words*:

> (4) Imagine a world where terrorists have access to weapons that could inflict mass destruction. (5) This prospect seems horrible to consider; however, to ignore a problem with potentially catastrophic consequences seems irrational. (6) Civilization must rehearse scenarios that provide calculated responses to terrorists who may inhabit a future world.

This paragraph has an interesting variety of sentence patterns. Think of these patterns as a *base* for sentence expansion.

Now look at the revised paragraph that follows (the expansions are in *italics*), and compare it with the original paragraph above. This revision has *78 words*. Which version do you prefer?

Revision

(4) Imagine a world where *a handful of crazed, renegade* terrorists have access to weapons that could inflict mass destruction, *particularly in densely populated urban areas*. (5) This *dreadful* prospect seems horrible to consider; however, to ignore a problem with potentially catastrophic consequences seems irrational—*like an ostrich sticking its head in the sand*. (6) Civilization *has no choice but to* rehearse scenarios that provide calculated—*even cunning*— responses to nuclear terrorists who may *try to hold a future world hostage*.

Is longer better? Not necessarily. In this case, however, you may well conclude that the revised paragraph—the 78-word version—makes a stronger, more emphatic case than the original version. This emphasis was achieved by sentence expansion, by elaborating the basic patterns.

In the SC exercises for Unit 4, feel free to expand sentences. Expanding sentences is a way to practice a revising skill that all successful writers consider basic to their craft. (Later, in Unit 5, you will practice another skill: trimming flab from overly long sentences.)

WORKSHOP PORTFOLIO FOR UNIT 4

In the SC exercises for Unit 4, you'll work on additions, sentence options, and expansions. These are important skills for shaping and revising text. The follow-up "Writing Invitations" that you accept after these SC exercises will add more pieces to your workshop portfolio. Let's consider how you can pull material from your portfolio to develop even further.

Option 1: A Personality Profile Examine your portfolio to find pieces related to people—either individuals or ethnic and cultural groups. Which writings interest you? Which can be expanded? Writing about others clearly, fairly, and informatively is a very important skill.

Decide whether you want to write about an individual or a group. If you are going to focus on an individual, you'll need to describe the person's appearance and character. If you are going to focus on a group, you'll need to describe typical characteristics (for example, how group members look and behave together). Ask yourself how the individual or the group is personally significant to you. Considering significance will help you find a way into your writing.

In addition to including details, you will probably make certain judgments about the individual or group you're discussing. Such statements of opinion may either precede or follow the examples you use. Remember that without specific examples, your judgments will seem hollow to your reader. Remember too that your judgments can reveal as much about *you* as they do about your subject.

Option 2: An "I Search" Report As you read your portfolio, you'll probably find several pieces that present information or explain ideas. Such writing may also analyze causes, classify experiences, or make comparisons. Which topics hold particular interest for you? Which ones would you like to know more about?

An "I search" report is a way of pursuing a topic that interests you. Basically, this kind of report is written as a story. Its focus, of course, is your search for information. It has a three-part form:

- (1) What you wanted to find out and why
- (2) What steps you took in searching
- (3) What you learned about your topic

Depending on your topic, you may want to interview experts, conduct an opinion poll or survey, or visit the library. Remember that an "I search" reveals your *process* of learning about your topic, not just your conclusions.

After selecting a topic, try to write the first section of your three-part paper. Get ideas from your response group on ways to collect information; then lay out a plan for your research. As you move forward with your research, be sure to keep notes of where, when, and what you learned. These notes will prove invaluable in writing the second and third sections of your "I search" report.

SC FOR UNIT 4

Directions These SC exercises are "open"—there are *no* "hints," "closure clues," or "target sentences." Work on your own or with a partner to combine each sentence cluster in various ways, exploring stylistic options. Select the sentences you prefer. Then compare your sentences with those written by others, and again make choices.

➡ *Nasty but Nice*

An effective description weaves together various strands of information. Work with the following "personality sketch."

1.1 Nasty is a house cat.
1.2 The house cat is supremely lazy.
1.3 The house cat has white fur.
1.4 The white fur is long.

2.1 She basks in the sun by the hour.
2.2 She surveys her domain with authority.
2.3 Her authority is queenly.

3.1 Her subjects fondle her.
3.2 Her subjects feed her.
3.3 Her subjects are well trained.
3.4 They cater to her every whim.

4.1 Something happens on occasion.
4.2 She rewards them with a low purr.
4.3 She rewards them with a yawn.
4.4 The yawn is bored but contented.

5.1 Chasing mice is beneath her dignity.
5.2 It is an insult to her station.

6.1 Loud music offends her sensibilities.
6.2 Her sensibilities are delicate.
6.3 Her sensibilities are feline.

7.1 All strangers must pay homage.
7.2 They comment on her stature.
7.3 Her stature is regal.

8.1 Her manner is haughty.
8.2 Her appearance is homely.
8.3 No cat could replace Nasty.
8.4 Nasty is one of a kind.

Writing Tip Cluster 4 offers you a chance to make an appositive. See "Appositives" in Part Two, Toolbox, Unit 7.

Invitation Create a "personality sketch" of someone you know, weaving together details of appearance, behavior, and qualities.

Stuck in Time

After high school, friends often go their separate ways to build their own lives. But some may remain behind, reliving the good old days.

1.1 Most of us remember Duane.
1.2 Duane was a star football player.
1.3 The memory is from our high school days.

2.1 He was tall and angular.
2.2 He ran with a loping stride.
2.3 The stride was relaxed.

3.1 The quarterback would send him downfield.
3.2 This was on crucial plays.
3.3 The football would spiral through the lights.
3.4 This brought the crowd to their feet.

4.1 Duane's hands would go up and out.
4.2 His hands were outstretched.
4.3 He scrambled with defenders.
4.4 The defenders clawed at his jersey.

5.1 He was always in the right place.
5.2 He was there at the right time.
5.3 He had incredible timing.

6.1 Now we all wonder about Duane.
6.2 His hair is beginning to thin.
6.3 His weight is creeping up each year.

7.1 He just hangs around town.
7.2 He does odd jobs.
7.3 He drinks more than he should.

8.1 You can see him in the evenings.
8.2 He sits alone in the bleachers.
8.3 He watches the school team practice.

Writing Tip For sentence variety, try opening cluster 2 with *tall* and *angular;* use *whose* as a connector for cluster 6. See "Adjectives" in Toolbox, Unit 6; and "Relative Clauses" in Unit 7.

Invitation Use "Stuck in Time" to open a brief essay that explains why some people have this problem. Or provide a similar character sketch of a person you know from school.

➔ A Favorite Place

Each of us has a favorite place, either in the present or in memory. Can you create the details of your favorite place for a reader?

1.1 This place is a sanctuary for birds.
1.2 This place is a sanctuary for deer.
1.3 It is nestled at a bend in the river.

2.1 The property slopes from road to river.
2.2 The property has been landscaped with boulders.
2.3 The boulders are massive.
2.4 The boulders are from the nearby mountains.

3.1 A silver-leaf maple dominates the yard.
3.2 The maple is enormous.
3.3 The maple has split trunks.
3.4 The maple provides summer shade.

4.1 Beyond the maple is a waterfall.
4.2 Beyond the granite boulders is a waterfall.
4.3 Its white sound fills the green air.

5.1 Beneath the waterfall is a waist-deep pool.
5.2 Brown trout live there in the shadows.
5.3 Their tails waver in the cold water.

6.1 Willows rise up beyond the river's edge.
6.2 Tall grasses rise up beyond the river's edge.
6.3 These provide cover for wildlife.

7.1 The place is quiet.
7.2 This is except for the waterfall.
7.3 This is except for occasional bird calls.

8.1 Come with me for a walk.
8.2 The walk will be along a path.
8.3 The path winds above the river.

Writing Tip Try opening cluster 2 with *sloping*; try adding an *-ing* ending to *waver* in sentence 5.3. See "Participle Phrases" and "Absolutes" in Toolbox, Unit 7.

Invitation Describe a favorite place where you enjoy spending time—or where you used to spend time. Focus on specific details of the place as you write about it.

➔ Student Hangout

Where do you hang out between classes? Sometimes people head for the same spot without really noticing what it looks like.

1.1 Something happens after lunch.
1.2 Signatures are everywhere.
1.3 The signatures are stained.
1.4 The signatures are greasy.

2.1 One table is stacked with a clutter.
2.2 The clutter is messy.
2.3 The clutter is dishes and cups
2.4 The clutter is used food cartons.

3.1 Off to one side is a pizza slice.
3.2 The pizza slice is half-eaten.
3.3 Black flies flit in a dance.
3.4 The dance is nervous.

4.1 A sign stands atop the trash.
4.2 The sign is ironic.
4.3 The sign is folded like a tepee.
4.4 It asks students to bus their own dishes.

5.1 On the counter squats an ashtray.
5.2 The ashtray is makeshift.
5.3 The ashtray is ugly.

6.1 It is a soup bowl.
6.2 Its insides are blackened with ashes.
6.3 The ashes are gray and feathery.

7.1 Into it have been heaped cigarettes.
7.2 Into it have been heaped bread crusts.
7.3 Into it have been heaped poems.
7.4 The poems are written on paper napkins.
7.5 It accepts with indifference.

8.1 "Souper Ashtray" is its label.
8.2 The label is hand-lettered.
8.3 The hand lettering is careful.

Writing Tip Try adding an *-ly* ending to *careful* in cluster 8. See "Adverbs" in Toolbox, Unit 6.

Invitation Describe a place that you often visit as a student—either to study or to socialize. Include details so that your reader can visualize the specific scene you're writing about.

Hand Jive

The United States has rich ethnic diversity. Because of that diversity, it's important to understand the messages that our hands may send.

1.1 Gestures like waves convey greetings.
1.2 Gestures like salutes convey respect.
1.3 Gestures like handshakes convey friendship.

2.1 Equally well known is the gesture of insult.
2.2 It is an extended middle finger.
2.3 This gesture lacks meaning in many countries.

3.1 Different cultures have different codes.
3.2 The codes communicate obscenity.
3.3 The codes communicate insults.

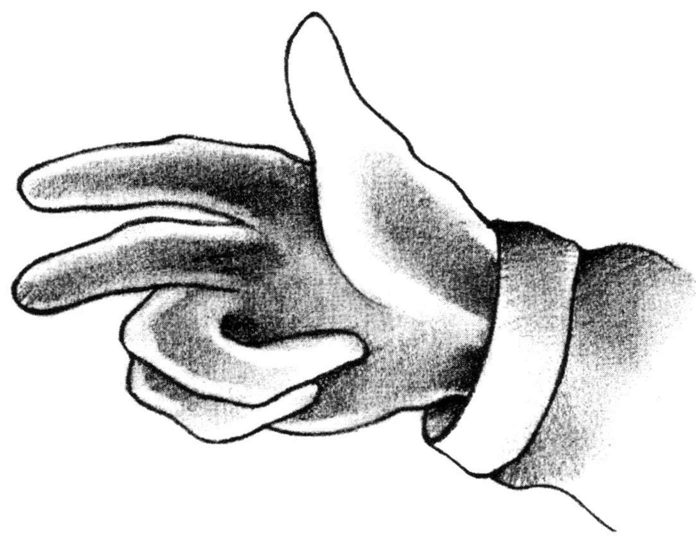

4.1 It is easy to offend others.
4.2 Our offense is unwitting.
4.3 We do not understand their cultural code.
4.4 We make inappropriate gestures.

5.1 The "OK" sign is okay in North America.
5.2 The "OK" sign is familiar.
5.3 The same gesture is "dirty" in Brazil.
5.4 It is "dirty" in many South American countries.

6.1 It is dangerous to extend one's thumb.
6.2 This is when hitchhiking in Sardinia.
6.3 An upturned thumb is considered obscene.
6.4 Motorists may be tempted to get revenge.

7.1 In Greece, don't tuck a thumb between two fingers.
7.2 One finger is your index finger.
7.3 The other is your middle finger.
7.4 This gesture may result in assault.

8.1 The same gesture is acceptable in Latin America.
8.2 The gesture is known as the sign of the "fig."
8.3 It wards off the effects of the evil eye.

Writing Tip Try an appositive—a renaming phrase like this—in cluster 2. See "Appositives" in Toolbox, Unit 7.

Invitation Describe a specific cultural gesture (for example, "high five") that you use regularly. What does this gesture mean to you and your friends?

➔ Opposite Views

When it comes to culture, most of us see our own way as "normal." But maybe our own way is all we know. Is ignorance bliss?

1.1 Most Americans go about their daily business.
1.2 Most Japanese go about their daily business.
1.3 They are unaware of striking contrasts.
1.4 The contrasts are in their cultural behavior.

2.1 Americans always mount horses from the left.
2.2 Japanese approach them from the right.
2.3 The approach is habitual.
2.4 The approach is successful.

3.1 Black is the color of mourning in the United States.
3.2 The color is traditional.
3.3 The Japanese wear white.
3.4 A loved one dies.

4.1 Americans use terms like *northwest* for locations.
4.2 Americans use terms like *southeast* for locations.
4.3 The same direction in Japan would be *westnorth*.
4.4 The same direction in Japan would be *eastsouth*.

5.1 Rowing teams in the United States use a backward motion.
5.2 The motion is for oar strokes.
5.3 Teams in Japan row in a forward direction.

6.1 An American host fills glasses to the rim.
6.2 This is to signal hospitality.
6.3 The same gesture in Japan is rude.
6.4 The same gesture in Japan is impolite.

7.1 American children count.
7.2 They start with a closed fist.
7.3 They extend their fingers in succession.
7.4 Japanese children start with an open hand.
7.5 They bend their fingers inward to count.

8.1 And Americans sit on toilets.
8.2 Their backs are to the water tanks.
8.3 Japanese usually take the opposite approach.
8.4 They face the back of the toilet.

Writing Tip Try using contrast words—*but, yet, however, still, although, while, whereas, conversely, in contrast, on the other hand*. Also, see "Semicolons" in Toolbox, Unit 9.

Invitation Is there a need for more tolerance among ethnic groups? Make your case in writing, using personal experience.

➡ Television Community

Television has changed us. Sometimes we know more about events thousands of miles away than we do about events next door.

1.1 Television enables us to experience history.
1.2 It brings events into our homes.
1.3 It dramatizes their significance.

2.1 Grief was shared by the nation during the 1960s.
2.2 Shame was shared by the nation during the 1960s.
2.3 John F. Kennedy was assassinated.
2.4 Martin Luther King, Jr. was assassinated.
2.5 Robert Kennedy was assassinated.

3.1 Then we experienced a great wave of pride.
3.2 Americans landed successfully on the moon.
3.3 Americans took the first lunar walk in 1969.
3.4 This was "a giant step" for mankind.

4.1 Something happened during the 1970s.
4.2 The Watergate hearings riveted Americans' attention.
4.3 The Iranian hostage crisis riveted Americans' attention.
4.4 These television events were unprecedented.

5.1 Television in the 1980s dramatized economic strife.
5.2 It dramatized the Challenger disaster.
5.3 It dramatized the collapse of communism.

6.1 Something happened during the 1990s.
6.2 Americans saw the beating of Rodney King.
6.3 Americans saw the riots in Los Angeles.
6.4 Americans saw the assault on Reginald Denny.

7.1 Television has made each viewer a participant.
7.2 The participant is a "witness to history."

8.1 Viewers may live thousands of miles apart.
8.2 They share a common core of knowledge.
8.3 The knowledge begins with images from television.
8.4 The images are flickering.

Writing Tip In clusters 3 and 7, you can make appositives. See "Appositives" in Toolbox, Unit 7.

Invitation Consider this sentence as an opener for follow-up writing: "And yet, despite the community of television, many Americans lack a sense of neighborhood or *personal* community."

➔ *Discount Store*

Satire is a writer's weapon for alerting us to the dark spots in a culture. Do you think discount stores provide a worthy target for satire?

1.1 Imagine a team of visitors.
1.2 The visitors are from another galaxy.
1.3 The visitors have been sent to earth.
1.4 Their purpose is to conduct observations.

2.1 What would they say about our discount stores?
2.2 People swarm in great hordes.
2.3 The hordes are jabbering.
2.4 People drag their children behind them.

3.1 They would see mobs of chunky women.
3.2 The women are middle-aged.
3.3 Their hair is in curlers.
3.4 The women claw through merchandise.
3.5 The merchandise is rumpled.

4.1 They would see out-of-shape men.
4.2 The men are looking at exercise equipment.
4.3 They will never use the equipment.

5.1 They would see young girls.
5.2 The girls lounge at cosmetic counters.
5.3 They would see young men.
5.4 The young men impulsively buy new CDs.

6.1 They would hear a voice barking at the crowd.
6.2 The bark comes every five minutes or so.
6.3 It announces "super specials."
6.4 They would see the crowd's movement.
6.5 The movement is toward a flashing light.

7.1 They would probably conclude this.
7.2 Our culture values things.
7.3 It promotes consumption of material goods.
7.4 The consumption is mindless.

8.1 And they would probably recommend this.
8.2 Communication with earth not be initiated.
8.3 The intelligence of our species is dubious.

Writing Tip Notice the parallelism—use of repeated sentence patterns—in this exercise. Also, as you combine clusters 7 and 8, see "Noun Substitutes" in Toolbox, Unit 7.

Invitation Try your hand at satire, using "Discount Store" as a model. Focus on another aspect of our culture that bothers you.

➔ *Drug Abuse*

Using statistics to "prove a point" is a common technique in arguments. Carefully evaluate the *logic* of what follows.

1.1 Many people talk about the evils of marijuana.
1.2 Few discuss the larger problem of alcohol.
1.3 Alcohol also represents a health hazard.
1.4 The health hazard is significant.

2.1 Consider the sobering statistics.
2.2 The statistics concern alcohol consumption.
2.3 The consumption is each year in the United States.
2.4 The consumption is for persons above age 14.

3.1 The statistics are based on reliable data.
3.2 Each person annually consumes 591 cans of beer.
3.3 This equates to 115 bottles of wine.
3.4 This in turn equals 35 fifths of 80-proof vodka.

4.1 One-third of Americans abstain from alcohol.
4.2 One fact seems obvious.
4.3 Drinkers consume much more than the average.
4.4 The average is per capita.
4.5 The average is cited above.

5.1 Consumption actually averages three drinks per day.
5.2 The consumption is for nonabstainers.
5.3 This is an astonishingly high rate.

6.1 Equally shocking is another fact.
6.2 One-tenth of the population consumes half the alcohol.

7.1 Something should come as no surprise.
7.2 Drinking leads to 30 percent of hospital admissions.
7.3 Drinking contributes to 40 percent of arrests.
7.4 The arrests are made by law officers.

8.1 Alcohol causes a liver disease called cirrhosis.
8.2 Cirrhosis is the nation's sixth leading killer.
8.3 Alcohol plays a role in damage to the brain.
8.4 The damage is irreversible.
8.5 It contributes to thousands of auto fatalities.
8.6 The auto fatalities are senseless.

9.1 These are the cold facts.
9.2 These are the indisputable facts.
9.3 Society continues to lecture pot smokers.
9.4 Society continues to stress marijuana's dangers.

10.1 A rational approach leads to one conclusion.
10.2 The conclusion is inescapable.
10.3 Marijuana should be decriminalized immediately.

Writing Tip In cluster 4, try *because* or *since* as an opener and an *it . . . that* construction as you combine. See "Noun Substitutes" in Toolbox, Unit 7.

Invitation This exercise concludes that marijuana should be decriminalized—but why? It might be an argument for making alcohol illegal, but what does it prove about marijuana? Rewrite the conclusion so that it logically follows from the preceding points.

➔ *Not Again*

We've all had one of *those* days—when nothing goes right. Recall one of yours to share with a partner. Then work with Mac's.

1.1 Mac pulled at the door handle.
1.2 It was hot chrome beneath his fingers.
1.3 The car door swung open.
1.4 It squeaked on its worn hinge.

2.1 He slid into the front seat.
2.2 He arched his back.
2.3 He rolled the window down in turns.
2.4 The turns were quick and jerky.

3.1 A glare made him frown into the sunlight.
3.2 The glare was blinding.
3.3 The sunlight was pounding.
3.4 He fumbled the key into the ignition.
3.5 He pumped the gas pedal once.
3.6 He listened to the whir of starter gears.
3.7 He listened to the engine's strain.

4.1 The engine coughed once.
4.2 The engine sputtered in protest.
4.3 The engine fell back to silence.

5.1 Mac was drenched in sweat.
5.2 Mac set his teeth.
5.3 Mac struggled not to lose his temper.
5.4 His struggle was valiant.

6.1 The battery was weak and fading.
6.2 The engine coughed once again.
6.3 The engine then died.

7.1 Mac's fingers twisted the key once more.
7.2 His fingers were tightening with nervousness.
7.3 This time the engine wheezed to life.
7.4 Its exhaust punched out blue smoke.
7.5 The smoke soiled the hot afternoon.

8.1 Exhilaration exploded in a shout.
8.2 The exhilaration was mixed with relief.
8.3 Mac fastened his seat belt.
8.4 Mac slipped the car into gear.
8.5 Mac stepped on the gas.

9.1 He anticipated cool relief.
9.2 The relief was from cooling breezes.
9.3 The car swerved to one side.
9.4 It made a repeated thumping sound.

10.1 "Not again!" Mac shouted.
10.2 His spare tire had just gone flat.

Writing Tip For sentence variety, try opening cluster 5 with *drenched*. In cluster 7, try to embed *tightening* after *fingers*. See "Participle Phrases" in Toolbox, Unit 7.

Invitation Using this exercise as a model, write about an experience in which you had a "not again!" feeling.

Word Power

An old saying claims that "sticks and stones will break your bones, but words will never hurt you." Do you believe it?

1.1 Words seem to have magical powers.
1.2 The powers control how we think.
1.3 The powers control how we act.

2.1 Words generate tensions.
2.2 The words are angry or insulting.
2.3 The tensions lead to physical conflicts.
2.4 The conflicts are between individuals.
2.5 The conflicts are between nations.

3.1 Other words enable people to show sympathy.
3.2 They enable people to overcome loneliness.
3.3 They enable people to express love.

4.1 Some words create blushes.
4.2 Some words create embarrassment.
4.3 The embarrassment is profound.
4.4 The words are vulgar or profane.

5.1 Others heal divisions among families.
5.2 Others join partners together in marriage.
5.3 Others unite people in common causes.
5.4 The causes transcend individual differences.

6.1 Legal words separate people through divorce.
6.2 Legal words create judgments for execution.
6.3 They also enact legislation for social progress.
6.4 They also enable people of color to organize.

7.1 It may appear that words themselves have power.
7.2 This is really an illusion.
7.3 Power resides with people.
7.4 The people understand how words work.

8.1 It is people who possess the power.
8.2 The people are knowledgeable.
8.3 The people are articulate.
8.4 It is not the words themselves.

Writing Tip This exercise works through a series of contrasts. As you combine, see "Relative Clauses" in Toolbox, Unit 7.

Invitation Describe a specific example from your own experience that reinforces the main point of "Word Power."

Native Talents

Our images of Native Americans are shaped by movies depicting the wild west. What do we know about twentieth-century Native Americans?

1.1 Many Native Americans possess talents.
1.2 The talents are unique and unsung.
1.3 These talents have helped build American cities.
1.4 These talents have helped win wars.

2.1 One example is the Mohawk Indians.
2.2 They often worked as construction laborers.
2.3 This was until supervisors saw their poise.
2.4 Their poise was catlike.
2.5 Their poise was in extremely high places.

3.1 High bridges were under construction.
3.2 Tall buildings were under construction.
3.3 Mohawks would walk out on narrow beams.
3.4 Mohawks would walk out on steel girders.
3.5 This was simply out of curiosity.
3.6 This was to see how work was progressing.

4.1 Soon Mohawks were in demand as riveters.
4.2 Their job was to work hundreds of feet up.
4.3 Their job was to join beams with metal bolts.
4.4 Their job was dangerous and high-paying.
4.5 The metal bolts were red-hot.

5.1 The grace of Mohawks became legendary.
5.2 The agility of Mohawks became legendary.
5.3 The fearlessness of Mohawks became legendary.
5.4 They worked on thousands of skyscrapers.
5.5 These included the Empire State Building.
5.6 These included the United Nations Building.

6.1 Navaho Indians proved to be equally gifted.
6.2 Their giftedness was in a different arena.
6.3 American security interests were threatened.
6.4 The threats were grave.
6.5 This was during World War II.

7.1 The Navaho language is so subtle.
7.2 The Navaho language is so complex.
7.3 It is virtually impossible to counterfeit.
7.4 It is virtually impossible to master as an adult.

8.1 Only a few non-natives spoke Navaho in 1942.
8.2 None of these persons was a German spy.
8.3 None of these persons was a Japanese spy.
8.4 American forces saw a way to ensure communications.
8.5 The communications would be safe.

9.1 A team of 420 Navahos became radio operators.
9.2 A team of 420 Navahos became "code talkers."
9.3 They played a role in the war effort.
9.4 The role was highly significant.
9.5 Their code could not be broken by enemies.
9.6 Their code could not be stolen by enemies.

10.1 American troops gained a great tactical advantage.
10.2 They could make quick changes in strategy.
10.3 They could communicate these by radio.
10.4 They could implement them immediately.

Writing Tip Try using *whose* as a connector in cluster 4. Try using *because* as a sentence opener in cluster 8.

Invitation The actor Marlon Brando once rejected an Academy Award—an "Oscar"—for Best Actor, protesting that moviemakers had harmed the identity of American Indians. Do you agree or disagree with Brando's claim? Explain your views in an opinion paper.

UNIT 5

Editing and Proofreading

The language must be careful and must appear effortless. It must not sweat.

—Toni Morrison

In Units 2, 3, and 4 you learned how to generate ideas, create drafts, and revise your work. Here, in Unit 5, we'll focus on strategies for improving the style of your writing and ensuring its correctness.

The process of improving your style is called ***editing.*** When you edit a text, you change the form of sentences to improve their readability. Although there are many ways to edit, we'll concentrate on tightening your language.

The related process of ensuring correctness is called ***proofreading.*** In proofreading, you are alert to details of punctuation, usage, and spelling. As you work with exercises in this unit, you'll improve your proofreading skills.

You probably don't need to be reminded that editing and proofreading are crucial steps in the writing process. Obviously, it would make little sense to generate, draft, and revise a text and then fail to take care of details such as awkward phrasing or punctuation errors.

APPROACHING EDITING

A Context for Editing

Have you ever handed in a paper and had it returned with editing marks—suggestions for changes—that you didn't understand? You thought your work was fine: you consulted a thesaurus to find elegant-sounding words, and you labored over phrases to dress up plain, simple sentences. Why didn't that approach work?

Perhaps you've developed the idea that extra words or polysyllabic words enhance writing. You may think that being "intellectual" means using big words and lots of them. Many student writers unthinkingly accept the notion that "bigger is better" and imitate the mind-numbing double-talk of pompous bureaucrats. Others hope that a patchwork of fancy words, quotations, and clichés will cover gaps in their research or analysis.

It's time to realize that this kind of thinking is wrong. The fact is that *lean, direct sentences* make for the best and strongest writing. Does this surprise you? Consider the matter from the reader's viewpoint. You probably get irritated when authors obfuscate the obvious, and you are grateful when authors don't waste your time.

One function of editing, therefore, is to achieve a lean, direct style. Editing helps you cultivate the habit of getting to the point—speaking your mind with grace, clarity, and intelligence.

To develop editing skills, try to see yourself as a "prose surgeon." Using a pencil or your computer's *delete* key, you'll cut away flab to communicate your message clearly. You'll rearrange sentences to emphasize active voice. You'll write mainly with nouns and verbs, not with adjectives, adverbs, or long strings of prepositional phrases. But you'll try to leave the structure of the text—its muscles and bones—intact.

When should you do your editing? According to the author James Moffett, "Sentences must grow rank before they can be trimmed back." Moffett contends that the analytic work of editing should occur *after* you've developed and organized your message—in other words, *after* you've generated and planned your writing, drafted it, and shaped it through revision. To edit before that point often leads only to a page full of cross-outs, and an upset stomach. Keep in mind that the preliminary stages of the writing process are quite different from editing.

Techniques for Editing

The late Peter De Vries—another author—knew what editing is all about. "When I see a paragraph shrinking under my eyes like a strip of bacon in a skillet," he once said, "I know I'm on the right track." For De Vries, like many other professional writers, editing often meant deleting extra words. His aim was not to write short sentences or short paragraphs. But, out of consideration for his readers, he got to the point by trimming "fat" or "flab" from his writing.

Getting to the point in writing is easier said than done. To begin with, though, you can get rid of redundant, or repetitive, words. The following phrases illustrate redundancy. In each case, instead of using a *pair* of words, you can use just one:

Redundant	*Lean*
each and every	each
hope and trust	hope
full and complete	complete
first and foremost	first
basic and fundamental	basic
totally and completely	completely

Redundancy often appears as unnecessary *categories*. *Huge in size* is one example; why not simply say *huge*? Here are a few more examples:

Redundant	*Lean*
blue in color	blue
period of time	period
modern world of today	modern world
complex set of factors	complex factors
few in number	few
various sorts of effects	various effects
odd type of behavior	odd behavior
kind of redundant phrase	redundant phrase

There are also redundant *modifiers*. For instance, since history is a record of past events, why say *past history?* Just saying *history* works fine. Try editing the phrases below, which contain other redundant modifiers:

Redundant	*Lean*
end result	____________
personal opinion	____________
final outcome	____________
basic essentials	____________
unintended accident	____________
repeat again	____________
future plans	____________
discarded litter	____________
unexpected surprise	____________
terrible tragedy	____________

Many *stock phrases* are redundant. To tighten your writing, why not substitute a single word for a stock phrase? For example, instead of saying *owing to the fact that*, try saying simply *because*. Here are some examples of stock phrases with one-word equivalents:

Redundant	*Lean*
the reason for this is	since
in view of the fact that	because
on the occasion of	when
the way in which	how
despite the fact that	although
come to the realization that	realize
is of the opinion that	thinks
is aware of the fact that	knows
at this point in time	now
at that point in time	then
make an adjustment in	adjust
come into contact with	meet
there is a need for	must
it is necessary that	must
there is a possibility that	may, might, could
has the ability to	can
for the purpose of	or, to
in close proximity to	near
concerns the matter of	about
to the effect that	that
as a matter of fact	actually

In addition to getting rid of redundancies, two other secrets of editing are *shortening noun phrases* and, if possible, *converting nouns into verbs*. Study these two examples:

Flabby

The results of the election for president in 1992 were an indication of the desire of the people for a new set of priorities at the federal level. *(28 words)*

Lean

The 1992 presidential election indicated the people's desire for new federal priorities. *(12 words)*

Flabby

The campaign that was waged with success by Bill Clinton was one that called for an end to the Reagan-Bush policies for the economy which had been in effect for 12 years. *(33 words)*

Lean

Bill Clinton's successful campaign called for an end to 12 years of Reagan-Bush economic policies. *(16 words)*

SC for Practice with Editing

Let's now practice editing with sentence combining (SC). The main editing technique you'll practice here is cutting away extra words. In each exercise, you'll see a sentence cluster and then a combined version labeled "Problem." For each problem sentence, you'll see a word count. Your challenge is to combine the cluster more clearly and directly, using *fewer words*. Compare your total words with the count for the problem sentence, with other students' sentences, and with the sentence given in the Answer Key or provided by your instructor. In this editing game, shorter is better. Remember: clarity, directness, and readability are your goals.

Here's the first cluster, followed by a problem sentence:

Example 1

Writing sentences is harder than it looks.
The sentences are clear.
The sentences are direct.
Writing sentences is not impossible.

↓

Problem The writing of sentences which not only are clear but also are direct is a task of considerable difficulty in spite of the fact that it may look rather easy; nevertheless, it is not an impossibility to construct sentences of this kind. *(42 words)*

If you reexamine the cluster in example 1, you'll be able to think of alternative ways to combine. Here's one alternative:

1x It is harder than it looks to write sentences that are clear and direct; however, the task is not impossible. *(20 words)*

Obviously, 1X represents a great improvement over the problem sentence. It communicates the same message in less than half as many words. However, let's see if we can do even more editing:

1y Writing clear, direct sentences is harder than it looks but not impossible. *(12 words)*

As you can see, this second stage of editing cuts away additional words and makes 1Y even easier to read than 1X.

Example 1 illustrates several important techniques in prose surgery. Notice, for instance, how clauses beginning with *which* or *that* are converted into single-word modifiers. Notice, too, how several empty phrases are eliminated from the problem sentence with no loss in meaning. You can apply these techniques to papers in your writing portfolio.

Here's a second cluster leading to a problem sentence:

Example 2

Extra words make writing difficult to read.

You should not overlook your responsibility.

The responsibility is for editing.

↓

> ***Problem*** Owing to the fact that large numbers of extra and redundant words can have the effect of making writing somewhat more difficult to read with good comprehension, it is your personal responsibility not to overlook the editing of the work that you have written. *(44 words)*

Look at the "flab" in this problem sentence! To edit this swollen monster, consider the following moves:

- Delete *owing to the fact that;* substitute *because.*
- Delete the empty phrase *large numbers of.*
- Delete *and redundant,* since this means *extra.*
- Delete *can have the effect of making;* substitute *make.*
- Delete the empty phrase *somewhat more.*
- Delete *with good comprehension,* since this is implied by *to read.*
- Delete *it is your personal responsibility not to;* substitute *you should not.*
- Delete *the editing of the work that you have written;* substitute *your editing responsibility.*

Here's the result; note that it has only 15 words, compared with 44 words in the problem sentence. Read it aloud to compare it with the problem sentence in terms of clarity:

> ***2x*** Because extra words make writing difficult to read, you should not overlook your editing responsibility. *(15 words)*

Obviously, 2X is not only leaner but much clearer. Could 2X be edited even further? Consider one more possibility:

> ***2y*** Extra words make writing difficult to read; therefore, don't overlook editing. *(11 words)*

You may, however, decide that 2Y is *too* lean. Keep in mind that editing is a process of clarifying sentences, not just shortening them. Is 2Y clear enough?

Now, here are some SC exercises to try on your own.

Directions Trim the flab from the problem sentence that follows each cluster. Check the Answer Key for odd-numbered exercises.

1.1 We have provided a full report.
1.2 We hope that it answers your questions.

Problem 1 We have provided a full and complete report that we sincerely hope and trust will answer each and every one of the questions you might possibly have. *(27 words)*

2.1 The weather was rainy.
2.2 Few football fans showed up at the game.

Problem 2 In view of the fact that the weather was rainy, the number of football fans who showed up at the game was few in number. *(25 words)*

3.1 Presently the lab is shut down.
3.2 It has not complied with safety standards.

Problem 3 At this point in time, the lab is in a standby mode of operation as a result of the fact that it is not in compliance with a variety of safety standards. *(32 words)*

4.1 Fred knew his assignment was late.
4.2 He decided to try a lame excuse.

Problem 4 Despite the fact that Fred knew his assignment was late, it was his decision to try an excuse that could only be characterized as lame. *(25 words)*

5.1 Technological change is accelerating.
5.2 This is in today's world.

Problem 5 It perhaps goes without saying that there is, in the modern world of today, an acceleration of the various aspects of technological change. *(23 words)*

6.1 I then realized something.
6.2 I wanted to be near her.

Problem 6 At that point in time, I came to the realization that I wanted to be in close proximity to her. *(20 words)*

7.1 Something is undeniable.
7.2 We must meet the deadline.
7.3 This is to keep our jobs.

Problem 7 It is an undeniable fact that there is a need for us to meet the deadline in order for us, both as individuals and as a group, to keep our jobs. *(31 words)*

8.1 Nelson Mandela's election opens a new era.
8.2 The era is in the history of South Africa.
8.3 It shows that democracy can work.

Problem 8 The end result of the election of Nelson Mandela may be viewed as the opening of a new era in the history of South Africa as well as an indication of the fact that democracy can work. *(37 words)*

9.1 This paper has an aim.
9.2 The aim is to interpret facts.
9.3 Others have verified the facts.

Problem 9 The basic and fundamental aim of this paper is to offer an interpretation of various sorts of facts that have undergone a process of verification by others. *(27 words)*

10.1 I have reached a conclusion.
10.2 Writing well takes time.
10.3 Writing well demands editing.

Problem 10 The conclusion that I have reached is that in order for writing to be done well there must be an expenditure of time, not to mention some attention to the various demands and aspects of editing. *(36 words)*

APPROACHING PROOFREADING

A Context for Proofreading

Proofreading is a special kind of reading that focuses on details of writing—on spelling, usage, and punctuation. Proofreading differs radically from revising. When you revise, you consider content, organization, and development. When you proofread, on the other hand, you focus strictly on details.

To understand the concept of proofreading, imagine yourself driving on a dark night, along an unlit, unfamiliar road. You're relaxed at first, but then you hit a pothole, and then another and another. Suddenly, your whole mood changes. What was an ordinary ride now becomes a tense, bone-jarring ordeal.

Something like this happens to readers when they encounter errors in writing. When readers are jarred by a misspelled word, a sentence fragment, or a run-on sentence, their whole mood changes. They tense up, like a driver waiting to hit the next pothole.

As a writer, therefore, try to think of proofreading as road patching. By finding and fixing the "potholes" in your text, you smooth the way for your readers, making their journey as trouble-free as possible.

For most students—and you may be one of them—problems in proofreading result mainly from carelessness, not from other deficits. Consider, for example, how adept you are at running up the score on computer games. Obviously, you attend to subtle cues on the video screen with great accuracy; obviously, too, you've *trained* yourself to pay attention to details that matter.

In proofreading, of course, it's very difficult to focus on details if you've revised so extensively that you've virtually memorized your paper. Try setting your text aside to "cool off" for a day or two—longer, if possible. When you come back to the paper, you may discover that it reads differently. You may also discover errors that you failed to notice earlier.

Techniques for Proofreading

There are three principles that will improve your proofreading. Let's look at each of them.

First, remember that your aim is *not* to change content or organization, since such changes have already been made at earlier stages of the writing process.

Second, understand that proofreading is done at a much slower rate than ordinary reading. The idea is to read at a snail's pace, not at your usual rate of 250 words or so per minute. By slowing down, you suddenly see more—and seeing more will lead, reliably, to small but important improvements in the papers you submit.

You may need to make a special effort to slow down. One strategy worth trying is a proofreading ***pacer***. A pacer can be a pointer (such as your finger), but a note card may be even better. Use the note card to cover up your text; then move the card to expose one line at a time. In this way, you'll force yourself to slow down dramatically.

Third, commit yourself to *repeated* readings of the text, with each reading focused on a different aspect of conventions. As beginning proofreaders, most of us make the same mistake. Even when we allow sufficient time for the task, we think that we can attend to several things at once. We could learn a lesson from aircraft pilots, who follow a step-by-step checklist in the cockpit: one point of the checklist is to make the pilot do *one thing at a time*.

The strategy of proofreading several times, each time with a single aim in mind, works something like this. Your first reading might focus exclusively on fragments or run-ons. Second, you might shift to verbs—consistency of tense and agreement with subjects—or to agreement of pronouns and antecedents. A third round of proofreading might deal with punctuation (apostrophes, commas, etc.). A fourth round might concentrate on capitalization or spelling. And so on. This strategy can yield surprising dividends.

To give you the idea of proofreading, here are a few examples to try. Proofread carefully and check off (✓) each error you find. Answers are given below.

- (1) If your a good profreader, you will spot three or fore mispelled words hear—or is it five?
- (2) to get better grades in english, find the three Errors in capitalization in this sentence.
- (3) Its not easy to find the four errors with apostrophe's shown here, but thats a writers task.
- (4) Finding a sentence fragment is not always easy either. Especially if you're in a hurry.
- (5) The comma splice, which joins independent sentences, can be tricky, it's quite often overlooked, in fact.
- (6) A related punctuation problem is the run-on sentence it needs your close attention as a proofreader.
- (7) Clauses in a compound sentence are usually separated by a comma but you may sometimes forget to put it in.
- (8) When you write a subordinate clause at the beginning of a sentence you may also overlook the comma accidentally.
- (9) A different sort of problem results from, leaving in extra commas, because you don't proofread with care.
- (10) If you drop word endings, as in this sentence, you will disrupt your reader concentration.
- (11) Similarly, if you switch verb tenses, as shown here, you confused your readers.
- (12) Listening to sentences where you proofread can help you avoid errors with connecting words like *when*, *while*, etc.
- (13) Writers which are not proofreading may misuse relative pronouns (like *who*, *whom*, *which*, *that*, *whose*).

- (14) A simple sentence is rather difficult to read that puts its modifiers in the wrong place.
- (15) Trying to make complex sentences, dangling modifiers can sometimes appear in your prose.
- (16) When you proofread, remember that each pronoun should agree with their antecedent.
- (17) Remember, too, that parallelism problems occur when you are focused on content, not to worry about proofreading.
- (18) On proofreading prepositions, make sure you have used the right word with the right spot.
- (19) Shifting one's point of view, as shown here, is a problem you should try to catch in proofreading.
- (20) A problem in subject-verb agreement, with a long series of intervening phrases, are sometimes difficult to spot.
- (21) Their are those beginning writers who overlook there responsibility to proofread easily confused words.
- (22) For others, a lapse of attention to exact words resorts in unintended humor that affects a reader's constipation.

Here are the answers: (1) Correct words are *you're*, *proofreader*, *four*, *misspelled*, *here*. (2) Corrections for capitalization are *To*, *English*, *errors*. (3) Corrections for apostrophes are *It's*, *apostrophes*, *that's*, *writer's*. (4) Fragment beginning with *especially* should be attached to the main sentence. (5) Comma splice after *tricky* should be changed to a semicolon. (6) To fix the run-on sentence, *it* should be changed to *which*. (7) Comma should be inserted after the word *comma*. (8) Comma should be inserted after the word *sentence*. (9) Both commas should be deleted. (10) Either *-'s* (singular possessive ending) or *-s'* (plural possessive ending) should be added to *reader*. (11) Verb *confused* should be changed to *confuse*. (12) Connector *where* should be changed to *when* or *while*. (13) Relative pronoun *which* should be changed to *who*. (14) Clause beginning with *that* should be placed after the word *sentence*. (15) Subject of the sentence should be *you* or *the writer*. (16) Pronoun *their* should be changed to *its*. (17) Phrase *to worry* should be changed to *worried*. (18) Prepositions *on* and *with* should be changed to *in*. (19) Pronouns should be either *one's* and *one*, or *your* and *you*. (20) Verb *are* should be changed to *is*. (21) Words *their* and *there* are each wrong in context. (22) Word *resorts* should be *results*, and *constipation* should be *concentration*. Consult the minilessons in Part Two, Toolbox, if you need information about any of these points.

As you practice proofreading, try to develop certain habits of mind. Attend *consciously* to the task, and take pride in your ability to spot mistakes quickly. Watch for common errors in the work of your writing partners or on bulletin boards around your school. Ask questions if you're unsure about details of usage or punctuation.

We'll now turn to some sentence-combining (SC) exercises involving proofreading. Before going on, remember: Proofreading matters—*make no misteak!*

(Did you catch that one?)

SC for Practice with Proofreading

For practice with proofreading, let's work on some clusters followed by problem sentences. Each problem sentence has *three errors*. Your challenge is to proofread the problem sentence, spot the three errors, and then use the cluster to write a *corrected* version.

With this kind of practice, you can train yourself in proofreading skills. You'll learn to spot spelling mistakes, errors in punctuation, usage problems, and nonstandard capitalization.

We'll start with an example. Try proofreading the problem sentence; it has three errors.

Example

It's not easy to spot three errors.
The errors are in sentences.
Learning to do so can improve your grades.

↓

Problem Its not easy to spot three errors in sentances, learning to do so can improve your grades. *(3 errors)*

What are the three errors? Notice the missing apostrophe for *it's*, the careless misspelling of *sentences*, and the comma splice (also called a *run-on sentence)* between the two independent clauses. Here's one possible corrected version of the problem sentence:

It's not easy to spot errors in sentences; however, learning to do so can improve your grades.

Of course, there are other ways to correct the problem sentence in this example. Here are two more possibilities:

> Although it's not easy to spot errors in sentences, learning to do so can improve your grades.
>
> *or*
>
> Spotting errors in sentences is not easy, but learning to do so can improve your grades.

Now, here are some SC exercises for you to do on your own.

Directions Proofread each problem sentence to find *three* errors. Recombine the original cluster, making the necessary corrections. Check your proofreading in the Answer Key (for odd-numbered exercises) or against answers provided in class by your instructor (for even-numbered exercises).

1.1 There are three proofreading problems.
1.2 We are going to spot them here.

Problem 1 Their are three proofreading problems that were going to spot hear. *(3 errors)*

2.1 Something is a fact of life.
2.2 Hurried proofreading can lower your grade.

Problem 2 Its a fact of life that hurried Proofreading can lower you're grade. *(3 errors)*

3.1 Serious errors stop the readers cold.
3.2 They create strong feelings of irritation.

Problem 3 Serious errors stop the reader's cold. Creating strong feelings off irritation. *(3 errors)*

4.1 Run-on sentences are especially common.
4.2 These result from joining two sentences with a comma.

Problem 4 Run-on sentences are especially common, these resulted form joining two sentences with a comma. *(3 errors)*

5.1 Other details can interrupt a reader's concentration.
5.2 These include missing apostrophes and commas.

Problem 5 Other details, such as missing apostrophe's and commas can interrupt a readers concentration. *(3 errors)*

6.1 Proofreading skill does not happen overnight.
6.2 It is something one must work at to improve.

Problem 6 Proofreading skill doesnt happen overnight, instead, its something one must work at to improve. *(3 errors)*

7.1 Exercises can build one's level of awareness.
7.2 Some writers are simply unwilling to proofread.

Problem 7 Exercises can build one's level of awareness, however, there is some writers which are unwilling to proofread. *(3 errors)*

8.1 Proofreading is actually a complex set of skills.
8.2 Each results from attention to detail.
8.3 Each builds on the others.

Problem 8 Proofreading is actually a complex set of Skills. Each resulting from attention to details. Each building on the others. *(3 errors)*

9.1 You are having trouble with proofreading.
9.2 A pacer can slow down your reading.
9.3 It can also focus your attention.

Problem 9 If your having trouble proofreading, a pacer can slow down your reading, and focusing your attention. *(3 errors)*

10.1 Toolbox minilessons will teach you skills.
10.2 Each minilesson is focused on a different topic.
10.3 You can apply skills to your own writing.

Problem 10 Toolbox minilessons—each focused on a different topic, will teach you skills, you can apply these skills to your own Writting. *(3 errors)*

Remember—as cluster 10 suggests—that you should consult Part Two, Toolbox, if you need information about any of these proofreading points. You'll find a quick reference guide to the Toolbox on page 13 and on the back cover.

WORKSHOP PORTFOLIO FOR UNIT 5

To apply editing and proofreading in your portfolio, you'll need to study your writing with a critical eye. Photocopy several selections and use these for practice, keeping an original copy for comparison. As your editing and proofreading skills improve over time, you'll have a clear and dramatic record of your growth as a writer. You can use this information as the basis for a personal essay focused on your own development.

As you consider your growth as a writer, look for patterns in your portfolio. Don't compare your writing with writing done by other students. The point, after all, is to document what *you* have done over the term or semester. By studying your own development in a serious, thoughtful way, you lay a foundation for future progress. Here are two possible writing assignments.

Option 1: A Progress Report Examine your portfolio to find pieces showing your growth as a writer. Choose one or two from early in the term or semester and one or two from later on. Are the more recent pieces longer, better developed, or more carefully organized? Do they contain fewer errors or more vivid examples? What specific features do you see in the writing itself?

Tell the story of your progress in this writing course. You may want to describe how you felt during the first class meetings or while adding pieces to your portfolio. Were you doubtful about the process, or did you feel confident and self-assured? Share an example from your portfolio that reflects your state of mind or your writing skills early in the course. Use one or more such examples as a "benchmark," or reference point, for comments about your subsequent growth in writing.

The examples you choose from midway or late in your writing course will probably be stronger in several ways. Identify these for the reader. Provide brief examples to support your assertions. Then try to explain the *reasons* for your growth as a writer. How and why have you made progress? What writing goals do you *now* have? How optimistic or pessimistic are you about achieving them?

Option 2: A Comparison-Contrast Analysis Find examples of successful and unsuccessful writing in your portfolio. Use your own judgment, the judgment of your response group, or feedback from your instructor—or all three—to identify these pieces. Of course, writing may be successful or unsuccessful for a variety of reasons. Write a comparison-contrast analysis in which you examine those reasons as carefully and thoughtfully as possible.

To begin your analysis, study each set of papers separately. Ask yourself about the *shared features* of each set. Are the successful papers all of one type? Do they share an organizational pattern or a particular voice? Is vivid language a shared feature? Repeat the process of questioning as you read the less successful pieces. Again, try to determine what characteristics these papers have in common. Don't overlook editing and proofreading.

Organize your comparison-contrast paper to focus on the main features of successful and unsuccessful writing in your portfolio. You'll want to use brief examples from each set of papers to support your assertions. Comparison and contrast transition words such as *similarly*, *in the same way*, *however*, and *on the other hand* will help you present your case. Conclude your paper by pointing out the significance of this analysis—what it means to you as a developing writer.

SC FOR UNIT 5

There are two groups of SC exercises in this section: the first group is for editing and the second for proofreading. Be sure to read the separate directions for *each* group.

Exercises for Editing

Directions In this first group of exercises—for editing—find ways to *tighten* each of the "problem" sentences; note the word counts. Check your editing work in the Answer Key (for odd-numbered exercises) or against answers provided by your instructor (for even-numbered exercises).

➔ *Still Life*

Nothing is more inevitable than death, and yet we are never ready for it. Sometimes, the world goes still.

1.1 The night had been cruel.
1.2 Now a man sat in a doorway.
1.3 The man was grieving.
1.4 The doorway was sunlit.

Problem 1 It was following the cruelty of the night that a man who was filled with grief stood in a doorway that was lit by the sun. *(26 words)*

2.1 His arms were folded.
2.2 A hat shaded his eyes.
2.3 He leaned to one side.

Problem 2 Perhaps the first thing that one noticed about him was the fact that his arms were folded and that a hat shaded his eyes as he leaned to one side. *(30 words)*

3.1 He wore bib overalls.
3.2 They were faded from washing.
3.3 They were shapeless from washing.
3.4 He wore a shirt.
3.5 It was made from blue denim.

Problem 3 His clothing consisted of a pair of bib overalls that were faded and rather shapeless from probably countless washings and a shirt that was made from blue denim. *(28 words)*

4.1 Sunlight glared against the white siding.
4.2 It did not penetrate the room behind him.
4.3 The room was heavy with shadows.
4.4 Its curtains were drawn.

Problem 4 Although there was the glare of sunlight against the white siding, the room behind him, which was heavy with shadows from the curtains that had been drawn, was not penetrated by it. *(32 words)*

5.1 Tears stained his face.
5.2 The tears were silent.
5.3 It was weathered by a lifetime of work.
5.4 The work was in the fields.

Problem 5 It was his face, which was weathered by a lifetime of work in the fields, that was stained by the silent tears. *(22 words)*

6.1 He cried without a sound.
6.2 He did not wipe his eyes.
6.3 He did not look back to the room.
6.4 He had spent so many years there.

Problem 6 No sound could be heard as he cried, nor did he make a gesture to wipe his eyes or to look back to the room where so many of the years of his life had been spent. *(37 words)*

7.1 His loved one was gone.
7.2 He had never felt so completely alone.

Problem 7 As a result of the fact that the one whom he had loved was gone, the aloneness that he felt was far more complete than anything he had ever before experienced. *(31 words)*

8.1 He felt stillness inside him.
8.2 It was like a smooth stone.

Problem 8 There was a stillness that he felt inside his being, which was like the smoothness of a stone. *(18 words)*

Invitation Extend this "Still Life" narrative by describing what happens next, what the man thinks, or simply the scene inside.

Health Care

Got a problem? Take it to the doctor! While this habit of mind is still popular, many people are beginning to take a new view.

1.1 Traditional medicine sees the body as a machine.
1.2 The machine is tremendously complicated.

Problem 1 In the traditional practice of the medical arts, the body is seen as a kind of machine, the workings of which are tremendously complex and complicated. *(26 words)*

2.1 Something goes wrong.
2.2 People take themselves to "shops."
2.3 Physicians work much like mechanics.
2.4 They search for the problem's cause.
2.5 The cause is isolated.

Problem 2 When some sort of problem or difficulty seems to arise, people take themselves to "shops"—and it is in the context of these facilities that physicians engage in activities much like those of mechanics, searching for the single cause, which is thought to be isolated. *(45 words)*

3.1 The problem is diagnosed.
3.2 The doctor removes the defective part.
3.3 The doctor repairs the defective part.
3.4 The doctor replaces the defective part.
3.5 Or the doctor may prescribe chemicals.
3.6 The chemicals treat the problem's symptoms.

Problem 3 After the diagnosis of the problem is completed, the defective part is removed, repaired, or replaced by the doctor; or, as an alternative approach, a prescription of chemicals may be initiated by the doctor, with the aim of treating the symptoms of the problem. *(44 words)*

4.1 The treatment centers on fixing problems.
4.2 It does not center on preventing them.
4.3 The responsibility lies mainly with the physician.
4.4 The responsibility is for a cure.
4.5 It does not lie with the patient.

Problem 4 The fixing of problems rather than the prevention of problems is the center of the treatment, and the responsibility for a cure is mainly that of the physician and not so much that of the patient. *(36 words)*

5.1 Holistic medicine takes a viewpoint.
5.2 The viewpoint is radically different.
5.3 It challenges traditional ideas about health.

Problem 5 A viewpoint that is somewhat different, perhaps radically so, is taken by holistic medicine in its challenge to the older or more traditional ideas about health care. *(27 words)*

6.1 Its practitioners see wellness as a harmony.
6.2 The harmony is between body and spirit.
6.3 Its practitioners see disharmony as a cause.
6.4 The disharmony is psychological.
6.5 The cause contributes to most illnesses.

Problem 6 Wellness is seen as a kind of harmony between the body and spirit by its practitioners; moreover, psychological disharmony is seen as a cause or at least as a contributing factor in most illnesses. *(34 words)*

7.1 Maladies are often caused by the way we live.
7.2 The maladies include arteriosclerosis.
7.3 The maladies include lung cancer.
7.4 The maladies include chemical dependencies.
7.5 They can often be cured by changes in lifestyle.

Problem 7 The cause of maladies, ranging from arteriosclerosis to lung cancer to chemical dependencies, is often a function of the way in which we live, and these maladies can often be cured as certain changes in our lifestyle are effected. *(39 words)*

8.1 Treatment often centers on diet.
8.2 Treatment often centers on exercise.
8.3 Treatment often centers on stress management.
8.4 Primary responsibility lies with individuals.
8.5 The responsibility is for good health.
8.6 It does not lie with doctors.

Problem 8 Various aspects such as proper diet, physical exercise, and the management of stress are what the treatment often centers on; however, the primary responsibility for the maintenance of good health is an individual one rather than a responsibility that lies with doctors. *(42 words)*

Invitation This paragraph *contrasts* two approaches to health care. How might you resolve this conflict in follow-up writing?

➔ Think about Writing

When we say that we "dig" for facts or "sift" through our notes, we're using metaphors—in this case, from mining—to describe our processes. Here are two additional metaphors for thinking about writing.

1.1 Think of writing as a conversation.
1.2 The conversation is "one-way."
1.3 The conversation is with an audience.
1.4 The audience is invisible but real.

Problem 1 It is possible to think of the act of writing as a "one-way" conversation that is with an audience which is invisible but nevertheless real. *(26 words)*

2.1 Your audience can hear words.
2.2 The words appear in your text.
2.3 Its members cannot question you.
2.4 Its members cannot request examples.

Problem 2 Although the various types of words that appear in the lines of your text can be heard by the members of your audience, they cannot ask questions of you nor can they make requests for examples. *(36 words)*

3.1 The implications are clear.
3.2 Paragraphs must be well organized.
3.3 Paragraphs must be carefully sequenced.
3.4 Readers can follow your discussion.
3.5 Readers can participate in it.

Problem 3 The implications of this are very clear: in order for readers not only to follow the progress of your discussion but also to participate in the experience, it is important that paragraphs be well organized and that their sequencing be carefully done. *(42 words)*

4.1 Readers have only your text to rely on.
4.2 Your words must address the readers' needs.
4.3 Your sentences must address the readers' needs.
4.4 Your paragraphs must address the readers' needs.

Problem 4 As a result of the fact that readers have only your text on which to rely, it should come as no surprise that your words, sentences, and paragraphs must address the needs of the readers you have. *(37 words)*

5.1 Or think of writing as mountain climbing.
5.2 You serve as a guide for readers.
5.3 You lead the way to the summit.

Problem 5 As an alternative mode of thinking about writing, there is the possibility of mountain climbing, with the service you render being that of guide for readers, which is to say leading the way to the summit. *(36 words)*

6.1 Your sentences are threads of meaning.
6.2 The threads are woven into paragraph "ropes."
6.3 The paragraph "ropes" are strong.
6.4 The "ropes" support the readers' ascent.

Problem 6 The sentences that are written by you are threads of meaning—threads that are woven into paragraph "ropes" which are hopefully strong enough to support the upward ascent of readers. *(30 words)*

7.1 You guide readers through territory.
7.2 The territory is potentially dangerous.
7.3 The territory is often slippery.
7.4 You try to keep your lines clear.
7.5 You try to ensure they don't get tangled.

Problem 7 As you guide the readers of your text through territory which is potentially dangerous, not to mention often slippery, an effort should be made both to keep your lines clear as well as to ensure that the lines don't get tangled up. *(42 words)*

8.1 A serious misstep means something.
8.2 Readers will drop away into the darkness.
8.3 They will not share your view from the summit.

Problem 8 The result of a serious misstep is that readers will not only fall away into the darkness but also will not share your view from the summit. *(27 words)*

Invitation Invent your own metaphor for describing the writing process as you understand it. Some starters might be photography, traveling, or gardening.

Laser Light

Laser light scans your groceries at the checkout counter and also the grooves in your CDs. How and why does laser light do its magic?

1.1 The laser beam differs from ordinary light.
1.2 It is a special kind of intense light.

Problem 1 The laser beam is not only different from ordinary light, but is also a special kind of intense light. *(19 words)*

2.1 Ordinary light has many colors.
2.2 Its waves move in many directions.
2.3 The movements are random.
2.4 Laser light is monochromatic.
2.5 Its waves move in a single direction.

Problem 2 Ordinary light has many colors, and its waves move randomly in many directions; in contrast, however, light from a laser is monochromatic, and the movement of these waves is in a single direction. *(33 words)*

3.1 Photons in ordinary light spread out.
3.2 They diffuse their energy.
3.3 Laser-beam photons are focused.
3.4 This concentrates their power.

Problem 3 In ordinary light, the photons spread out, which causes them to diffuse their energy, whereas the photons in laser beams are focused, and this fact enables them to concentrate their power. *(31 words)*.

4.1 Laser rays have exactly the same wavelength.
4.2 Laser rays all vibrate together.
4.3 Laser rays produce beams of intensity.
4.4 The intensity is very great.

Problem 4 As a result of the same wavelength that laser rays have and the fact that laser rays all vibrate together, they produce beams whose intensity is, to say the least, very great. *(32 words)*

5.1 These narrow beams may be continuous.
5.2 These narrow beams may be pulsing.
5.3 They may also be visible.
5.4 They may also be invisible.

Problem 5 These narrow beams may be continuous, or they may be pulsing; in addition, they may be visible, but they may also be invisible. *(23 words)*

6.1 Lasers provide results of high quality.
6.2 The lasers emit visible light.
6.3 They are used in digital recording.
6.4 They are used in fiber-optic communications.
6.5 They are used in distance measurement.

Problem 6 Results of high quality in a variety of areas such as digital recording, fiber-optic communications, and the measurement of distances are provided by lasers that emit visible light. *(29 words)*

7.1 But infrared lasers can cut metal.
7.2 Infrared lasers can pierce armor.
7.3 They are invisible to human eyes.
7.4 This makes them military weapons.
7.5 The weapons are enormously potent.

Problem 7 Infrared lasers, which are not visible to the eyes of human beings, have the ability to cut metal and to pierce armor, which makes them military weapons of enormous potency. *(30 words)*

8.1 A laser can weld retinas.
8.2 The retinas have loosened from the eye.
8.3 Welding does not destroy the tissue.
8.4 Infrared lasers can also be used as gunsights.
8.5 The sights help soldiers kill in the dark.

Problem 8 On the one hand, a laser can weld retinas that have loosened from the eye, and the act of welding does not result in the destruction of the tissue; but on the other hand, infrared lasers can also be used as sights for guns, and this fact helps soldiers to kill in the dark. *(54 words)*

9.1 Lasers now carry TV signals.
9.2 Lasers now carry telephone communications.
9.3 This same technology could also be based in space.
9.4 It might serve as a destructive tool.
9.5 This would be in the future.

Problem 9 TV signals and telephone communications can be carried by lasers, but this same technology could also be based in space, and there it might serve as a tool of destruction at some future point in time. *(36 words)*

10.1 Something seems clear.
10.2 Laser light is not ordinary.
10.3 Its uses are not ordinary.

Problem 10 It seems clear that not only is laser light not ordinary but its uses are not ordinary either. *(18 words)*

Invitation Notice the use of *contrast* in sentences above. Using this principle of development, focus on a topic with positive and negative points—for example, political campaigns or fast foods.

➔ Hopi Way

Maybe you've seen T shirts that say "Don't worry—be Hopi!" While humorous, the slogan does suggest a Native American point of view.

1.1 The Hopi are a remarkable culture.
1.2 The culture lives on a mountainous reservation.
1.3 The reservation is in the Arizona desert.

Problem 1 It is on a reservation, located in the mountains and the desert of Arizona, that there lives a rather remarkable culture known as the Hopi. *(25 words)*

2.1 The word *Hopi* means "peaceful."
2.2 The word *Hopi* means "happy."
2.3 These are good descriptions for people.
2.4 The people do not value competition.
2.5 The people do not value materialism.
2.6 The materialism is crass.

Problem 2 A translation for the word *Hopi* is "peaceful" or "happy," and this is indeed a good and useful description for people who do not tend to value either competition or what can only be termed crass materialism. *(37 words)*

3.1 The Hopi are like other Native Americans in North America.
3.2 The Hopi have a strong sense of family.
3.3 The family is "extended."
3.4 This means a love for other Hopi.
3.5 This means a love for their heritage.
3.6 This means a love for ceremonies.

Problem 3 Like other Native Americans in North America, the Hopi have a strong sense of "extended" family, and this may be defined more operationally as a love not only for other Hopi but also for their heritage and for the ceremonies of their culture. *(43 words)*

4.1 But the Hopi differ from the Navaho.
4.2 The Navaho are more aggressive.
4.3 The Navaho are widely dispersed on a reservation.
4.4 The reservation surrounds Hopi lands.

Problem 4 But the Hopi are somewhat different in orientation as compared with tribes like the Navaho, who are known to be somewhat more aggressive and are also widely dispersed on a reservation that surrounds Hopi lands. (35 *words*)

5.1 The family teaches the "Hopi way."
5.2 This is a system of values.
5.3 This is a system of behavior.
5.4 The system runs deeply through the culture.

Problem 5 It is by imparting a system of values and a system of behavior that runs deeply though the culture that the family teaches the "Hopi way." (26 *words*)

6.1 Families belong to clans.
6.2 The clans extend over a wide territory.
6.3 The clans create a network of associations.
6.4 The clans create a network of relationships.
6.5 The network is intricate.

Problem 6 Families belong to clans, and it is these clans, extending as they do over a wide range of territory, that serve to create a network of associations and relationships that can only be described as intricate. (36 *words*)

7.1 The society is matriarchal.
7.2 It is not patriarchal.
7.3 The mother's family represents lineage.
7.4 The mother's family represents authority.

Problem 7 The organization of the society is matriarchal, rather than patriarchal in its structure, with the family of the mother representing lineage as well as authority. (25 *words*)

8.1 The chief functions as a counselor.
8.2 The counselor is for the village.
8.3 The counselor helps people follow precepts.
8.4 The precepts are ancient.
8.5 He does not issue orders.
8.6 He does not possess power.

Problem 8 The chief, functioning as a kind of counselor for the village, helps the people to follow precepts that can only be described as ancient; however, it is not his task to issue orders, nor are there any sorts of power in his possession. *(43 words)*

Invitation Imagine yourself as a Hopi visiting the place where you live. What would you probably notice about social or cultural patterns?

➡ Hopi Values

What beliefs and behaviors shape Hopi values? Is there something we can learn from Hopi philosophy?

1.1 The Hopi learn self-discipline as children.
1.2 The Hopi learn restraint as children.
1.3 The Hopi learn concern for others as children.
1.4 The others are in the extended family.

Problem 1 As children, the Hopi learn the values of self-discipline, of restraint, and of concern for others in the extended family of which they are a part. *(27 words)*

2.1 Hopi children share responsibilities.
2.2 The responsibilities are economic.
2.3 The responsibilities are for the family.
2.4 They learn to work without urging.
2.5 Work is part of their family ties.

Problem 2 The economic responsibilities for the family are shared by Hopi children. What they learn about work is that because it is part of their ties to the family, it is done without urging. *(33 words)*

3.1 All work has worth to the Hopi.
3.2 It is not to be dreaded.
3.3 It is not to be done for rewards.

Problem 3 As an activity, work is worthwhile in and of itself to the Hopi; it is not to be dreaded, on the one hand—or done for rewards, on the other. *(30 words)*

4.1 The Hopi also see nature as continuity.
4.2 The Hopi believe something.
4.3 Forces manifest themselves through reality.
4.4 The forces are spiritual.
4.5 The reality is physical.

Problem 4 The continuity of nature is something that the Hopi also see; in addition, they believe that the forces of the spirit are made manifest through a physical sort of reality. *(30 words)*

5.1 They view "things" as processes.
5.2 The processes are dynamic.
5.3 Their prayer is an exercise of will.
5.4 It is not a supplication to a higher being.

Problem 5 It is their view that "things" may be regarded as processes, which are dynamic, and that their prayer is in many ways an exercise of personal will rather than an act of supplication to a higher being, or deity. *(39 words)*

6.1 The Hopi believe something.
6.2 Human beings cause change.
6.3 Change results from an act of will.

Problem 6 There is a belief among the Hopi that the cause of change is human beings and that change itself is the result of an act of will. *(27 words)*

7.1 Each Hopi is thus responsible.
7.2 The responsibility is to direct thoughts.
7.3 The direction is toward constructive ends.
7.4 The direction is away from destructive aims.

Problem 7 Each and every Hopi thus has a personal responsibility to direct thoughts toward ends which are constructive and to direct them away from aims which are destructive. *(27 words)*

8.1 Thoughts are turned toward health.
8.2 Thoughts are turned toward strength.
8.3 Thoughts are turned toward happiness.
8.4 One is following the "Hopi way."
8.5 It is the way of harmony.

Problem 8 It is when thoughts are turned toward health, toward strength, and toward happiness that one can be said to be following the "Hopi way," which is the way of harmony. *(30 words)*

Invitation Do you see Hopi values as practical for your personal philosophy of life or for American culture generally? Make your case in follow-up writing.

Exercises for Proofreading

Directions In this second group of SC exercises—for proofreading—find *three errors* in each problem sentence. Then recombine the original cluster, making the necessary corrections. Remember to refer to the Toolbox minilessons as necessary. Check your proofreading work in the Answer Key (odd-numbered exercises) or against answers provided by your instructor (even-numbered exercises).

➜ *Inversions*

As the name implies, inversions turn people's lives "upside down." Let's consider causes and effects of this weather phenomenon.

1.1 Inversions occur.
1.2 Fog hangs in mountain valleys.
1.3 It is trapped by frigid air.
1.4 The frigid air is at higher elevations.

Problem 1 Inversion occur when fog hangs in mountain valleys, it is trapped by frigid air, at higher elevations. *(3 errors)*

2.1 The cold air is like a lid on a container.
2.2 The lid is invisible.
2.3 The cold air tends to sink.
2.4 This prevents circulation.

Problem 2 Like a invisible lid on a container, the cold air naturally tends to stink, which prevent air circulation. *(3 errors)*

3.1 Trees become coated with frost.
3.2 Bushes become coated with frost.
3.3 The frost gathers in heavy layers.

Problem 3 Trees and brushes, they become coated with frost, that gathers in heavy layers. *(3 errors)*

4.1 The damp air becomes gray.
4.2 The damp air becomes opaque.
4.3 It is like an icy veil.
4.4 The veil diffuses the light.

Problem 4 The damp air becomes gray and opaque, it is like an icey veil that diffused the light. *(3 errors)*

5.1 The fog mixes with smoke.
5.2 The fog mixes with other pollutants.
5.3 It becomes choking.
5.4 It becomes oppressive.

Problem 5 The fog, mixing with smoke and other polutants becomes choking and oppresive. *(3 errors)*

6.1 An inversion blurs the edges of reality.
6.2 It erases all sharpness of visual form.

Problem 6 In it's blurring of realitys edges, an Inversion erases all sharpness of visual form. *(3 errors)*

7.1 It lasts for several days or weeks.
7.2 It can become a serious health threat.
7.3 This is especially for those with problems.
7.4 The problems relate to respiration.

Problem 7 When it lasts for several days or weeks, it can become a serious health threat. Especially for those with perspiration problem's. *(3 errors)*

8.1 For others it serves as a reminder.
8.2 Clean air is one of life's gifts.
8.3 We take the gift for granted.

Problem 8 For others it serves as a reminder, clean air is one of lifes gifts that we take for granite. *(3 errors)*

Invitation Make a transition to another of "life's gifts" that we ignore until it is taken away or threatened. Write about this gift.

➡ *Slavery Today*

Most of us take for granted the personal freedoms we enjoy. Can you imagine a person as property—in the twentieth century?

1.1 Most Americans value human worth.
1.2 Most Americans value individual dignity.
1.3 Few realize how such values are abused.
1.4 The abuse occurs in third world countries.

Problem 1 Most americans value human worth and individual dignity, few realize how such values are abuse in third world countries. *(3 errors)*

2.1 The Anti-Slavery Society uses United Nations guidelines.
2.2 The Anti-Slavery Society is based in London.
2.3 The Anti-Slavery Society estimates something.
2.4 There are over 220 million slaves in today's world.

Problem 2 Using United Nations guidelines the London-based Anti-Slavery Society estimates that there is over 220 million slaves in todays world. *(3 errors)*

3.1 This figure exceeds the workforce of Canada.
3.2 This figure exceeds the workforce of the United States.
3.3 This figure exceeds the workforce of Mexico.
3.4 This figure is astonishing.
3.5 This figure is apparently reliable.

Problem 3 This figure—astonishing but apparently reliable, excedes the combined workforce of Canada, the United States, and mexico. *(3 errors)*

4.1 The vast majority of slaves are women.
4.2 The vast majority of slaves are children.
4.3 The women are defenseless.
4.4 The children are innocent.
4.5 They are used for sexual exploitation.

Problem 4 The vast majority of slaves, they are defenseless woman and innocent children, which are used for sexual exploitation. *(3 errors)*

5.1 This happens in impoverished countries.
5.2 Slave traders abduct children.
5.3 Slave traders trick young women.
5.4 Slave traders cut deals with parents.
5.5 The parents are desperate.
5.6 The parents sell family members into captivity.

Problem 5 In impoverish countries, slave traders abduct children trick young women and cut deals with desperate parents who sell family members into captivity. *(3 errors)*

6.1 A major slave route begins in Asian nations.
6.2 It ends in the middle east.
6.3 Slaves are used in local brothels there.
6.4 Slaves are sold to European pornographers.

Problem 6 A major slave route begins in Asian nations, it ends in the middle east; where slaves are used in local brothels or sold to european pornographers. *(3 errors)*

7.1 These women experience abuse.
7.2 These children experience abuse.
7.3 They are often forced into prostitution.
7.4 The abuse is unthinkable.

Problem 7 Because they are often forced into Prostitution these women and children experiencing unthinkable abuse. *(3 errors)*

8.1 A pornography industry supports slavery.
8.2 This industry is worldwide.
8.3 It produces films and videos.
8.4 These products are immensely profitable.
8.5 Slave victims serve as unwilling actors.

Problem 8 A worldwide pornography industry that supports slavery because it produces immensely profitable films and videos; in which slave victims serve as unwilling actor's. *(3 errors)*

Invitation To combat third world slavery, would you support national laws to prohibit pornographic films and videos in the United States? Develop your views in a follow-up paragraph.

➔ The Nerd

Perhaps you know people who don't "fit in" socially. Do they have a problem, or does society have the problem? Take the nerd, for example.

1.1 The nerd is a nonconformist.
1.2 The nerd wears baggy clothes.
1.3 The nerd wears white socks.
1.4 He often has his fly unzipped.

Problem 1 The nerd is a nonconformist who wears baggy clothes, and white socks, he often had his fly unzipped. *(3 errors)*

2.1 His shirt is mustard-stained.
2.2 His shirt is untucked.
2.3 His pants are usually too short.
2.4 His shoelaces flap wildly.
2.5 His shoelaces are untied.

Problem 2 His untuck shirt is mustard-stained, his pants are usually to short, and his untied shoelaces flaps wildly. *(3 errors)*

3.1 He walks into walls.
3.2 He loses his glasses.
3.3 He falls asleep in class.
3.4 He always carries several pens.
3.5 The pens don't work.
3.6 He always carries textbooks.
3.7 The textbooks are badly tattered.

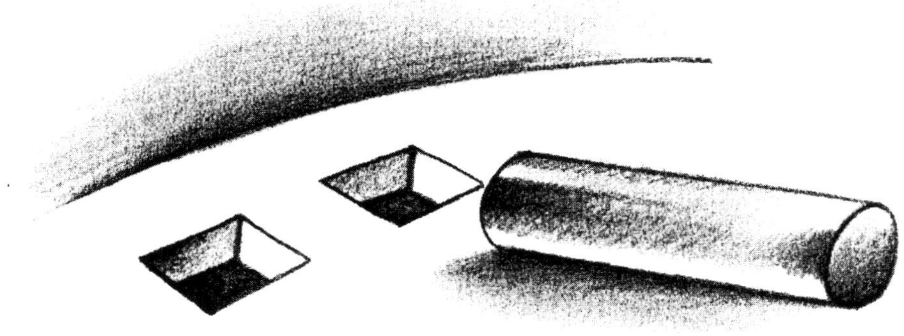

Problem 3 He walks into walls, looses his glasses, falls asleep in class, and always carries badly tattered textbook's and several pens that dont work. *(3 errors)*

4.1 His fingernails are dirty.
4.2 His fingernails are well chewed.
4.3 His hair glistens with a hair oil.
4.4 The hair oil is heavy-scented.
4.5 The hair oil attracts flies.

Problem 4 His dirty fingernails are well chewed, his hair glistened with a heavy-scented, hair oil that attracts flies. *(3 errors)*

5.1 His appearance is different.
5.2 His behavior is different.
5.3 The nerd's life is one of ridicule.
5.4 The nerd's life is one of loneliness.
5.5 The loneliness is aching.

Problem 5 Because his appearance and behavior is different the nerds life is one of ridicule and aching loneliness. *(3 errors)*

6.1 Others mimic his walk.
6.2 His walk is stumbling and uncoordinated.
6.3 Others groan at his answers in class.
6.4 Others single him out as a target for jokes.

Problem 6 Other's not only mimic his stumbling uncoordinated walk; but also groan at his answers in class and single him out as a target for jokes. *(3 errors)*

7.1 They put gum in his books.
7.2 They add taco sauce to his milk.
7.3 They write passionate love notes.
7.4 They attach his name to the notes.

Problem 7 They put gum in his books added taco sauce to his milk, and write passionate love notes; to which his name is attached. *(3 errors)*

8.1 The nerd takes the teasing with a smile.
8.2 The smile is stiff-lipped.
8.3 No one really knows what he is thinking.
8.4 No one really knows what he is feeling.

Problem 8 Although the nerd takes the teasing with a stiff-lipped smile no-one really knows what he is thinking. Or what he is feeling. *(3 errors)*

Invitation Write about "How the Nerd Feels," "Why People Pick on Nerds," or "Why Nerds Have the Last Laugh." Or switch focus to describe the rally queen, the macho man, or the brown-noser.

Ski with Me

Here's an invitation from a good friend to hit the slopes together. After a description like this, how can you resist?

1.1 Come with me to the mountain.
1.2 The early morning air is calm there.
1.3 The early morning air is clear there.
1.4 The early morning air is cold there.
1.5 Fresh snow lies in drifts there.
1.6 The drifts are untracked.

Problem 1 Come with me to the mountain, there the early morning air is calm and clear and cold. Fresh snow lying in untracked drift's. *(3 errors)*

2.1 Snow will crunch beneath our skis.
2.2 Snow will squeak beneath our skis.
2.3 We head toward our first run.
2.4 It is a steep and bowl-shaped area.
2.5 The area is called "Widow-Maker."

Problem 2 Snow will crunch and squeak beneath our skis as we heads toward our first run. A steep, bowl-shaped Area called "Widow-Maker." *(3 errors)*

3.1 You'll look out over the valley below.
3.2 Fir trees stand like sentinels.
3.3 Each wears a white mantle.
3.4 Aspen huddle in groves.
3.5 The aspen are slender and bare-limbed.
3.6 The groves are quiet.

Problem 3 You'll look out over the valley below, were fir trees stand like sentinels. Each wearing a white mantle. Aspen huddled in quiet groves, slender and bare-limbed. *(3 errors)*

4.1 You'll take a deep breath.
4.2 You'll flex your knees.
4.3 You'll choose your line of attack.
4.4 It is the first of the morning.
4.5 It is through powder snow.
4.6 The powder snow is thigh-high.

Problem 4 Taking a deep breath and flexing your knees, you'll choose you're line of attack. The first of the Morning through thigh-high powder snow. *(3 errors)*

5.1 And then you'll push off like a bird.
5.2 You'll let gravity take you on a flight.
5.3 The flight is swooping and breathless.
5.4 The flight is down the mountain's face.

Problem 5 And then you'll push off like a bird letting gravity take you on a swooping breathless flight down the mountains face. *(3 errors)*

6.1 You'll hear your skis click.
6.2 You'll hear your skis chatter.
6.3 Your body dips in turn after turn.
6.4 Your body soars in turn after turn.
6.5 Your legs flex with the bumps.
6.6 The flexing is rhythmic.

Problem 6 You'll here your skis click and chatter; as your body dips and soars in turn after turn. Your legs flexing with the rhythmic bumps. *(3 errors)*

7.1 Clouds of snow will follow your path.
7.2 The snow is bright and swirling.
7.3 Your path is birdlike.
7.4 Their crystals glitter in the sun.

Problem 7 Clouds of snow, bright and swirling will follow your birdlike path; their crystal's glittering in the sun. *(3 errors)*

8.1 Come with me to the mountain.
8.2 The mountain is snow-covered.
8.3 We can break loose from routine.
8.4 We can enjoy a day of freedom.
8.5 You will always remember the day.

Problem 8 Come with me to the snow-covered mountain so that we can brake lose from routine, and enjoy a day of freedom that you will always remember. *(3 errors)*

Invitation Using the "come with me" format shown above, describe an activity *(or place)* that you especially enjoy. Choose details that will persuade a friend to accompany you.

➡ Stereotyped Thinking

The term *stereotype* originated in printing shops, where it referred to something cast in metal from a mold. Today's mindless stereotypes are also ready-made.

1.1 Stereotyping is a way of thinking.
1.2 The thinking is about groups of people.
1.3 It emphasizes similarities in groups.
1.4 It ignores differences among group members.

Problem 1 Stereotyping, a way of thinking about groups of people, it emphasizes similarities in group's but ignored differences among group members. *(3 errors)*

2.1 Typical stereotypes suggest something.
2.2 Red-haired people are hot-tempered.
2.3 Scottish people are stingy.
2.4 Stereotyping ignores something.
2.5 Many redheads are even-tempered.
2.6 Many Scots are generous.

Problem 2 Typical stereotypes suggests that red-haired people have hot tempers and that Scottish people are stingy; however stereotyping ignores that many redheads are even-tempered and that many scots are generous. *(3 errors)*

3.1 . Stereotyping also stresses differences.
3.2 The differences are between groups.
3.3 Stereotyping ignores a group's similarities.
3.4 The similarities are to other people.

Problem 3 Stereotyping also stresses differences between groups, and ignore a groups similarities to other people. *(3 errors)*

4.1 It ignores something.
4.2 Blond-haired people lose their temper.
4.3 Black-haired people lose their temper.
4.4 It overlooks something.
4.5 Many Americans are stingy.
4.6 Many Brazilians are stingy.
4.7 Many Cambodians are stingy.

Problem 4 It ignores that blond-haired and black-haired people loose their temper; and it overlooks that many Americans, Brazilians, and cambodians, are stingy. *(3 errors)*

5.1 A stereotype for redheads does little harm.
5.2 A stereotype for Scots does little harm.
5.3 It typically leads only to jokes.
5.4 It typically leads only to kidding.
5.5 The kidding is good-natured.
5.6 Such thinking also has its dangers.

Problem 5 While a Stereotype for redheads and Scots does little harm and typically leads only to jokes and good-natured kidding. Such thinking also has it's dangers. *(3 errors)*

6.1 The danger lies in exaggerating differences.
6.2 The differences are in ethnicity.
6.3 The differences are in nationality.
6.4 The differences are in religious beliefs.

Problem 6 The danger that lies in exaggerating differences in ethnicity nationality and religious beliefs. *(3 errors)*

7.1 We exaggerate our differences.
7.2 We ignore what we share as human beings.
7.3 We inevitably become narrow-minded.
7.4 We inevitably become prejudiced.

Problem 7 By exaggerating our differences, we ignore what we share as human being's and inevitably become narrow-minded, and prejudice. *(3 errors)*

8.1 Prejudice is an emotion.
8.2 The emotion is profoundly negative.
8.3 The emotion bears the fruit of hatred.
8.4 Prejudice grows out of exaggeration.
8.5 Prejudice is nourished by fear.

Problem 8 Prejudice, which grows out of exageration and is nourished by fear is a profoundly negative emotion that bares the fruit of hatred. *(3 errors)*

Invitation Everyone has stereotypes and prejudices. In follow-up writing, examine one of yours to determine whether it grew out of a ready-made stereotype or resulted from your own experience.

➔ Racial Stereotypes

The world community has applauded social progress in South Africa. Closer to home, however, racial stereotypes still exist.

1.1 An extreme form of prejudice is racism.
1.2 The prejudice is destructive.
1.3 Racism can lead to violence.
1.4 The violence is physical.
1.5 The violence is psychological.

Problem 1 A extreme form of destructive prejudice is Racism, it can lead to physical and psychological violence. *(3 errors)*

2.1 Racists can be any color.
2.2 They can be black
2.3 They can be white.
2.4 They can be brown.
2.5 They can be yellow.
2.6 They can be red.

Problem 2 Racist's can be any color—black or white brown or yellow or red. *(3 errors)*

3.1 Whites show racist leanings.
3.2 The whites think something.
3.3 Blacks are all alike.
3.4 So do blacks show racist leanings.
3.5 The blacks think something.
3.6 Koreans are all alike.

Problem 3 Whites which think that blacks are all alike show racist leanings; and so do blacks which think that koreans are all alike. *(3 errors)*

4.1 A Hispanic is racist.
4.2 The Hispanic thinks something.
4.3 Native Americans are all alike.
4.4 So is a Chinese racist.
4.5 The Chinese thinks something.
4.6 Whites are all alike.

Problem 4 A Hispanic who think that Chinese are all alike is a racist; and so is a Native American, who thinks that whites is all alike. *(3 errors)*

5.1 Racism knows no ethnic boundaries.
5.2 Racism requires only a target.
5.3 The target can be ridiculed.
5.4 The target can be discriminated against.
5.5 The target can be attacked.

Problem 5 Knowing no ethnic boundaries racism require only a target, that can be ridiculed, discriminated against, or attacked. *(3 errors)*

6.1 A fear of differences motivates such attacks.
6.2 Intolerance motivates such attacks.
6.3 The intolerance is antidemocratic.
6.4 The attacks are unfair and damaging.

Problem 6 A fear of differences, and antidemocratic intolerance, motivates such unfair and damaging attacks. *(3 errors)*

7.1 Attacks are expressed in labels.
7.2 The labels include *chink*.
7.3 The labels include *nigger*.
7.4 The labels include *honky*.
7.5 The labels include *wop*.
7.6 The labels include *spic*.
7.7 The labels include *kike*.
7.8 The labels include *gook*.

Problem 7 Attack's expressed in lables like *chink*, *nigger*, *honky*, *wop*, *spic*, *kike*, and *gook*. *(3 errors)*

8.1 Such is the power of stereotyping.
8.2 Stereotyping is a style of thinking.
8.3 The style is simpleminded.
8.4 The thinking is negative.

Problem 8 Such is the power of stereotyping; a simple, minded style of Negative thinking. *(3 errors)*

Invitation Describe a specific incident in which you or a friend felt the sting of racism or stereotyped thinking. How have you resolved the incident in your own mind and learned from it?

PART TWO

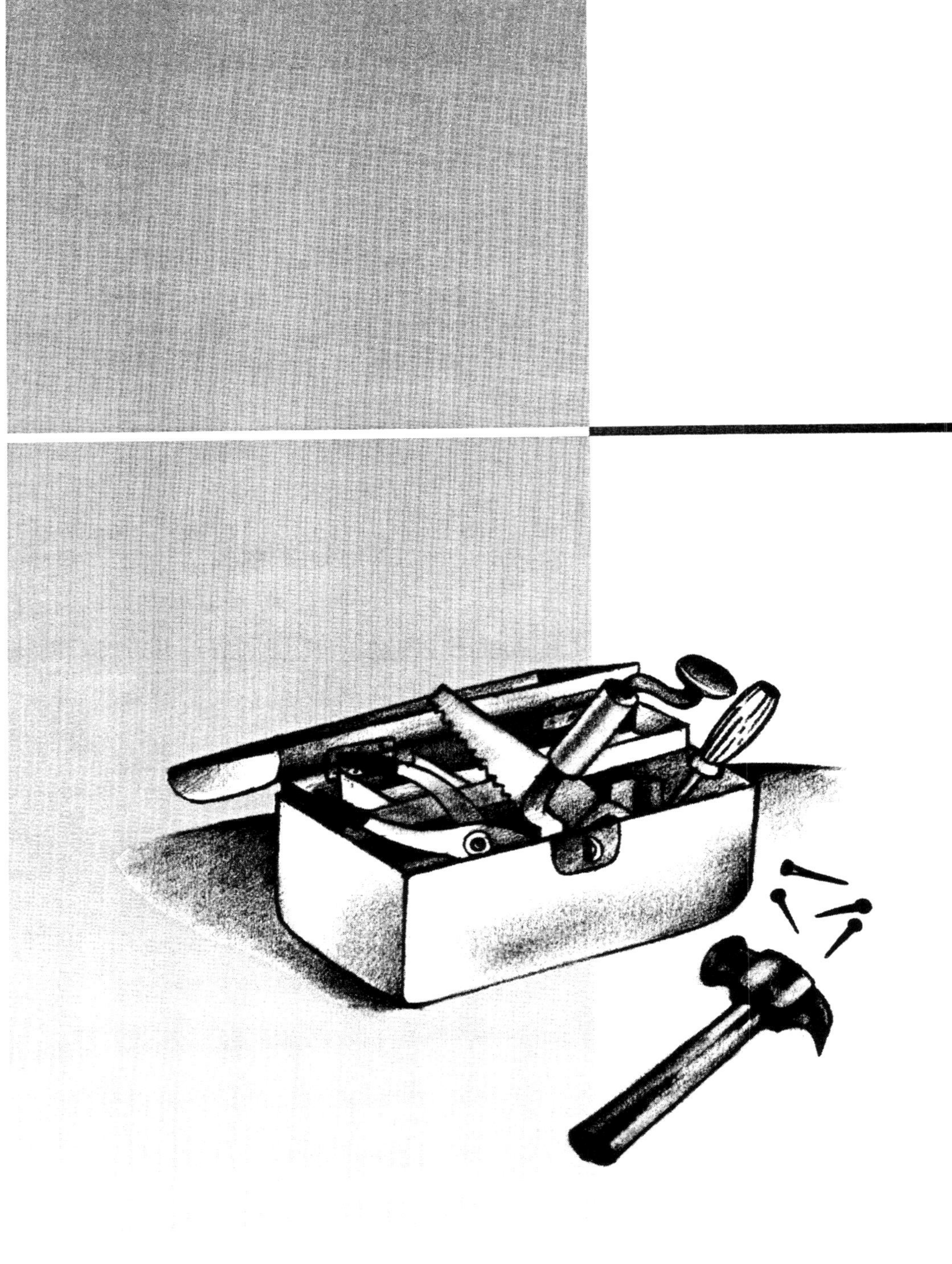

PART TWO

Toolbox

MINILESSONS AND PRACTICE

UNIT 6

Tools of Basic Grammar

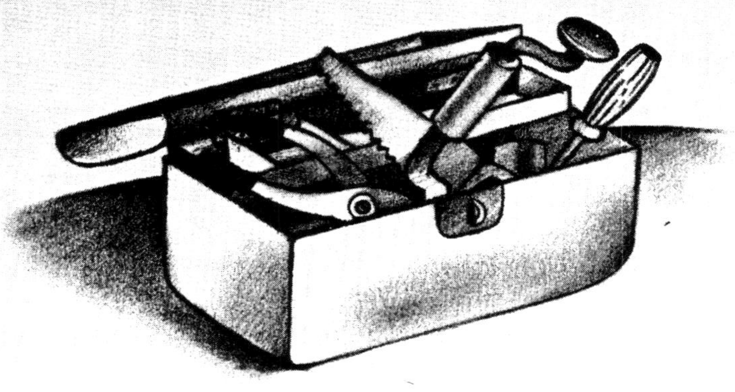

NOUNS

If you can't remember the definition of a ***noun***—that it names a person, place, thing, or idea—cheer up. The following cluster of unusual sentences is just for you.

Example

Tucker was a trucker.
Tucker was out of luck.
He was stuck in the muck.
He was near Winnemucca.

Notice that this cluster first names a *person* in two different ways (*Tucker* and *trucker*). Then it goes on to name a *place* (*Winnemucca*, a town in Nevada), a *thing* (*muck*), and even an *idea* (*luck*—what Tucker is out of). All the words in italics are nouns. Notice, too, that the cluster contains a *pronoun* (*he*), which is used twice to refer to the noun *Tucker*.

As we combine sentences, we'll move nouns around and sometimes use connectors like *and*, *who*, or *when*. We'll also delete repeated nouns (like *Tucker*) and pronouns (like *he*). And later we'll change nouns into other parts of speech—like adjectives or adverbs.

Here are three possible combined sentences to get us started:

A Tucker was an out-of-luck trucker *who* was stuck in the muck near Winnemucca.

or

B Near Winnemucca, a trucker named Tucker was out of luck *and* stuck in the muck.

or

C *When* Tucker the trucker was muck-stuck near Winnemucca, he was out of luck.

Sentences A, B, and C are all "right answers," of course. They illustrate the *flexibility* of nouns in English—the way nouns can occupy different "slots" in a sentence.

You can put these nouns into different arrangements by using other connectors and by changing word order. Here are just a few possibilities:

D Stuck in the muck and out of luck, Tucker the trucker was near Winnemucca.

or

E A trucker named Tucker, out of luck near Winnemucca, was stuck in the muck.

or

F It was near Winnemucca that Tucker, an out-of-luck trucker, was stuck in the muck.

or

G Not only was trucker Tucker stuck in the muck near Winnemucca, but he was also out of luck.

As you learned above, nouns can also change form and become new parts of speech. For example, we can convert a noun phrase (like *out of luck)* into an adjective (like *luckless* or *unlucky*). Such an adjective, in turn, can then become an adverb (like *lucklessly* or *unluckily*). Watch these processes: nouns becoming adjectives and adjectives becoming adverbs.

H Tucker, a *luckless* trucker, was stuck in the muck near Winnemucca.

or

I Near Winnemucca was where a trucker named Tucker was *unluckily* stuck in the muck.

or

J *Unlucky* Tucker, the trucker, was muck-stuck near Winnemucca.

What about a phrase like *muck-stuck* above? Once again, it shows the flexibility of nouns. In addition, the words *muck* and *stuck* can team up in other creative ways, without a hyphen. Here's one way that might make a telegram:

> *K* Muck stuck unlucky Trucker Tucker near Winnemucca.

Sentence K is mostly nouns—*muck, Trucker, Tucker, Winnemucca.* The sentence has one verb *(stuck)*, one adjective *(unlucky)*, and one preposition *(near)*. Or, even more economically, we might send this:

> *L* Winnemucca's muck stuck luckless Tucker's truck.

Sentence L, with only six words, has four nouns. By now, you should have little trouble spotting them.

Besides naming people, places, things, and ideas, it's clear that nouns do other things as well. For example, they sometimes change into adjectives (for example, *unlucky* and *luckless*). They sometimes team up with other words to become modifiers (such as *muck-stuck*). They sometimes modify other nouns (such as *out-of-luck trucker* or *Trucker Tucker*). And, to show possession, they sometimes take on an ending: *-'s* (for example, *Winnemucca's muck* and *Tucker's truck)* or *-s'*.

But the main job of nouns is to name things and *rename* each other. For example, we can take a perfectly good sentence like M:

> *M* Tucker was an unlucky trucker who was stuck in Winnemucca's muck.

and make it a tighter, more direct sentence like N:

> *N* Tucker, an unlucky trucker, was stuck in Winnemucca's muck.

Notice that N puts a noun phrase *(an unlucky trucker)* close to the noun it describes *(Tucker)*. (For more on this strategy, see the Toolbox lesson on appositives in Unit 7.)

The same approach also works with adjectives, as is shown below, in sentence O:

O Trucker Tucker, luckless and muck-stuck, was near Winnemucca.

You'll learn how nouns and adjectives team up in the Toolbox lesson on adjectives, later in this unit. Until then, think "Tucker" when you think of nouns!

 SC with Nouns

Directions Focus on nouns as you combine sentences. Then check your work (odd-numbered exercises) in the Answer Key. Imitate at least five of these sentences, using your own content.

1.1 Matt was a fat cat.
1.2 He sat on his hat.
1.3 He made it flat.

2.1 Mark was in a dark park.
2.2 Clark was in a dark park.
2.3 They heard dogs bark.

3.1 Sue heard from you.
3.2 She felt somewhat blue.
3.3 She ordered a brew or two.
3.4 She decided to start anew.

4.1 Gwen was a Zen comedienne.
4.2 She had no friends.
4.3 She developed a yen for Ben.
4.4 Ben was an Italian "specimen."

5.1 The dentist testified in a lawsuit.
5.2 The dentist was nicely dressed.
5.3 She swore to tell the whole tooth.
5.4 She swore to tell nothing but the tooth.

6.1 A bachelor sailor is a fellow.
6.2 The fellow is footloose.
6.3 The fellow is fiancée-free.
6.4 The fellow has a yacht to offer.

7.1 Our ranch offers an environment for horses.
7.2 The environment is stable.
7.3 It includes groom and board.
7.4 It even features a Bridle Suite.

8.1 A crematorium guard made a cryptic remark.
8.2 The remark was to a grave mortician.
8.3 "We'll furnace the ashes."
8.4 "You'll have to urn your own way."

9.1 The surgeon made a cutting remark.
9.2 The surgeon was the knife of the party.
9.3 "I removed the comedian's appundix."
9.4 "He had an infectious sense of humor."

10.1 Bird lovers have four beliefs.
10.2 "Nothing vultured, nothing gained."
10.3 "Ostrich in time saves nine."
10.4 "One good tern deserves another."
10.5 "Toucan live as cheaply as one."

VERBS

Like small engines, ***verbs*** provide power for every sentence you speak or write. Without verbs, your sentences go nowhere. To help you remember that verbs create the energy for expression, let's consider a pair of sentences dealing with engines—sentences in which *shuddered* and *sputtered* are the verbs.

Example 1

The engine shuddered.
The engine sputtered.

To combine these sentences, you could use *and* or *then* as connectors:

1A The engine shuddered *and* sputtered.

or

1B The engine shuddered, *then* sputtered.

But you could also change the *form* of the verbs so that each one becomes a modifier for the noun *engine*. Notice what happens to each verb's ending.

1C The *shuddering* engine sputtered.

or

1D The *sputtering* engine shuddered.

When verbs become noun modifiers, as shown in sentences 1C and 1D, they're called *participles*. For more about one-word participles, see the Toolbox lesson on adjectives, below.

In the next cluster (example 2), you see more verbs, just waiting to be combined. How will you handle this cluster?

Example 2

Mechanic Cutter muttered under her breath.
Mechanic Cutter uttered an oath.
Mechanic Cutter puttered on the carburetor.

Because the sentences in example 2 have the same subject—*Mechanic Cutter*—you'd probably make a series of verb phrases:

2A Mechanic Cutter *muttered* under her breath, *uttered* an oath, and *puttered* on the carburetor.

With this strategy, one noun *(Mechanic Cutter)* works with three verbs. Notice how commas separate the verb phrases in a series.

Another approach to combining example 2 is to use connecting words like *after* and *before*. This approach forces you to add an *-ing* ending to verbs as you combine:

2B *After muttering* under her breath and *uttering* an oath, Mechanic Cutter puttered on the carburetor.

or

2C *Before puttering* on the carburetor, Mechanic Cutter muttered to herself and uttered an oath.

The *-ing* verb phrases in 2B and 2C are like the one-word participles you saw modifying nouns above—they perform a similar task.

So far, you've seen the flexibility of verbs. You can link them in pairs or in a series; you can make them into noun modifiers by changing their endings; and you can make them into verb phrases (participle phrases) that add variety to sentences. For more on this topic, see the Toolbox lesson on participle phrases in Unit 7.

Let's now add two new sentences to example 2:

Example 2 (continued)

The oath was stuttering.
The carburetor was cluttered.

Watch what happens to *stuttering* and *cluttered* as we combine:

2D Mechanic Cutter muttered under her breath, uttered a *stuttering* oath, and puttered on the *cluttered* carburetor.

One-word modifiers like those in sentence 2D—one with an *-ing* ending, the other with an *-ed* ending—modify nouns such as *oath* and *carburetor*.

Let's now put verb phrases in the *middle* of a basic sentence, between the noun subject *(Mechanic Cutter)* and the main verb *(puttered)*:

> *2E* Mechanic Cutter—*muttering* under her breath, then *uttering* a stuttering oath—*puttered* on the cluttered carburetor.

It's important to emphasize here that *-ing* verb phrases don't stand by themselves as sentences. Such pieces of sentences are called *sentence fragments*. Note, for instance, the fragment below (2F), which lacks a main verb. It is labeled "Problem" to signal what you *shouldn't* do in your writing. Say fragment 2F aloud, noticing how it sounds unfinished and "up in the air."

> *2F—Problem* Mechanic Cutter *muttering* under her breath, *uttering* a stuttering oath, and *puttering* on the cluttered carburetor.

How do you fix such a fragment? At least one of the verb phrases must be switched from the *-ing* form to an *-ed* form. Sentence 2G shows one possible solution to the problem in 2F:

> *2G* Mechanic Cutter *puttered* on the cluttered carburetor—*muttering* under her breath and *uttering* a stuttering oath.

If you have problems with fragments, pay attention to verbs. If you get the verbs straight, things generally fall into place.

Finally, how about transforming verbs into nouns? Can it be done? Let's give it a try:

> *2H* Mechanic Cutter's *under-her-breath muttering* and *uttering of a stuttering oath* were followed by *cluttered carburetor puttering*.

This transformation of verbs into noun phrases (in italic) in sentence 2H shows the flexibility of verbs. They can modify nouns—as we saw earlier—but they can also *become* nouns.

For work on subject-verb agreement, see "Coordinators" later in this unit and "Subject-Verb Agreement" in Unit 8.

 SC with Verbs

Directions Focus on verbs as you combine sentences. Create plural verb forms for *is*, *was*, *does*, and *has*. Then check your work (odd-numbered exercises) in the Answer Key. Imitate at least five of these sentences, using your own content.

1.1 Alex crossed the finish line.
1.2 Alex raised a fist in victory salute.

2.1 Ruth demanded a raise from her employer.
2.2 Ruth received a severance notice.

3.1 Seijo turned to head downstairs.
3.2 Seijo faced a gang of armed thugs.

4.1 Geri nodded gravely to her supporters.
4.2 Geri understood what was expected of her.

5.1 Elden was asked to retake the exam.
5.2 Henry was asked to retake the exam.

6.1 Yuki is considered part of our family.
6.2 Elsa is considered part of our family.

7.1 Jake does not know how to handle compliments.
7.2 Fred does not know how to handle compliments.

8.1 Rose has been offered a tuition scholarship.
8.2 Anna has been offered a tuition scholarship.

9.1 The proposxal introduced the problem.
9.2 The proposal reviewed previous research.
9.3 The proposal outlined a new methodology.

10.1 In a secret meeting the competitors met.
10.2 In a secret meeting the competitors fixed prices.
10.3 In a secret meeting the competitors drank a toast.

ADJECTIVES

If you're a "Peanuts" fan, you probably know the first (and only) line of Snoopy's great American novel:

> It was a dark and stormy night.

What you may not know is that Madeline L'Engle used exactly the same words to open her award-winning classic, *A Wrinkle in Time*.

This sentence uses adjectives—*dark* and *stormy*—to establish mood. ***Adjectives*** modify, or describe, nouns; in this case, they modify the word *night*, which is a noun.

The following example shows other ways to position adjectives in a sentence.

Example 1

It was a dark and stormy night.
Night fell on our village.

↓

1A It was a *dark*, *stormy* night that fell on our village.

or

1B A *dark*, *stormy* night fell on our village.

or

1C *Dark and stormy*, the night fell on our village.

or

1D The night, *dark and stormy*, fell on our village.

Notice that sentences 1A and 1B have a comma between *dark* and *stormy*. And remember this: If you can put *and* between two adjectives, you put a comma between them in a series. Notice also that the phrase *dark and stormy* can go in front of *night* (1C) or after it (1D). Sentences 1A, 1B, 1C, and 1D are all correct, but each has its own distinctive rhythm. Experiment with such patterns when combining sentences or revising your own writing.

Here's a second example:

Example 2

Gusts of wind blew across the lake.

The wind was icy.

The wind was from the arctic.

↓

2A Gusts of icy arctic wind blew across the lake.

but not

2B—Problem Gusts of icy, arctic wind blew across the lake.

Why shouldn't sentence 2B be punctuated as shown above? The answer is that you probably wouldn't say "icy and arctic wind." (Technically speaking, the words *icy* and *arctic* come from different word classes.)

Let's see what happens when we add a new sentence to example 2:

Example 2 (continued)

The wind snarled.

2C Gusts of *icy* and *snarling* arctic wind blew across the lake.

or

2D Gusts of *icy*, *snarling* arctic wind blew across the lake.

Notice first that the verb *snarled* has become *snarling* (a type of adjective called a *participle*). Notice also that a comma appears between *icy* and *snarling* in 2D because of the "and" rule you learned earlier.

While it's possible to load up adjectives in front of a noun, the sentence may begin to sound awkward. An alternative approach is to position adjectives (or participles) *after* the noun. Let's add two more sentences to example 2:

Example 2 (continued)

The wind was mixed with sleet.
The sleet chilled our bones.

Two possible combinations, 2E and 2F, are interesting to read:

2E Gusts of *snarling, icy* arctic wind, *mixed with bone-chilling sleet,* blew across the lake.

or

2F Gusts of arctic wind—*icy, snarling, and mixed with bone-chilling sleet*—blew across the lake.

A modifier like *bone-chilling* in 2E and 2F is especially powerful because it packs the meaning of an entire sentence—*The sleet chilled our bones*—into a succinct phrase.

Here's another example focusing on modifiers that precede and follow a noun, in this case *fireplace*. Notice the punctuation patterns.

Example 3

My family huddled in front of a fireplace.
The fireplace was made of stone.
The fireplace was drafty.
The fireplace blazed.
The fireplace was stocked well.

↓

3A My family huddled in front of a *drafty, blazing, and well-stocked* stone fireplace.

or

3B My family huddled in front of a stone fireplace—*drafty, blazing, and well-stocked.*

Sentences 3A and 3B are both effective, though different in their rhythms. To choose one, you would depend on a larger context, the paragraph as a whole.

Adjectives don't always come as single words, of course. Sometimes you'll have adjective phrases that you can work with:

Example 4

We hung together spiritually.
We were secure and warm.
We were frightened by the storm's fury.

↓

4A *Secure and warm, but frightened by the storm's fury,* we hung together spiritually.

Using what you have learned, try two *other* placements for the italicized adjective phrases in 4A:

4B ____

4C ____

SC with Adjectives

Directions Focus on adjectives as you combine sentences. Then check your work (odd-numbered exercises) in the Answer Key. Imitate at least five of these sentences, using your own content.

1.1 Theo found a slice of pizza in his backpack.
1.2 The slice of pizza was forgotten.
1.3 The pizza was greasy.

2.1 A team of agents nailed the drug pushers.
2.2 The team was swift and silent.
2.3 The drug pushers were sleeping.

3.1 The class turned to Sabrina for answers.
3.2 The class was frustrated.
3.3 The answers would be helpful.

4.1 Sounds of music reverberated in the stadium.
4.2 The music was loud and brassy.
4.3 The stadium was packed.

5.1 The path led toward a view of the lake.
5.2 The view was stunning and unobstructed.
5.3 The lake was shimmering.

6.1 A group of children watched the potter's hands.
6.2 The children were inquisitive but shy.
6.3 The hands were sure and practiced.

7.1 Kwan Ho strode toward the speaker's platform.
7.2 Kwan Ho was confident.
7.3 Kwan Ho was thoroughly prepared.

8.1 Anna watched the garden shadows.
8.2 The shadows were cool and inviting.
8.3 The shadows were filled with mosquitoes.

9.1 Mark sold his bracelet for tuition.
9.2 The bracelet was crafted by hand.
9.3 The bracelet was studded with turquoise.

10.1 Rufina's dark eyes expressed her emotion.
10.2 Her eyes filled with tears.
10.3 Her emotion was heartfelt.

ADVERBS

Probably, you remember ***adverbs*** from seventh grade; but if not, just focus on the word that opens this sentence. We'll consider modifiers like *probably* because they're so useful for adding texture to sentences.

Here's an example:

Example 1

The boss studied her company's balance sheet.
Her study was thoughtful.

1A The boss *thoughtfully* studied her company's balance sheet.

Notice that the adjective *thoughtful* takes an *-ly* ending to become a different part of speech—an adverb. This adverb modifies a verb, *studied*.

One interesting feature of adverbs is that you can move them around. Sentence 1A might be written as follows:

1B *Thoughtfully*, the boss studied her company's balance sheet.

or

1C The boss studied her company's balance sheet *thoughtfully*.

Each version creates a slight change in emphasis. Experiment with positioning adverbs in your own sentences.

Let's focus on a *pair* of adverbs in example 2. Once again, watch how adjectives take *-ly* endings to become adverbs.

Example 2

She had reorganized the firm.
Her reorganization had been swift.
Her reorganization had been decisive.
The results were still disappointing.

↓

2A She had *swiftly* and *decisively* reorganized the firm, but the results were still disappointing.

or

2B She had reorganized the firm *swiftly* and *decisively*, but the results were still disappointing.

Whisper sentences 2A and 2B aloud. Notice that 2B has adverbs at the *end* of a main clause—this gives them emphasis.

Another way to give adverbs emphasis is through punctuation, as shown in example 3:

Example 3

She had argued for radical change.
Her arguments were persuasive.
Her arguments were successful.
She had then implemented new policies.
Her implementation was single-handed.

↓

3A After arguing *persuasively* and *successfully* for radical change, she had implemented new policies *single-handedly*.

For added emphasis, you might set off the paired adverbs in 3A between two commas or a pair of dashes:

3B After arguing—*persuasively* and *successfully*—for radical change, she had implemented new policies *single-handedly*.

Now that you see how adverbs modify verbs, let's consider another use for them. In example 4, watch how an adverb is used to modify the adjective *professional*.

Example 4

Her approach had been professional.
Her professionalism was complete.

↓

Her approach had been *completely* professional.

Unlike other adverbs we've seen, *completely* here cannot be moved. It's tied to the adjective it modifies.

Here's another example of the same pattern. Notice how adverbs modify the adjective *simple* and the participle *detailed*; a third adverb modifies the verb *informed*. As you will see, the third adverb is movable, whereas the other two are not.

Example 5

She had developed a simple but detailed plan.
Its simplicity was elegant.
Its detail was thorough.
She had informed workers of her intentions.
Her informing was forceful.

↓

5A She had developed an *elegantly* simple but *thoroughly* detailed plan and had *forcefully* informed workers of her intentions.

or

5B She had developed an *elegantly* simple but *thoroughly* detailed plan and had informed workers, *forcefully*, of her intentions.

As you can see here, adverbs add texture and richness to phrasing in a sentence. Notice particularly how punctuation adds emphasis.

Here's a final example of adverbs in action:

Example 6

She considered the firm's bottom line.
Her consideration was nervous.
She felt uneasy about the future.
Her uneasiness was vague.

↓

6A *Nervously* considering the firm's bottom line, she felt *vaguely* uneasy about the future.

or

6B Feeling *vaguely* uneasy about the future, she *nervously* considered the firm's bottom line.

Once you discover the power of adverbs, you may be tempted to overuse them. Resist this temptation. Like rich chocolate cake, an occasional adverb—used *caringly* and *sparingly*—achieves a more satisfying result than adverbs used *mindlessly*. In fact, adverbs sometimes become a crutch for writers who are too lazy to find vivid, specific verbs. So use them—but don't abuse them.

 SC with Adverbs

Directions Focus on adverbs as you combine sentences. Then check your work (odd-numbered exercises) in the Answer Key. Imitate at least five of these sentences, using your own content.

1.1 Hector reviewed the lesson on adverbs.
1.2 His review was careful.

2.1 Jennifer submitted her research paper.
2.2 Her submission was confident.

3.1 They left the cafe after their argument.
3.2 Their leaving was quiet.
3.3 Their leaving was unobtrusive.

4.1 We welcomed the newcomers to town.
4.2 Our welcome was warm.
4.3 Our welcome was enthusiastic.

5.1 The security man checked in at midnight.
5.2 This was customary.
5.3 His check-in was sleepy.

6.1 The committee meeting dragged on.
6.2 This was typical.
6.3 The dragging on was endless.

7.1 The storm's fury moved inland.
7.2 This was ironic.
7.3 The movement was unexpected.

8.1 We argued a problem that was complex.
8.2 Our arguments were loud.
8.3 The complexity was bewildering.

9.1 The detailed analysis of results arrived.
9.2 The detail was rich.
9.3 Its arrival was belated.

10.1 A disgusted parent barked her disapproval.
10.2 Her disgust was thorough.
10.3 Her bark was sharp.

COORDINATORS

You're an expert in ***coordination.*** Why? As a child, you mastered this combining strategy first. Specifically, you used coordinators (like *and*, *but*, *for*, *nor*, *so*, *yet*) to join words, phrases, and sentences.

Let's review how coordination works.

Example 1

The Rodney King videotape was a traumatic event.
The trial of four policemen was a traumatic event.
The aftermath was an American catastrophe.

↓

The Rodney King videotape *and* the trial of four policemen were traumatic events, *but* the aftermath was an American catastrophe.

Notice how the verb *was* changes to *were* as sentences are combined. Joining two sentences with *and* creates a *compound subject* for the first clause. The second clause is connected by *but* plus a comma. The result shown above is called a ***compound sentence.***

Here's another example of the compound sentence pattern:

Example 2

Los Angeles exploded into flames.
Los Angeles exploded into violence.
Los Angeles exploded into both of the above.
The urban shame of the United States could no longer be ignored.

Los Angeles exploded into flames *or* violence *or* both, *and* America's urban shame could no longer be ignored.

Here, once again, you see a compound sentence with standard punctuation—a coordinator *(and)* plus a comma. The first clause of the combined sentence has a *compound predicate* with words joined by *or*.

Of course, coordination may involve more than a pair of words, phrases, or sentences. Sometimes these elements occur in a series of three or more, as shown in example 3:

Example 3

The riots resulted from poverty.
The riots resulted from lack of jobs.
The riots resulted from lack of hope.
The riots resulted from racial tensions.

The riots resulted from poverty, lack of jobs and hope, *and* racial tensions.

When you put items in a series—whether they are words, phrases, or sentences—you separate them by commas as shown above; notice that the sentence you are *now* reading also illustrates a series.

Besides the basic coordinators, several other types of *paired coordinators* are useful to you. These include the following:

either . . . or
neither . . . nor
whether . . . or
both . . . and
not . . . but (only)
not only . . . but (also)

The *not only . . . but (also)* pattern is shown in example 4. Watch how it works and notice the sophisticated effect it creates.

Example 4

Many leaders called for restraint.
Rodney King called for restraint.

↓

4A *Not only* did many leaders call for restraint, *but* so did Rodney King.

Of course, we can add information to example 4:

Example 4 (continued)

Some leaders were black.
Other leaders were white.

The result, using another type of paired coordinator *(both . . . and)*, might look like this:

4B Many leaders, *both* black *and* white, called for restraint, *and* so did Rodney King.

Sentence 4B shows a paired coordinator, but it also shows something else—the use of *interruption*. By interrupting a pattern of coordination, you can achieve special emphasis. You achieve emphasis by altering the rhythm and "pointing" the reader's attention with subtle cues. Notice that, in example 5, sentence 5A uses a paired coordinator *(whether . . . or)* to make its statement; 5B uses interruption for added emphasis. Stylistically, which of the two do you prefer?

Example 5

The United States can choose to address its urban problems.
The United States can choose to ignore its urban problems.
The choice may well determine our nation's future.

↓

5A *Whether* the United States chooses to address its urban problems *or* to ignore them may well determine our nation's future.

or

5B Whether the United States chooses to address its urban problems—*or* to ignore them—may well determine our nation's future.

As shown in 5B, dashes can provide strong interruption in the flow of a sentence. But you can also interrupt a compound sentence with a semicolon, to achieve more emphasis (and more formality) than the standard comma gives.

To review coordination, study example 6:

Example 6

We may differ in skin color.
Our shared dreams can unite us as citizens.
Our shared dreams can rebuild our city's skylines.
Our shared dreams are for peace, respect, and opportunity.

↓

We may differ in skin color; *but* our shared dreams—for peace, respect, and opportunity—can *not only* unite us as citizens *but also* rebuild our city's skylines.

 SC with Coordinators

Directions Focus on coordination as you combine sentences. Then check your work (odd-numbered exercises) in the Answer Key. Imitate at least five of these sentences, using your own content.

1.1 Wan Su was among the first to be honored.
1.2 Sung Ho was among the first to be honored.

2.1 Jenny has asked for help with coordination.
2.2 Marie has asked for help with coordination.

3.1 Benito recently bought a stereo for his car.
3.2 Benito recently bought new tires for his car.
3.3 Benito recently bought a battery for his car.

4.1 Celia first went to the day care center.
4.2 Celia then stopped for gas and groceries.
4.3 Celia finally ended up at the College Center.

5.1 The restaurant's food was delicious.
5.2 The restaurant's food was satisfying.
5.3 The restaurant's food was much too expensive.

6.1 The new neighbors seem cordial.
6.2 The new neighbors seem very helpful.
6.3 The new neighbors seem extremely nosy.

7.1 You may work on coordination.
7.2 You may do 100 sit-ups.
7.3 You may do 50 push-ups.

Note Use *either . . . or* in cluster 7.

8.1 Michelle likes to play soccer.
8.2 Michelle likes to play volleyball.
8.3 Michelle really prefers track competition.

Note Use *both . . . and* in cluster 8.

9.1 The concert was sold out.
9.2 All the rooms in town were booked.
9.3 All the rooms for miles around were booked.

Note Use *not only . . . but also* in cluster 9.

10.1 Citizens can choose to use drugs.
10.2 Citizens can turn away from them.
10.3 This choice has far-reaching implications.

Note Use *whether . . . or* in cluster 10.

SUBORDINATORS

A subordinate clause is part of a larger sentence. Such a clause is always introduced by a ***subordinator,*** a word that "points" the sentence in a specific logical direction. Compare the different meanings of the two combined sentences in example 1:

Example 1

Some young adults risk long-term injury with steroids.
Many schools provide weak programs in health education.

↓

1A *Although some young adults risk long-term injury with steroids*, many schools provide weak programs in health education.

or

1B *Because many schools provide weak programs in health education*, some young adults risk long-term injury with steroids.

The subordinators above are *although* and *because*. By attaching them to a complete sentence, you create a subordinate clause (shown in italic). Notice that this clause cannot stand alone; it depends on another sentence, an independent (or main) clause.

As you see, positioning a subordinate clause "up front" in a sentence creates interest. However, subordinate clauses can also *follow* a main clause, as shown in sentence 1C:

1C—Some young adults risk long-term injury with steroids *because many schools provide weak programs in health education*.

Notice that although an "up front" subordinate clause takes a comma, no comma is needed in sentence 1C. This pattern is an important one to remember.

Here's another example of subordinate clauses. Once again, pay attention to the punctuation pattern.

Example 2

Steroids have physical and mental side effects.
A million Americans ignore the serious dangers.
They want to look like their fantasy heroes.

↓

Although steroids have physical and mental side effects, a million Americans ignore the serious dangers *because they want to look like their fantasy heroes*.

This sentence has two subordinate clauses (in italic) and one main clause (in regular type). As you can see, the "point" of the total sentence is in the main clause. The "up front" subordinate clause is again set off by a comma.

So far, we've looked at two subordinators—*although* (which expresses contrast) and *because* (which expresses cause). Let's now consider subordinators that express other meanings.

Example 3

Young men go to popular "action films."
They see larger-than-life figures like the Terminator.

↓

3A *When young men go to popular "action films,"* they see larger-than-life figures like the Terminator.

or

3B Young men go to popular "action films" *where they see larger-than-life figures like the Terminator*.

Sentence 3A shows a subordinator that expresses time or condition *(when)*; 3B shows a subordinator that expresses place *(where)*. The punctuation patterns are like those you've already seen.

Following is a list of common subordinators by category. You can refer to this list when you're unsure about the specific subordinator you need.

Contrast

although
even though
whereas
while

Cause

as
because
since
so that

Time

after
as soon as
before
since
until
when
whenever
while

Condition

as if
assuming that
if
in case
provided that
unless
when
whether

Place

where
wherever

Degree

inasmuch as
to the extent that

For a final example of subordination, consider this:

Example 4

Steroids are now found in elementary schools.
They can stunt growth and cause deformities.
Young children look up to teenage users.

4A *Because young children look up to teenage users*, steroids are now found in elementary schools, *where they can stunt growth and cause deformities*.

In 4A, one subordinate clause begins with *because*, the other with *where*. Notice that each subordinate clause is positioned close to the material it modifies. Such positioning makes the sentence clear.

Here's the same sentence pattern with different subordinators:

4B *Since young children look up to teenager users*, steroids are now found in elementary schools—*despite the fact that they can stunt growth and cause deformities*.

In 4A and 4B, both final clauses *do* have internal punctuation—for special emphasis!

SC with Subordinators

Directions Focus on subordinators as you combine sentences. Then check your work (odd-numbered exercises) in the Answer Key. Imitate at least five of these sentences, using your own content.

1.1 The morning paper had arrived.
1.2 Julian was ready to begin his routine.

Note Use *after* in cluster 1.

2.1 The Orchard Society met each month.
2.2 Hilda made sure her voice was heard.

Note Use *when* in cluster 2.

3.1 Friendships take years to build.
3.2 They can be wrecked with a few careless remarks.

Note Use *although* in cluster 3.

4.1 I didn't turn in this lottery number.
4.2 Five million dollars went unclaimed last week.

Note Use *because* in cluster 4.

5.1 Maxine gets some kind of job.
5.2 Maxine cuts her monthly expenses.
5.3 Her parents are reluctant to buy her a Porsche.

Note Use *until* in cluster 5.

6.1 You may have extra time on your paper.
6.2 It is turned in by 5 P.M. Friday.
6.3 You buy pizza for our final class meeting.

Note Use *provided that* in cluster 6.

7.1 The weather began to turn cold.
7.2 We took one last camping trip into the hills.
7.3 We hope to build a cabin there someday.

Note Use *before* and *where* in cluster 7.

8.1 A full moon peeks through the clouds.
8.2 We are sure to see an unusually high tide.
8.3 The laws of the universe still work.

Note Use *if* and *assuming that* in cluster 8.

9.1 Senior citizens are a powerful voting bloc.
9.2 Most politicians are reluctant to cut entitlements.
9.3 Everybody wants to reduce the deficit.

Note Use *because* and *although* in cluster 9.

10.1 Many apply for jobs with the CIA.
10.2 Few are able to pass the rigorous security requirements.
10.3 They are highly patriotic Americans.

Note Use *while* and *even though* in cluster 10.

PREPOSITIONAL PHRASES

Prepositional phrases are word groups, some expressing *time* or *place*, others expressing *how* or *why* things happen, and still others expressing what things are *like*. Here are some prepositional phrases, in italic:

> *Before the Challenger disaster*, shuttle launches seemed almost routine; but *after the explosion*, Americans knew the risks.
>
> Today, we remember where we were—*at school*, *on the patio*, or *by the kitchen window*—when we first saw the tragic videotape.
>
> *In our mind's eye*, we can still see the rocket's liftoff *into a blue Florida sky*, *with all systems "go."*

Each prepositional phrase consists of a preposition—a word like *before*, *after*, *at*, *on*, *by*, *in*, *into*, or *with*—plus a noun or noun phrase (the "object" of the preposition). English has dozens of prepositions.

To learn how prepositional phrases are embedded into sentences, let's consider some examples. In example 1, notice that the combined sentences highlight a series of three phrases—beginning, respectively, with *in*, *to*, and *of*.

Example 1

The Challenger carried a female teacher.
The teacher was Christa McCullough.
This was in addition to its crew.
The crew was six male astronauts.

1A *In addition to its crew of six male astronauts*, the Challenger carried a female teacher, Christa McCullough.

or

1B The Challenger, *in addition to its crew of six male astronauts*, carried a female teacher, Christa McCullough.

1C The Challenger carried a female teacher, Christa McCullough, *in addition to its crew of six male astronauts*.

As you can see, prepositional phrases often team up to make a "train" of modifiers. Moreover, the "train" of phrases can do its work at the beginning, middle, or end of a sentence.

Prepositional phrases are so plentiful—and so movable—that you can often use them to create *sentence variety*. For example, if you spot several sentences with the same boring pattern, it's usually easy to move a phrase or two, thus improving the "flow" of the paragraph. Such tinkering puts you in control of your writing.

Here's another example to study:

Example 2

Christa McCullough's children were there watching.
The scene took on tragic dimensions.

2A *Because Christa McCullough's children were there watching*, the scene took on tragic dimensions.

or

2B *Because of Christa McCullough's watching children*, the scene took on tragic dimensions.

Sentence 2A illustrates a full subordinate clause; sentence 2B illustrates a subordinator *(because)* plus a prepositional phrase. In some contexts, 2B might be more effective because of its brevity. Which do you prefer?

Let's now see how to position prepositional phrases at other points in a sentence. Whisper the combined sentences below to yourself.

Example 3

The children's joy was transformed into shocked horror.
The joy was in the wake of a thundering liftoff.
Their horror was like ours.
Their horror was much worse.

3A The children's joy, *in the wake of a thundering liftoff*, was transformed *into shocked horror—like ours, except much worse*.

In 3A, the prepositional phrase is embedded in the *middle* of the sentence; but notice that it can also *open* the sentence:

3B *In the wake of a thundering liftoff*, the children's joy was transformed *into shocked horror—like ours, except much worse*.

You can also use prepositional phrases to set up dramatic and effective contrasts:

At first, we experienced grief; but *over time*, we became numb.

Here the contrasting prepositional phrases work with the coordinator *but* to make a point forcefully and succinctly.

One problem with prepositional phrases is that they sometimes "pile up" like rush-hour traffic. To prevent such gridlock from slowing your reader, you can sometimes *combine* meanings so that each phrase does more work. Combining works just like car-pooling. If you make each phrase carry one or two others, you clear out the congestion. Sentence 4A below is a problem; it is long (23 words) and hard to read. Sentence 4B, which is shorter (19 words), clears up the congestion, solving the problem.

Example 4

This happened despite the reality of the disaster.
Our emotions were anesthetized by imagery.
The imagery was in slow motion.
The imagery was from countless replays.
The replays were Challenger's last moments.

↓

4A—Problem *Despite the reality of the disaster*, our emotions were anesthetized *by imagery in slow motion from the countless replays of Challenger's last moments*.

↓

4B *Despite the disaster's reality*, our emotions were anesthetized *by slow-motion imagery*—the countless replays *of Challenger's last moments*.

For more about prepositional phrases, see the material on editing in Unit 5.

 SC with Prepositional Phrases

Directions Focus on prepositional phrases as you combine sentences. Then check your work (odd-numbered exercises) in the Answer Key. Imitate at least five of these sentences, using your own content.

1.1 Andy felt confident and prepared.
1.2 This was before the exam.

2.1 Megan began arguing with her boyfriend.
2.2 This was after an expensive supper.

3.1 Sol understood what he had to do.
3.2 This was in his "heart of hearts."

4.1 Luisa treated herself to a new outfit.
4.2 This was because of her promotion.

5.1 Leroy stood at the edge of the crowd.
5.2 Leroy stood with a toothpick in his mouth.

6.1 Tina was like a roller derby queen.
6.2 Tina pushed her way into our conversation.

7.1 Everyone attended the poetry reading.
7.2 The reading was at a neighborhood cafe.
7.3 This was except for Mark and Michelle.

8.1 Grandpa's friends came from miles around.
8.2 The friends were from years gone by.
8.3 This was in order to pay their respects.

9.1 A compost pile helps reduce pressure on landfills.
9.2 The compost pile is for grass clippings and leaves.
9.3 This is in our nation's suburban communities.

10.1 The committee's report was quietly shelved.
10.2 This was toward the close of the legislative session.
10.3 This was despite the protests of activists.

UNIT 7

Tools of Advanced Grammar

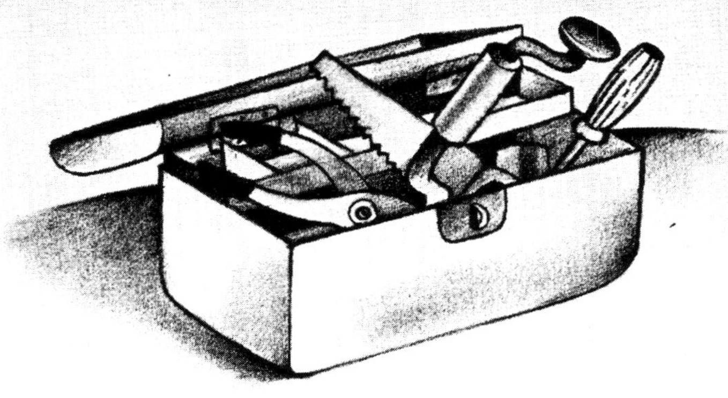

RELATIVE CLAUSES

What is a ***relative clause?*** To answer this question, let's consider three examples; the relative clauses are in italic:

Example 1

Tirebiter stood up abruptly.
Tirebiter was running for class president.

Tirebiter, *who was running for class president*, stood up abruptly.

Example 2

He made an impassioned speech.
The speech argued for longer lunches.

He made an impassioned speech *that argued for longer lunches*.

Example 3

His words were fiery and dramatic.
His words inspired bursts of applause.

3A His words, *which inspired bursts of applause*, were fiery and dramatic.

or

3B His words, *which were fiery and dramatic*, inspired bursts of applause.

Relative clauses—all of which modify nouns—provide a smooth, mature way to combine sentences. Although you don't want to overuse relative clauses, they can help you move beyond the "and, and, and" style of writing that you mastered in elementary school.

The examples above show relative clauses that use connectors such as *who*, *that*, or *which*. Notice that these connectors substitute for nouns and phrases such as *Tirebiter*, *speech*, and *his words*. Certain connectors (*who*, *that*, *whom*, *whose*) replace nouns that refer to people; other connectors (mainly *that* and *which*) replace nouns that refer to things, animals, and ideas. Relative clauses can also team up with prepositions—words like *by*, *for*, *in*, *of*, *to*, and *with*—as well as phrases such as *many of*, *some of*, or *none of*.

Note that the connectors need not always be used. In the following examples, any connector in parentheses is *optional*. Omitting such connectors results in an informal writing style.

Example 4

In the doorway stood Tirebiter's teacher.
The doorway opened to the hall.
Tirebiter's teacher appeared deeply unamused.

In the doorway *that opened to the hall* stood Tirebiter's teacher, *who appeared deeply unamused*.

Example 5

The students turned back to their assignments.
Tirebiter had entertained the students.
One of the assignments was due in a few minutes.

The students *(whom) Tirebiter had entertained* turned back to their assignments, *one of which was due in a few minutes*.

Example 6

The teacher shuffled to a cluttered desk.
Her attitude looked dangerous.
The desk was near the windows.

↓

The teacher—*whose attitude looked dangerous*—shuffled to a cluttered desk *that was near the windows.*

Example 7

The smile had become a serious frown.
She usually wore a smile.
Tirebiter had deep respect for the frown.

↓

7A The smile *(that) she usually wore* had become a serious frown, *for which Tirebiter had deep respect.*

or

7B The smile *she usually wore* had become a serious frown, *which Tirebiter had deep respect for.*

As you study the examples above, you can see the *flexibility* of relative clauses. Remember, however, that a relative clause carries *less emphasis* than the sentence in which it is embedded. Therefore, you should put what you want to emphasize in the main sentence, not in a relative clause.

Punctuating relative clauses can be tricky. Looking over the examples, you will see that some clauses use commas and dashes while others don't. Remember to *whisper sentences aloud and trust your ear.* Many writers also use this rule of thumb: *When in doubt, leave it out.*

To learn more about punctuation of relative clauses, consider example 8 on the opposite page. Read aloud sentences 8A and 8B, and think about the two different meanings.

Example 8

Tirebiter glanced at his friends.
Friends giggled at the back of the room.

↓

8A Tirebiter glanced at his friends *who giggled at the back of the room.*

or

8B Tirebiter glanced at his friends, *some of whom giggled at the back of the room.*

Sentence 8A focuses on a specific group—only those at the back of the room. There's no pause and therefore no comma. In 8B, however, Tirebiter looks at *everybody* in the room—they're *all* his friends—and sees some of them giggle.

Such differences are subtle, even for experienced writers, but don't let them throw you. You can learn the punctuation you need from paying attention to good writing. Pick up a book and find connectors like *who, that,* and *which;* then watch the punctuation! See "Commas" and "Dashes" in Unit 9 for more on punctuation.

SC with Relative Clauses

Directions Focus on relative clauses as you combine sentences. Then check your work (odd-numbered exercises) in the Answer Key. Imitate at least five of these sentences, using your own content.

1.1 George asked for help from his instructor.
1.2 She set up an appointment after class.

2.1 Helen prepared a detailed budget plan.
2.2 It was adopted by the Advisory Board.

3.1 Phil took a coffeepot to the office.
3.2 It had been salvaged from the trash.

4.1 Kim asked her boyfriend for a loan.
4.2 He had just borrowed money from his mom.

5.1 On the same lot, we looked at two cars.
5.2 Both of them seemed to be in good shape.

6.1 In the storm's wake were hundreds of victims.
6.2 Many of them needed food and medical care.

7.1 The young couple finally found an apartment.
7.2 The couple had camped in our living room.
7.3 The apartment is located just down the street.

8.1 The iced cappuccino was served in tall glasses.
8.2 We drank it on a bright and sunny lanai.
8.3 The glasses had been imported from Denmark.

9.1 The park's superintendent hired six workers.
9.2 He was subsequently fired for misconduct.
9.3 All of them were relatives or family members.

10.1 The paper's conclusion led to a failing grade.
10.2 The conclusion was completely plagiarized.
10.3 The grade seemed fair under the circumstances.

APPOSITIVES

An ***appositive*** adds information to a noun or noun phrase. Here's an example; appositives are highlighted in combined sentences 1A and 1B:

Example 1

Clarence Thomas was the Bush nominee to the Supreme Court.
Clarence Thomas was a staunchly conservative black judge.

↓

1A Clarence Thomas, *a staunchly conservative black judge*, was the Bush nominee to the Supreme Court.

or

1B Clarence Thomas—*the Bush nominee to the Supreme Court*—was a staunchly conservative black judge.

Both appositives tell more about a noun phrase, *Clarence Thomas*. The first appositive (*a staunchly conservative black judge*) identifies Thomas; the second (*the Bush nominee to the Supreme Court*) identifies his political connections.

To make an appositive, you first need to target the words that follow verbs such as *is*, *are*, *was*, *were*. Second, you attach this information to another sentence.

Example 2

Anita Hill was a law professor in Oklahoma.
Anita Hill was a woman of high moral character.
Anita Hill was a witness at the Senate hearings.

↓

2A Anita Hill—*a witness at the Senate hearings*—was a law professor in Oklahoma and a woman of high moral character.

or

2B Anita Hill, *a law professor in Oklahoma and a woman of high moral character*, was a witness at the Senate hearings.

Generally, words in an appositive carry less force than words in a complete sentence. Therefore, *put what you want to emphasize in the complete sentence*.

In the preceding examples, appositives appear in the *middle* of sentences. However, you can also make an appositive at the *beginning* or *end* of a sentence:

Example 3

The respected professor was a former colleague of Thomas.
The respected professor provided shocking testimony.
Her testimony was an accusation of sexual harassment.

↓

A former colleague of Thomas, the respected professor provided shocking testimony—*an accusation of sexual harassment*.

While most appositives *follow* nouns or noun phrases, you can create sentence variety by occasionally using an appositive as a sentence opener, as in example 3.

How else can you use appositives? Let's consider three strategies for integrating appositives into your writing:

- Negative appositives
- Adjectives that work as appositives
- Connecting words that introduce appositives

Example 4 shows an appositive in ***negative form.*** Notice the dramatic effect.

Example 4

Hill appeared to be a highly credible witness.
She was not a woman interested in sensational publicity.

Hill appeared to be a highly credible witness, *not a woman interested in sensational publicity*.

Following is an example of ***paired adjective phrases*** that work as appositives. Again, the effect is dramatic.

Example 5

Thomas was clearly shaken by Anita Hill's allegations.
Thomas was visibly angered by Anita Hill's allegations.
Thomas stuck to his story under questioning.

↓

Clearly shaken and visibly angered by Anita Hill's allegations, Thomas stuck to his story under questioning.

Finally, ***connecting words and phrases*** can introduce appositives. Such "renaming" connectors include words like *namely*, *especially*, and *mainly*; and phrases like *for example* and *in other words*. Here's an example:

Example 6

Thomas denied Hill's dramatic charges.
The charges included those confirmed by other witnesses.
Thomas was eventually appointed to the Supreme Court.

Thomas denied Hill's dramatic charges—*including those confirmed by other witnesses*—and was eventually appointed to the Supreme Court.

As you can see, commas and dashes are the main punctuation marks for appositives. However, the colon is also useful:

Example 7

The Senate hearings drew attention to an important issue.
The Senate hearings were controversial and divisive.
The issue was sexual harassment in the workplace.

While controversial and divisive, the Senate hearings drew attention to an important issue: *sexual harassment in the workplace*.

In punctuating appositives, use commas for clear, low-key emphasis. Use dashes for longer, more dramatic pauses. Reserve the colon for particularly serious or formal writing. For more on commas, dashes, and colons, see Unit 9.

SC with Appositives

Directions Focus on appositives as you combine sentences. Then check your work (odd-numbered exercises) in the Answer Key. Imitate at least five of these sentences, using your own content.

1.1 We hope to open a computer dating service.
1.2 This is not a commuter dating service.

2.1 The evaluators asked about office morale.
2.2 They did not ask about office morals.

3.1 Two new students joined our writing group.
3.2 They are Toshio Goya and Marita Rivera.

4.1 In my backpack two items were missing.
4.2 They were a calculator and a tape player.

5.1 Mike is a hardworking and talented artist.
5.2 Mike recently won a major regional prize.
5.3 It was one that carried a cash award.

6.1 Tonya is now the clerk in a law firm.
6.2 Tonya wants to become a children's advocate.
6.3 She will be a clear voice in their defense.

7.1 Anthony was relaxed and self-assured.
7.2 Anthony waited for his job interview.
7.3 It was a culmination of years of work.

8.1 Malee was upset but not discouraged.
8.2 Malee headed for the Writing Center.
8.3 It was a place where tutors provided help.

9.1 For dessert we had expected cannoli.
9.2 Cannoli are cream-filled pastries.
9.3 We had not expected cannelloni.
9.4 Cannelloni are a type of pasta.

10.1 The challenge for the United States seems quite clear.
10.2 The challenge is especially in technology.
10.3 The challenge is to move ahead aggressively.
10.4 The challenge is not to lose further ground.

PARTICIPLE PHRASES

Participle phrases are easy to use. They offer another alternative to "and, and, and" sentences and also add energy to your writing.

To understand how participle phrases work, consider the following cluster:

Example 1

Hurricane Andrew cut a swathe through Florida.
Hurricane Andrew left hundreds of thousands homeless.
Hurricane Andrew caused billions in property damage.

One simple approach to combining would be a series:

1A Hurricane Andrew cut a swathe through Florida, left hundreds of thousands homeless, and caused billions in property damage.

But another approach—one you might prefer—is to make participle phrases, as shown in italic in sentences 1B, 1C, and 1D.

1B *Cutting a swathe through Florida*, *causing billions in property damage*, Hurricane Andrew left hundreds of thousands homeless.

or

1C Hurricane Andrew—*cutting a swathe through Florida* and *leaving hundreds of thousands homeless*—caused billions in property damage.

or

1D Hurricane Andrew cut a swathe through Florida, *leaving hundreds of thousands homeless* and *causing billions in property damage*.

As you can see, participle phrases in sentences 1B, 1C, and 1D begin with a verb ending in *-ing*—a ***present participle.*** Notice how flexible these phrases are. They can be positioned at the beginning, middle, or end of a sentence.

Another type of participle phrase—a ***past participle***— has a verb ending in *-ed:*

Example 2

Tremendous winds tore at rooftops.
Tremendous winds flattened trees.
Tremendous winds were clocked at over 170 miles per hour.

↓

2A *Clocked at over 170 miles per hour*, tremendous winds tore at rooftops and flattened trees.

or

2B Tremendous winds—*clocked at over 170 miles per hour*—tore at rooftops and flattened trees.

Of course, you can also combine example 2 using present participles, as in 2C:

2C *Tearing at rooftops* and *flattening trees*, tremendous winds were clocked at over 170 miles per hour.

To use participle phrases skillfully, put what you want to emphasize in the *main sentence*. And in longer sentences, make sure to put participle phrases close to the key words they describe. In example 2, *tremendous winds* are the key words. Notice that in example 3, the key words are *mobile homes*. Whisper sentences 3A and 3B, to hear differences in emphasis.

Example 3

Mobile homes rolled and cartwheeled in Andrew's path.
Mobile homes shattered into fragments of lethal aluminum.

↓

3A *Rolling and cartwheeling in Andrew's path*, mobile homes shattered into fragments of lethal aluminum.

or

3B Mobile homes rolled and cartwheeled in Andrew's path, *shattering into fragments of lethal aluminum*.

Of course, we can add participle phrases to the description, thus enriching its detail.

3C *Upended by the winds* and *crushed like beer cans*, mobile homes rolled and cartwheeled in Andrew's path, *shattering into fragments of lethal aluminum*.

Participle phrases are remarkably flexible. But remember the "key words" principle. In example 4, the key word is *Floridians*. Watch what happens in 4A, 4B, and 4C.

Example 4

Floridians emerged from overnight shelters.
Floridians were stunned by the total devastation.

4A *Emerging from overnight shelters*, Floridians were stunned by the total devastation.

or

4B Floridians emerged from overnight shelters, *stunned by the total devastation*.

but not

4C—Problem *Emerging from overnight shelters*, the total devastation stunned Floridians.

Study sentence 4C carefully. Notice that the word order for the main sentence has been reversed. The result makes no sense: it says that *total devastation emerged from overnight shelters*. What's the problem? If you look carefully, you'll see that the participle phrase describes *total devastation* rather than *Floridians*. You might call this problem "not keeping track of key words." But most instructors call it a *dangling modifier* or *dangling participle*.

Here's another problem, with its solution:

Problem *Draped from broken poles*, people stared at downed power lines.

Solution People stared at downed power lines, *draped from broken poles*.

Don't let worries about dangling participles scare you away from participle phrases. By keeping track of "key words," you can easily edit any problems that come up. For more on dangling modifiers, see Unit 8.

SC with Participle Phrases

Directions Focus on participle phrases as you combine sentences. Then check your work (odd-numbered exercises) in the Answer Key. Imitate at least five of these sentences, using your own content.

1.1 Marcus stood on the deck of the boat.
1.2 Marcus raised one hand to shade his eyes.

2.1 Lucy sat in the tired, drafty courtroom.
2.2 Lucy felt a flood of tears behind her eyes.

3.1 Sam was relieved that his friends were safe.
3.2 Sam gave each of them a bear hug.

4.1 Carmen attended her church's Christmas pageant.
4.2 She was pleased that her son was participating.

5.1 The batter stepped up to the plate.
5.2 The batter pulled nervously at his cap.
5.3 The batter squinted into the afternoon sun.

6.1 The young lawyer held her voice steady.
6.2 The young lawyer began her summation.
6.3 The young lawyer showed poise and intelligence.

7.1 We were offended by the loud music.
7.2 We headed for another part of the beach.
7.3 We did not want to cause a scene.

8.1 We sat in the front row near the stage.
8.2 We were amused by the comedian's quickness.
8.3 We were concerned that he might focus on us.

9.1 A crowd swept past the security guards.
9.2 A crowd fanned out through the store.
9.3 A crowd searched for December 26 bargains.

10.1 The employer was impressed by my poise.
10.2 The employer was pleased that I could write.
10.3 The employer decided to hire me.

TRANSITIONS

To make a move is to make a transition. And the same idea applies to writing. You can make a transition within sentences or between sentences; you can also make a paragraph transition that links large chunks of text.

Let's consider a special group of words and phrases that serve as the "movers" for such a transition. Textbooks often call these words *conjunctive adverbs*, but the term ***transitions*** may work just as well. We'll study transitions in sentences, but remember that they also link paragraphs.

One kind of transition expresses ***contrast*** between ideas. For example, we might have a pair of sentences like these, expressing a contrast:

Example 1

Ross Perot energized voters in 1992.
Few political analysts saw him as a winner.

After combining this cluster with a contrast transition word like *however*, our results look like this:

1A Ross Perot energized voters in 1992; *however*, few political analysts saw him as a winner.

or

1B Ross Perot energized voters in 1992; few political analysts, *however*, saw him as a winner.

or

1C Ross Perot energized voters in 1992; few political analysts saw him as a winner, *however*.

Of sentences 1A, 1B, and 1C, the weakest is probably 1C. The reason is that, as readers, we like clear signals about where a sentence is headed—and the long-delayed *however* in 1C doesn't offer us that.

Now notice the punctuation patterns in example 1. The transition may immediately follow a semicolon; on the other hand, it may also be embedded, with commas, into the second sentence—or it may even end the sentence.

Other contrast transitions include *instead, rather, conversely, in contrast, on the contrary*, and *on the other hand*.

A second kind of transition expresses ***addition.*** Thus, if you've made one point and want to add a second point, you would use words and phrases like *also, in addition, furthermore, likewise, similarly, moreover.* And if you've made a point and want to reinforce it, you would use words like *indeed, in particular, in fact, more (or most) important*, and *above all*. Here's an example of an addition transition:

Example 2

Perot's no-nonsense approach appealed to many people.
He often scored points with quick one-liners.

2A Perot's no-nonsense approach appealed to many people; *also*, he often scored points with quick one-liners.

or

2B Perot's no-nonsense approach appealed to many people; he often scored points, *in addition*, with quick one-liners.

or

2C Perot's no-nonsense approach appealed to many people; he often scored points with quick one-liners, *in particular*.

Once again, notice the punctuation pattern: a semicolon in all three sentences and commas to signal pauses. Please note that *these patterns work for all transition words and phrases*.

A third kind of transition expresses ***reasons*** and ***results***—what we might call ***cause and effect.*** Words and phrases in this group include: *thus, therefore, consequently, hence, as a result*. Let's combine some more sentences, noting a familiar pattern of punctuation for cause-effect transitions.

Example 3

Perot financed his own campaign.
He could say anything he wanted.

↓

3A Perot financed his own campaign; *as a result*, he could say anything he wanted.

or

3B Perot financed his own campaign; *consequently*, he could say anything he wanted.

or

3C Perot financed his own campaign; he could, *therefore*, say anything he wanted.

Although sentence 3C is completely correct, there is another correct version, one without commas. When you whisper sentence 3D, you hear no pauses around *therefore*.

3D Perot financed his own campaign; he could *therefore* say anything he wanted.

The point with regard to 3D is that when you move the transition word in *front* of the verb and don't hear pauses, you can forget the commas.

A fourth kind of transition serves to ***rename*** or ***reassert*** earlier points. Included in this useful group are words and phrases like *namely, specifically, that is, for example, for instance, in other words*. Following is an example of a reassertion transition.

Example 4

What bothered many voters was Perot's quirkiness.
He entered the race, withdrew, and then reentered.

4A What bothered many voters was Perot's quirkiness; *that is*, he entered the race, withdrew, and then reentered.

or

4B What bothered many voters was Perot's quirkiness; *for example*, he entered the race, withdrew, and then reentered.

Finally, let's briefly note a fifth and sixth kind of transition. Words like *previously*, *meanwhile*, *in the meantime*, and *subsequently* enable you to express ***time.*** And words like *finally*, *thus*, *then*, *in conclusion*, *in summary* enable you to make a ***summary.*** Time and summary transitions are both very useful to you as a writer.

SC with Transitions

Directions Focus on transitions as you combine sentences. Then check your work (odd-numbered exercises) in the Answer Key. Imitate at least five of these sentences, using your own content.

1.1 Sasha is only 5 feet, 6 inches tall.
1.2 He wants to play professional basketball.

Note Use a *contrast* transition in cluster 1.

2.1 Fran asked for help on her research paper.
2.2 She asked for an extension of the deadline.

Note Use an *addition* transition in cluster 2.

3.1 Konomu recently emigrated from rural Japan.
3.2 He has struggled to understand American customs.

Note Use a *cause-effect* transition in cluster 2.

4.1. Renae is interested in regional folklore.
4.2 She has a collection of "Bigfoot" legends.

Note Use a *reassertion* transition in cluster 4.

5.1 Our writing instructor gets cooperation.
5.2 She held a black belt in karate.

Note Use a *time* transition in cluster 5.

6.1 All of the facts have been set forth.
6.2 We must make our recommendation for action.

Note Use a *summary* transition in cluster 6.

7.1 The auto had sustained serious body damage.
7.2 The car dealer concealed that fact from us.

8.1 The weather forecast looked promising.
8.2 We decided to ride our bikes in the country.

9.1 Our entree consisted of rich French food.
9.2 We had heavy chocolate cake with whipped cream.

10.1 Mormons have a strong interest in genealogy.
10.2 They conduct research into family history.

Note For clusters 7 through 10 above, decide on an appropriate transition.

NOUN SUBSTITUTES

Skilled writers have secrets. One secret they guard closely is the trick of substituting whole *clusters* of words for a single word like *this* or *something*.

Consider example 1:

Example 1

Tony refused to share his pizza.
This upset me.

To combine this cluster, some people will play it safe:

1A Tony refused to share his pizza, *and* this upset me.

But skilled writers—and those of us who like to take chances—will see the word *this* as an opportunity for ***noun substitutes*** (or ***noun clauses***). Here are some examples of noun clauses:

1B It upset me *that Tony refused to share his pizza.*

or

1C *That Tony refused to share his pizza* upset me.

or

1D *The fact that Tony refused to share his pizza* upset me.

or

1E *Tony's refusal to share his pizza* upset me.

or

1F *What* upset me was *Tony's refusal to share his pizza.*

There are other possibilities, too—but you get the idea.

Let's try another cluster. This time we'll substitute clusters of words in the "slot" occupied by the word *something*.

Example 2

He told me something.
His only interest was my well-being.
Pizza would give me zits.

2A He told me *that his only interest was my well-being* and *that pizza would give me zits*.

Do you notice how the connector *that* keeps showing up? This is a key observation, because *that* enables you to move complete sentences (as shown above) *into* another sentence.

Of course, the word order of sentence 2A can also be reversed. Whisper 2B:

2B *That his only interest was my well-being*—and *that pizza would give me zits*—was what he told me.

Although 2B looks complicated, it's actually simple to make. First you make a noun clause using *that;* then you flip-flop the word order. Result? Instant sophistication in your syntax.

Of course, complication for its own sake is clutter. Noun substitutes can be elegant, but they can also sound awkward and contrived. What really matters is *emphasis*—being able to craft a sentence to your advantage, to fill a specific need.

Here's another example of noun substitutes in action:

Example 3

Something seemed callous.
Tony was insensitive to my hunger.

3A It seemed callous *that Tony was insensitive to my hunger.*

or

3B It seemed callous *for Tony to be insensitive to my hunger.*

Notice that you can reverse word order and create new sentences opening with *that*, *for*, or *the fact that*.

You can also use other approaches:

3D *Tony's insensitivity to my hunger* seemed callous.

or

3E *The insensitivity of Tony to my hunger* seemed callous.

or

3F What seemed callous was *Tony's insensitivity to my hunger.*

Contrast the "feel" of 3D, 3E, and 3F with the "feel" of 3G. Which do you prefer?

3G Tony was insensitive to my hunger, *and* this seemed callous.

What counts is knowing your options and making a choice.

A special kind of noun clause begins with words like *who*, *what*, *when*, *where*, *how*—plus several others like *whose*, *which*, *why*. Such words are found in *questions*, of course. The trick is to convert a question into a statement, as shown in examples 4, 5, and 6.

Example 4

Tony knew this.
Whose feelings had he devastated?

↓

Tony knew *whose feelings he had devastated.*

Example 5

Why did he choose to withhold his pizza?
This still puzzles me.

↓

Why he chose to withhold his pizza still puzzles me.

Example 6

I sometimes wonder this.
Will Tony and I again be friends?

I sometimes wonder *whether Tony and I will again be friends*.

You can convert virtually any question (including the yes-no type in example 6) into a statement that acts as a noun clause. The trick is to rearrange verbs and then to use some type of *wh-* word (like those above) as a connector. The *wh-* clause then goes into the noun "slot" held by the word *this* or *something*.

SC with Noun Substitutes

Directions Focus on noun substitutes as you combine sentences. Then check your work (odd-numbered exercises) in the Answer Key. Imitate at least five of these sentences, using your own content.

1.1 Ralph asked to borrow my term paper.
1.2 This surprised me.

2.1 Jane wore an engagement ring to the office.
2.2 This aroused envy among certain coworkers.

3.1 Something seemed rather rude.
3.2 Danny ignored his instructor's apology.

4.1 Something proved very entertaining.
4.2 We acted on Marsha's "food fight" idea.

5.1 Willy clearly understood something.
5.2 Whose paragraphs were judged superior?

6.1 Angela often wonders this.
6.2 Will she meet her writing group's standards?

7.1 In our paper we argued this.
7.2 Cartoons for children contain much violence.
7.3 Advertising for children preys on young minds.

8.1 This report will contend something.
8.2 Deficit reduction must be a high priority.
8.3 All citizens must be prepared to make sacrifices.

9.1 The proposal's opponents wondered something.
9.2 Why had their concerns not been addressed?
9.3 What provisions would be made for public safety?

10.1 A seminar on sexual harassment taught us this.
10.2 How can such behavior occur in the workplace?
10.3 Whom might we hire to train our employees?

ABSOLUTES

Movies and TV programs often begin with a panoramic scene—a landscape, say, or perhaps a tall office building. Then the camera moves in closer, focusing on details. This same approach—a long shot followed by one or more closeups—also works well in writing. One effective way to do this at the sentence level is to use ***absolutes.***

Consider example 1:

Example 1

The afternoon was hot and bright.
The sky was cloudless.

A simple approach is to use *and* as a connector:

1A The afternoon was hot and bright, *and* the sky was cloudless.

But you might prefer a more sophisticated strategy—the absolute, as shown in *italic* in sentence 1B.

1B The afternoon was hot and bright, *the sky cloudless*.

Notice how the absolute is made: In this case, you delete the verb *was* and attach the remaining words to the other sentence. You thus create a clear, correct sentence with two parts.

Here's another example of the same principle—a long shot (complete sentence) followed by a closeup (absolute) that adds detail. Once again, the absolute is italicized:

Example 2

Far out from the beach were sailboats.
Their sails were white against a blue sky.

Far out from the beach were sailboats, *their sails white against a blue sky*.

As before, in example 2 the absolute was formed by dropping a verb (in this case, *were*).

You can also *change* the verb to create an absolute:

Example 3

A line of palms stood at the water's edge.
Green fronds shimmered in the light breeze.

A line of palms stood at the water's edge—*green fronds shimmering in the light breeze*.

The verb *shimmered* was changed to *shimmering* to create an absolute; the absolute was then attached to the main sentence with a dash—a more emphatic punctuation mark than the comma.

You can create a *series* of absolutes to focus on different aspects of a subject: say, *elderly tourists*. Example 4 shows two absolutes in a series:

Example 4

Elderly tourists strolled the boardwalk.
Their eyes were shielded from the sun.
Their cameras were ready.

4A Elderly tourists strolled the boardwalk—*their eyes shielded from the sun, their cameras ready*.

Now use the same pattern to create a third absolute; then add it to the sentence about elderly tourists. Your absolute could be any specific image describing what elderly tourists do—for example, *their handbags clutched to one hip*.

4B Elderly tourists strolled the boardwalk—*their eyes shielded from the sun, their cameras ready*, ____________________________________.

Let's try absolutes in a series again. Think about routine beach scenes and the details you might add to example 5. Make sure to stick with the pattern shown:

Example 5

The scene on the beach was routine.
Sea gulls circled.
Dogs raced into the surf.
Young men preened and flexed.
Young women pretended not to notice.

5A The scene on the beach was routine: *sea gulls circling, dogs racing into the surf, young men preening and flexing, and young women pretending not to notice.*

5B The scene on the beach was routine: *sea gulls circling, dogs racing into the surf, young men preening and flexing, young women pretending not to notice,* ____.

In 5A, notice that the absolutes follow a colon. Notice also that the "punch" comes at the end of the series—where it should. In 5B, put what you want to emphasize last.

Absolutes don't come just at the end of sentences, though that is their usual position. You can add an absolute in the middle of a sentence, following a noun.

Example 6

A siren's shriek was a shock.
Its wail rose.
Its wail fell.
No one expected the shock.

↓

A siren's shriek—*its wail rising and falling*—was a shock that no one expected.

You can even use an absolute to open a sentence. Notice how the preposition *with* helps smooth out the combined sentence in example 7:

Example 7

Hands were raised in salute.
Everyone pointed toward a shark fin.
Its shape was dark against the blue water.

With hands raised in salute, everyone pointed toward a shark fin, *its shape dark against the blue water*.

The absolute is a versatile tool—one that can add variety and sophistication to your writing. Perhaps the only caution with regard to absolutes is not to overdo them once you've learned to make them. For more on commas, dashes, and colons, see Unit 9.

SC with Absolutes

Directions Focus on absolutes as you combine sentences. Then check your work (odd-numbered exercises) in the Answer Key. Imitate at least five of these sentences, using your own content.

1.1 Mark stood on the library steps.
1.2 His hand was lifted to shade his eyes.

2.1 Theresa sat in the first row.
2.2 Her pencil was poised to jot down notes.

3.1 A small dog huddled in a roadside ditch.
3.2 Its wet body trembled with fear and cold.

4.1 The black sedan roared out of the darkness.
4.2 Its rear wheels fishtailed from side to side.

5.1 Nate sized up the situation in a glance.
5.2 His eyes darted toward the inflatable raft.
5.3 His left hand scooped up a yellow life vest.

6.1 Marita rode the bus from work to school.
6.2 Her collar was turned up against the cold.
6.3 A book bag was nestled between her feet.

7.1 The team members rushed from the locker room.
7.2 Their fists were raised in salute.
7.3 Their voices were united in a cheer.

8.1 A freak storm came from the south.
8.2 Dark clouds scudded along the horizon.
8.3 Its wind thrashed everything in its path.

9.1 A young salesman stood at the door.
9.2 His face was scrubbed and earnest.
9.3 A nervous smile creased his mouth.

10.1 The last voter to register was Inez.
10.2 Her body was bent and frail.
10.3 Her face was determined.

UNIT 8

Tools of Usage

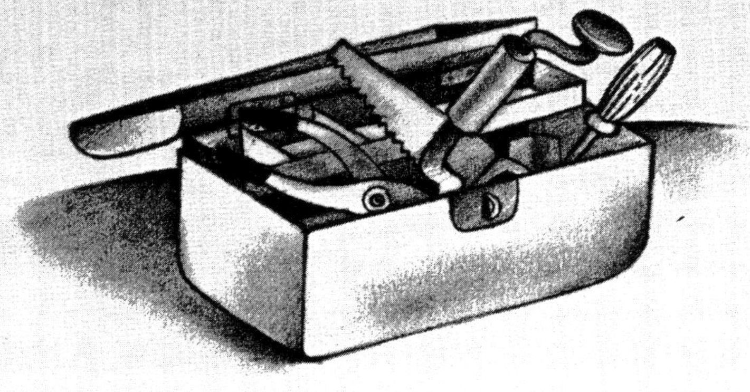

SENTENCE FRAGMENTS

Let's define a ***sentence fragment***—also called simply a ***fragment***—by contrasting it with a complete sentence. Whisper the following pairs to yourself, listening for *completeness*. Fragments are labeled.

Here is the first pair:

> This sentence expresses a complete thought.
>
> This fragment, which is long but incomplete. *(Fragment)*

The sentence above has a subject *(this sentence)* and a verb phrase *(expresses a complete thought)*. The fragment, by contrast, lacks a verb phrase; to complete its meaning, it needs an idea such as *does not express a complete thought)*.

Now study another pair:

> Recognizing fragments can be tricky.
>
> Especially for writers who fail to proofread. *(Fragment)*

The fragment here differs from the first one, which was missing a verb phrase. This fragment adds information to the complete sentence; however, the added information cannot stand by itself. Words that add information—like *also, and, besides, especially, except, for example, including,* and *such as*—demand close proofreading. Shown below is one way to fix the added-information fragment. Do you see another way?

> Especially for writers who fail to proofread, recognizing fragments can be tricky.

A fragment usually depends on a complete sentence to make sense. This fact makes fragments difficult to spot when you're reading quickly. In the Toolbox minilessons on subordinators (Unit 6) and relative clauses (Unit 7), you'll find common connecting words that make one statement depend on another. Here are some of the connectors that introduce dependent clauses:

after	before	that	whenever
although	if	unless	whether
as	since	until	which
because	so, so that	when	who

Let's now consider some examples of fragments in SC exercises. In example 1, the cluster consists of two complete sentences, but notice that a fragment beginning with *because* is produced in 1A. Two ways to fix this fragment are then shown (1B and 1C).

Example 1

Students sometimes write choppy sentences.
They are afraid of writing fragments.

↓

1A—Problem Students sometimes write choppy sentences. Because they are afraid of writing fragments. *(1 fragment)*

↓

1B Students sometimes write choppy sentences because they are afraid of writing fragments.

or

1C Because they are afraid of writing fragments, students sometimes write choppy sentences.

Here's another example to illustrate how a dependent clause, this one beginning with *which*, cannot stand by itself (as in 2A). Again, note the two different corrections of the fragment (2B and 2C):

Example 2

Ad writers often use fragments for emphasis.
This may lead students to write them unwittingly.

↓

2A—Problem Ad writers often use fragments for emphasis. Which may lead students to write them unwittingly. *(1 fragment)*

↓

2B Ad writers often use fragments for emphasis, which may lead students to write them unwittingly.

or

2C Ad writers, who often use fragments for emphasis, may lead students to write them unwittingly.

Example 3 shows two different kinds of fragments. One type has an *-ing* word (see "Participle Phrases" in Unit 7); another type has a verb phrase beginning with the word *to* or *and*. In example 3, one fragment (3A) begins with *making*, the other (3B) with *to*. Study how corrections are made in each case (3C and 3D).

Example 3

You should whisper sentences to yourself.
You should make sure that each one is complete.

↓

3A—Problem You should whisper sentences to yourself. Making sure that each one is complete. *(1 fragment)*

and

3B—Problem You should whisper sentences to yourself. To make sure that each one is complete. *(1 fragment)*

↓

3C You should whisper sentences to yourself, making sure that each one is complete.

or

3D To make sure that each sentence is complete, you should whisper sentences to yourself.

As you have seen, you can often fix a fragment by attaching it to a complete sentence. Use this strategy in example 4—you can easily fix the two fragments in 4A simply by applying what you have learned.

Example 4

In your portfolio are sentence fragments.
You can fix them with ease.
Simply apply what you have learned.

4A—Problem In your portfolio are sentence fragments. Ones that you can fix with ease. Simply by applying what you have learned. *(2 fragments)*

4B ____

____

One way to proofread a paper for fragments is to read it aloud. Read *backward*—from the last sentence to the first. Watch for groups of words that don't seem to contain a complete thought. Be alert to common fragments discussed in this lesson.

SC with Fragments

Directions Focus on sentence fragments as you combine sentences to solve each of the problems below. Then check your work (odd-numbered exercises) in the Answer Key. Imitate at least five of the *corrected* sentences, using your own content.

1.1 Michael ducked his head at the corner.
1.2 He did not want to be noticed by his parents.

Problem 1 Michael ducked his head at the corner. Not wanting to be noticed by his parents. *(1 fragment)*

2.1 Laura pulled an outrageous practical joke.
2.2 Laura is very quiet and unassuming.

Problem 2 Although Laura is very quiet and unassuming. She pulled an outrageous practical joke. *(1 fragment)*

3.1 Let's suppose you forget to proofread.
3.2 This is often the case among students of writing.

Problem 3 Let's suppose you forget to proofread. Which is often the case among students of writing. *(1 fragment)*

4.1 The sentence fragment is a serious error.
4.2 It is one clear indicator of careless writing.

Problem 4 The sentence fragment is a serious error. One clear indicator of careless writing. *(1 fragment)*

5.1 We celebrated together after final exams.
5.2 We ordered a big plate of Chinese appetizers.
5.3 Everyone soon devoured them.

Problem 5 After final exams we celebrated together. And ordered a big plate of Chinese appetizers that everyone soon devoured. *(1 fragment)*

6.1 The contract was written in plain English.
6.2 This was except for small print near the bottom.
6.3 Both of us neglected to read the small print.

Problem 6 The contract was written in plain English. Except for small print near the bottom that both of us neglected to read. *(1 fragment)*

7.1 Fragments are like potholes in a road.
7.2 Fragments provide a major nuisance for readers.
7.3 The nuisance usually makes them angry.

Problem 7 Like potholes in a road. Fragments provide a major nuisance for readers. One that usually makes them angry. *(2 fragments)*

8.1 Proofreading takes time and effort.
8.2 Some students avoid the task altogether.
8.3 Some students do it halfheartedly.

Problem 8 Because proofreading takes time and effort. Some students avoid the task altogether. Or do it halfheartedly. *(2 fragments)*

9.1 It was a festive Thanksgiving.
9.2 The meal brought loved ones together.
9.3 This included the ones who didn't deserve love.

Problem 9 It was a festive Thanksgiving. A meal that brought loved ones together. Including the ones who didn't deserve love. *(2 fragments)*

10.1 Tom's father stood at the curb.
10.2 One hand was waving in farewell.
10.3 The other hand shaded his eyes.

Problem 10 At the curb stood Tom's father. One hand waving in farewell. The other hand shading his eyes. *(2 fragments)*

RUN-ON SENTENCES

Run-on sentences—or ***run-ons*** for short—are common errors in writing. One type of run-on results from combining two or more complete clauses with a comma (a weak mark of punctuation); this type is known as a ***comma splice.*** Another type of run-on results from combining complete clauses with no punctuation whatsoever; this is called a ***fused sentence.***

Let's look at these two types of run-ons in example 1. Both errors are labeled.

Example 1

The comma splice is one type of run-on.
A fused sentence is another type of run-on.

↓

1A—Problem The comma splice is one type of run-on, a fused sentence is another type of run-on. *(Comma splice)*

and

1B—Problem The comma splice is one type of run-on a fused sentence another type of run-on. *(Fused sentence)*

In the comma splice (1A), two complete clauses are joined by a comma. The fused sentence (1B) is even more problematic; it has no internal punctuation and is therefore very difficult to read. Here are possible corrections:

1C The comma splice is one type of run-on, and a fused sentence is another type.

or

1D The comma splice is one type of run-on, a fused sentence another type.

Now consider example 2, which shows both a comma splice and a fused sentence:

Example 2

Comma splices are burdens for the reader.
Fused sentences are burdens for the reader.
The burdens are unnecessary and unwelcome.

2A—Problem Comma splices are burdens for the reader, so are fused sentences the burdens are unnecessary and unwelcome. *(Comma splice and fused sentence)*

There are several ways to fix the two problems in 2A. Perhaps the simplest solution is to combine the ideas in a more mature way than simply running them together:

2B Comma splices and fused sentences are unnecessary and unwelcome burdens for the reader.

Let's now consider a third example of the comma splice and the fused sentence, to see how these errors can be corrected in several different ways.

Example 3

The comma splice joins two clauses with a comma.
A fused sentence usually has no punctuation.
This makes it especially difficult to read.

3A—Problem The comma splice joins two sentences with a comma, a fused sentence usually has no punctuation this makes it especially difficult to read. *(Comma splice and fused sentence)*

To correct a *comma splice* like the one in 3A, you can work in five different ways: (1) Change the comma to a period and start a new sentence. (The period is a strong mark of punctuation.) (2) Use an appropriate connector, plus a comma. (3) Replace the comma with a semicolon (which is also a strong punctuation mark). (4) Use a semicolon plus an appropriate connector. (5) Rewrite the ideas, using subordination.

To correct a *fused sentence* like the one in 3A, there are also five methods: (1) Insert a comma and an appropriate connector. (2) Reword, using a comma and an *-ing* verb phrase. (3) Reword, using a comma and a relative term like *which*. (4) Reword, using an appositive. (5) Insert a period and start a new sentence.

Sentences 3B through 3F show how 3A can be corrected using the methods for both errors in turn:

> *3B* The comma splice joins two sentences with a comma. A fused sentence usually has no punctuation, and this makes it especially difficult to read. *(Method 1)*
>
> *or*
>
> *3C* The comma splice joins two sentences with a comma, but a fused sentence usually has no punctuation, making it especially difficult to read. *(Method 2)*
>
> *or*
>
> *3D* The comma splice joins two sentences with a comma; a fused sentence usually has no punctuation, which makes it especially difficult to read. *(Method 3)*
>
> *or*
>
> *3E* The comma splice joins two sentences with a comma; however, a fused sentence usually has no punctuation, a fact that makes it especially difficult to read. *(Method 4)*
>
> *or*
>
> *3F* Although the comma splice joins two sentences with a comma, a fused sentence usually has no punctuation. This makes it extremely difficult to read. *(Method 5)*

In spotting and correcting run-on sentences, your aim is to make your text easy to read. Spotting run-ons depends on your ability to recognize ***independent clauses*** (what you see in clusters); fixing run-ons depends on your ability to mark clause boundaries with appropriate punctuation and connectors.

The secret to spotting run-ons lies in reading your text aloud and hearing your voice "drop." For example, if you read this paragraph aloud, you'll hear yourself making different kinds of pauses for commas and periods. The key is to match periods (or sometimes semicolons) with the "full stops" that you hear as you read aloud.

Like sentence fragments, comma splices and fused sentences are serious errors, which can lower a reader's opinion of the ideas in your paper. For additional help on run-ons, see the Toolbox minilessons on coordinators (Unit 6), transitions (Unit 7), and commas and semicolons (Unit 9). Other minilessons on punctuation in Unit 9—for example, dashes and colons—will strengthen your understanding of clauses.

 SC with Run-Ons

Directions Focus on run-ons as you combine sentences to solve each of the problems below. Then check your work (odd-numbered exercises) in the Answer Key. Imitate at least five of the *corrected* sentences, using your own content.

1.1 The sun rose on the eastern horizon.
1.2 It made clouds the color of apricot.

Problem 1 The sun rose on the eastern horizon, it made clouds the color of apricot.

2.1 The motorcycle gang parked their machines.
2.2 Then they headed for the town cafe.

Problem 2 The motorcycle gang parked their machines then they headed for the town cafe.

3.1 Kim chee is a popular Korean side dish.
3.2 It consists of spicy marinated cabbage.

Problem 3 Kim chee is a popular Korean side dish, it consists of spicy marinated cabbage.

4.1 A civil rights leader spoke to the crowd.
4.2 This seemed to ease some of the tension.

Problem 4 A civil rights leader spoke to the crowd this seemed to ease some of the tension.

5.1 Old friends arrived on Sunday afternoon.
5.2 We had not heard from them in years.
5.3 They were looking for a bed and a meal.

Problem 5 Old friends, whom we had not heard from in years, arrived on Sunday afternoon, they were looking for a bed and a meal.

6.1 Television shapes values.
6.2 Parents should monitor what children see.
6.3 This doesn't mean making choices for them.

Problem 6 Because television shapes values, parents should monitor what children see this doesn't mean making choices for them.

7.1 The brown envelope was from the IRS.
7.2 This caused a wave of panic in Mark.
7.3 He doubted that it was a refund check.

Problem 7 The brown envelope was from the IRS, which caused a wave of panic in Mark, he doubted that it was a refund check.

8.1 Copying was easier than paraphrasing.
8.2 Sandra took a shortcut to her goal.
8.3 This was completing her term paper.

Problem 8 Copying was easier than paraphrasing, so Sandra took a shortcut to her goal, this was completing her term paper.

9.1 Driving to work is one thing.
9.2 Driving to the ocean is another.
9.3 One's attitude is so different.
9.4 Attitude refers to a feeling of anticipation.

Problem 9 Driving to work is one thing driving to the ocean another, one's attitude, or feeling of anticipation, is so different.

10.1 Look for run-ons in rough drafts.
10.2 These may have been written hurriedly.
10.3 Then make the appropriate corrections.
10.4 This is just as you have practiced here.

Problem 10 Look for run-ons in rough drafts, these may have been written hurriedly, then make the appropriate corrections, just as you have practiced here.

SUBJECT-VERB AGREEMENT

Think about marriage. For a marriage to work, the partners have to agree. The same idea holds for sentences. For sentences to work, subjects have to agree with verbs. A singular subject takes a singular verb; a plural subject takes a plural verb. When subjects and verbs disagree, serious problems result.

Let's consider singular and plural in more detail.

Example 1

Gino plays tennis. *(Singular subject and verb)*
Teri plays tennis. *(Singular subject and verb)*

↓

Gino and Teri play tennis. *(Plural subject and verb)*

When the cluster in example 1 is combined, the subject phrase is *Gino and Teri*. Because this refers to more than one person, the verb phrase must be a plural form *(play tennis)*.

Example 2 illustrates the same principle:

Example 2

Gino is very competitive. *(Singular subject and verb)*
Teri is very competitive. *(Singular subject and verb)*

↓

Both are very competitive. *(Plural subject and verb)*

For more on compound subjects like those in examples 1 and 2, see the Toolbox minilesson on coordinators (Unit 6).

A subject is often separated from its verb by several words or phrases. Such an interruption may create problems with subject-verb agreement. Here's an example:

Example 3

The shrillness of their debates offends others.
The shrillness of their disagreements offends others.

↓

3A—Problem The shrillness of their debates and disagreements offend others.

In 3A, the subject is *shrillness*. It is separated from the verb by a long phrase with plural nouns *(debates and disagreements)*. However, since the subject is singular, the correct choice remains a singular verb—in this case, *offends:*

3B The shrillness of their debates and disagreements offends others.

Example 4, on the following page, is similar.

Example 4

The disagreement even affects their marriage.
The disagreement is between Gino and Teri.
The disagreement is in their tennis matches.

↓

4A—Problem The disagreement between Gino and Teri in their tennis matches even affect their marriage.

Notice that in 4A the subject is *disagreement*, and it is singular. It is followed by two phrases—*between Gino and Teri* and *in their tennis matches*—both of which are plural. Does this mean we should choose a plural verb? Absolutely not! Because the subject is singular, the correct verb choice is *affects*, the singular verb.

4B The disagreement between Gino and Teri in their tennis matches even affects their marriage.

Subject-verb agreement can be tricky in another context—when a verb comes before the subject. Consider example 5:

Example 5

Why is Gino so contentious? *(Singular subject and verb)*
Why is Teri so contentious? *(Singular subject and verb)*

↓

5A—Problem Why is Gino and Teri so contentious?

Notice in 5A that combining creates a compound subject—*Gino and Teri*. Because the compound subject is plural, the correct verb is also plural—in this case, *are:*

5B Why are Gina and Terry so contentious?

In sentences that begin with *there* and *here*, you'll often find verbs coming before the subject. For instance:

> There *(seems to be? seem to be?)* clear reasons for their behavior.

Here, the word *reasons* is the subject. It is plural, of course. Therefore, the verb must also be plural. In this case, then, the correct choice is *seem to be*.

Following is a case that may require a second look. If you need help figuring this one out, refer to the preceding case:

> Here *(is? are?)* one of several possible reasons.

Ask yourself: What is the subject? Is it *one* or is it *reasons?* If you answered *one*, you're right. And because *one* is a singular subject, you should choose *is*, a singular verb. Whisper the correct sentence to yourself a few times.

Certain words—like *one*—always take singular verbs. These ***indefinite pronouns*** are listed below for easy reference:

-one pronouns	-body pronouns	-thing pronouns
one	nobody	nothing
anyone	anybody	anything
everyone	everybody	everything
someone	somebody	something

In addition, three other words take singular verbs: *each*, *either*, *neither*. On the other hand, the word *both* always takes a plural verb.

Use this information to answer the following questions:

> Both Gino and Teri *(is? are?)* stubborn; each *(believes? believe?)* that winning is everything; and neither *(is? are?)* willing to give an inch.

Here are the correct verbs, in order of appearance in the sentence: *are*, *believes*, *is*. Once again, whisper the correct sentence to yourself.

Sometimes you'll find subjects joined by pairs of words—for example, *either . . . or*, *neither . . . nor*, *not only . . . but also*. When this happens, the verb always agrees with the subject *closer* to the verb:

Neither their children nor anyone else (*wants? want?*) to see their disagreements continue.

Here, *anyone* is closer to the verb than *children*; and because *anyone* is singular, the correct verb is singular: *wants*.

 SC with Subject-Verb Agreement

Directions Focus on subject-verb agreement as you combine sentences to solve each of the problems below. Then check your work (odd-numbered exercises) in the Answer Key. Imitate at least five of the *corrected* sentences, using your own content.

1.1 George's friendly manner makes him a good choice.
1.2 George's upbeat attitude makes him a good choice.

Problem 1 George's friendly manner and his upbeat attitude (*makes? make?*) him a good choice.

2.1 Trudy seems like a very effective administrator.
2.2 Helen seems like a very effective administrator.

Problem 2 Trudy and Helen (*seems? seem?*) like very effective administrators.

3.1 Racism needs to be addressed in a positive way.
3.2 It affects the lives of all our children.

Problem 3 Racism, which affects the lives of all our children, (*needs? need?*) to be addressed in a positive way.

4.1 One of the coaches was picked up by police.
4.2 He had bet several hundred dollars on the games.

Problem 4 One of the coaches who had bet several hundred dollars on the games (*was? were?*) picked up by police.

5.1 Each of the magazines appeals to sleazy interests.
5.2 The magazines have high distribution figures.

Problem 5 Each of the magazines that have high distribution figures *(appeals? appeal?)* to sleazy interests.

6.1 Everybody was upset about the negotiations.
6.2 This included managers and workers alike.

Problem 6 Everybody, including managers and workers alike, *(was? were?)* upset about the negotiations.

7.1 There was a feeling of anger that evening.
7.2 There was a feeling of sadness that evening.

Problem 7 There *(was? were?)* feelings of anger and sadness that evening.

8.1 On the counter was a bowl of fruit.
8.2 On the counter were several bottles of soda.

Problem 8 On the counter *(was? were?)* a bowl of fruit and several bottles of soda.

9.1 Neither of the men was elected to office.
9.2 Their campaign posters were everywhere.

Problem 9 Neither of the men—whose campaign posters were everywhere—*(was? were?)* elected to office.

10.1 Jill's husband does not know about the surprise.
10.2 Her children do not know about the surprise.

Problem 10 Neither Jill's husband nor her children *(knows? know?)* about the surprise.

MISPLACED MODIFIERS

Humor is created when things are out of place—for example, when you see a monkey in an executive's chair or hear a symphony orchestra playing "Old McDonald Had a Farm." The same principle applies to sentences. When modifiers are misplaced, unintended humor often results.

Study the examples of misplaced modifiers below, and examine the corrected versions.

Example 1

Tina couldn't pound nails.
Tina had a sore hand.

↓

1A—Problem Tina couldn't pound nails with a sore hand. *(Misplaced modifier)*

No wonder her hand was sore. Sentence 1B is a corrected version:

1B Because of a sore hand, Tina couldn't pound nails.

Doesn't 1B make more sense?

Example 2

The newlyweds were on the ski lift.
The newlyweds were thinking about sex.

↓

2A—Problem The newlyweds were thinking about sex on the ski lift. *(Misplaced modifier)*

How interesting for the other skiers! Try 2B:

2B The newlyweds on the ski lift were thinking about sex.

One more example:

Example 3

Andy put a pizza in the garbage.
He was cooking it for supper.

↓

3A—Problem Andy put a pizza in the garbage he was cooking for supper. *(Misplaced modifier)*

Sorry we can't join you tonight, Andy. Here's a corrected version:

3B Andy put a pizza he was cooking for supper into the garbage.

You can easily revise sentences with misplaced modifiers. As you can see from 1B, 2B, and 3B, the key is to put the modifier *close* to the word it modifies. As the modifier moves close to the word it modifies, ambiguity is eliminated—and the unintended humor vanishes.

Let's study more examples of misplaced modifiers so that you'll understand how to revise such sentences.

Example 4

Edgar was in the bathroom.
Edgar thought about his job interview.

Sentences 4A and 4B are two possibilities for the cluster in example 4. Let your smile point to the one with the misplaced modifier, and label it "Problem."

4A— ________ Edgar thought about his job interview in the bathroom.

or

4B— ________ In the bathroom Edgar thought about his job interview.

By positioning *in the bathroom* close to *Edgar*, you get the modifier in its proper place (4B).

Look for a potential problem in example 5:

Example 5

Hikers made their way toward the dogs.
The hikers had not eaten for days.

Once again, it should be easy for you to pick out the sentence with a misplaced modifier. Label this sentence "Problem":

5A— ________ Hikers who had not eaten for days made their way toward the dogs.

or

5B— ________ Hikers made their way toward the dogs who had not eaten for days.

Here's another example to consider. Once again, look for a potential source of mischief as you combine ideas:

Example 6

Velma showed her car to a friend.
The car was equipped with dual exhausts.

You've probably already constructed the following two sentences—6A with a misplaced modifier and 6B with a correctly placed modifier:

6A—Problem Velma showed her car to a friend equipped with dual exhausts. *(Misplaced modifier)*

6B Velma showed her car, equipped with dual exhausts, to a friend.

As you have seen, some misplaced modifiers result from prepositional phrases. Consider example 7:

Example 7

Sitting near the clock was a beggar.
The clock had a blank face.
The clock has broken hands.

↓

7A—Problem Sitting near the clock was a beggar with a blank face and broken hands. *(Misplaced modifier)*

To correct 7A, you would move the prepositional phrase *with a blank face and broken hands* next to the word *clock:*

7B Sitting near the clock with a blank face and broken hands was a beggar.

Other problems result from relative clauses or from participle phrases:

Example 8

The judge gave a blue ribbon to the pig.
The judge wore a straw hat.
The judge wore a big grin.

↓

8A—Problem The judge gave a blue ribbon to the pig wearing a straw hat and a big grin.

You have two options for correcting 8A. Both solutions put the modifier *wearing a straw hat and a big grin* close to the word *judge:*

8B Wearing a straw hat and a big grin, the judge gave a blue ribbon to the pig.

or

8C The judge, wearing a straw hat and a big grin, gave a blue ribbon to the pig.

To better understand such modifiers, see the Toolbox minilessons on prepositional phrases (Unit 6), relative clauses (Unit 7), participle phrases (Unit 7), and dangling modifiers (below).

SC with Misplaced Modifiers

Directions Focus on misplaced modifiers as you combine sentences to solve each of the problems below. Then check your work (odd-numbered exercises) in the Answer Key. Imitate at least five of the *corrected* sentences, using your own content.

1.1 The used car had a 1,000-mile warranty.
1.2 The used car came with a pair of fuzzy dice.

Problem 1 The used car came with a pair of fuzzy dice, which had a 1,000-mile warranty.

2.1 Thad was in the dentist's chair.
2.2 Thad thought about his recent love affair.

Problem 2 Thad thought about his recent love affair in the dentist's chair.

3.1 A zookeeper approached the escaped monkey.
3.2 The zookeeper held a large capture net.

Problem 3 A zookeeper approached the escaped monkey holding a large capture net.

4.1 A lifeguard spotted a tiger shark.
4.2 The lifeguard had a pair of binoculars.

Problem 4 A lifeguard spotted a tiger shark with a pair of binoculars.

5.1 Melanie left school with her dog.
5.2 Melanie did not want to see the place again.

Problem 5 Melanie left school with her dog not wanting to see the place again.

6.1 Simpson was in a smoky and noisy barroom.
6.2 Simpson talked about his grade school years.

Problem 6 Simpson talked about his grade school years in a smoky and noisy barroom.

7.1 Students considered the problem of snoring.
7.2 This was during their psychology exam.

Problem 7 Students considered the problem of snoring during their psychology exam.

8.1 Diane put her blouse on a hangar.
8.2 The blouse needed ironing.

Problem 8 Diane put her blouse on a hangar that needed ironing.

9.1 Jason picked a tattoo from the computer.
9.2 The tattoo was shaped like a dumbbell.

Problem 9 Jason picked a tattoo from the computer shaped like a dumbbell.

10.1 Sheryl sat on the wooden dock.
10.2 Sheryl looked toward her future marriage.

Problem 10 Sheryl looked toward her future marriage on the wooden dock.

DANGLING MODIFIERS

How can a modifier "dangle"? The term ***dangling modifiers*** refers to phrases and clauses that serve as sentence openers but accidentally point to the wrong word in an independent clause. Thus dangling modifiers present a special kind of ungrammatical awkwardness.

Here's an example of a dangling modifier:

Example 1

My baby daughter sat with me in the front seat.
This was while I was driving around the island in a convertible.

1A—Problem While driving around the island in a convertible, my baby daughter sat with me in the front seat. *(Dangling modifier)*

As written, sentence 1A suggests that the baby was driving. The opening modifier—*While driving around the island in a convertible*—"dangles" because it refers to *baby*, not to the real (and logical) driver.

To fix 1A, you could rewrite as follows:

1B While driving around the island in a convertible, I had my baby daughter in the front seat with me.

or

1C While I was driving around the island in a convertible, my baby daughter sat in the front seat with me.

Notice that 1B and 1C solve the problem of a dangling modifier in different ways. Yet both make clear (by adding the pronoun *I*) who was doing the driving—that is, each of them clarifies the logical subject.

Let's consider further examples of dangling modifiers.

Example 2

Marcus worked on his paper in the library.
The afternoon seemed to fly by.

↓

2A—Problem Working on his paper in the library, the afternoon seemed to fly by.

The afternoon was working on the paper? Compare 2A with the corrected version:

2B As Marcus worked on his paper in the library, the afternoon seemed to fly by.

Now look at example 3:

Example 3

Millie studied her boyfriend's photo.
It was squeezed into a junk drawer.

↓

3A—Problem Squeezed into a junk drawer, Millie studied her boyfriend's photo.

Millie was squeezed into a junk drawer? Here's a corrected version:

3B Squeezed into a junk drawer was a photograph of Millie's boyfriend, which she studied.

Next, consider example 4, which is somewhat more subtle:

Example 4

You must always welcome change.
This is to achieve success in life.

↓

4A—Problem To achieve success in life, change must always be welcomed.

Can *change* achieve success in life? Sentence 4A would be clearer as follows:

4B To achieve success in life, you must always welcome change.

Each of the dangling modifiers in the preceding examples was fixed with a bit of rearranging. Let's see how this works.

Dealing with dangling modifiers is a two-part process, involving spotting them and fixing them. You'll spot dangling modifiers by proofreading, using a "read aloud" approach. As you think about the meanings you read, you may note problems similar to the examples here.

To fix a dangling modifier, first determine the logical subject of the sentence you're revising. To do this, ask *Who?* or *What?* When you've answered that question, you can make your correction. You'll put the logical subject within or near the modifier to solve the construction problem; sometimes, too, you'll add a *subordinator* (like *when*, *while*, or *as*) to the modifier. (See Unit 6 for a minilesson on subordinators.) As you make your correction, be sure that the logical subject is the grammatical subject of your main clause.

To practice these steps, consider example 5. Read the phrase that opens the problem sentence; then ask *Who was listening—a stomach?* Note the corrected versions, 5B and 5C:

Example 5

I listened to the world-famous speaker.
I heard my stomach begin to growl.

↓

5A—Problem Listening to the world-famous speaker, my stomach began to growl.

↓

5B While I listened to the world-famous speaker, my stomach began to growl.

or

5C Listening to the world-famous speaker, I heard my stomach begin to growl.

Let's now consider further examples of dangling modifiers, making sure we understand how to correct them. In each case, the problem sentence could be corrected in different ways, though only one correction is given as a sample:

Example 6

A mosquito stung Mona.
This was while she slept on the couch.

↓

6A—Problem While sleeping on the couch, a mosquito stung Mona.

↓

6B While sleeping on the couch, Mona was stung by a mosquito.

Example 7

I watched the fawn stumble and fall.
It was tired from running.

↓

7A—Problem Tired from running, I watched the fawn stumble and fall.

↓

7B Tired from running, the fawn stumbled and fell as I watched.

Example 8

Sunday afternoon was enjoyable.
We were in a relaxed mood.

↓

8A—Problem In a relaxed mood, Sunday afternoon was enjoyable.

↓

8B In a relaxed mood, we enjoyed Sunday afternoon.

Example 9

Politicians' values must be compromised.
This is in order for politicians to get elected.

↓

9A—Problem To get elected, politicians' values must be compromised.

↓

9B To get elected, politicians must compromise their values.

Example 10

Ted's head was in his hands.
He was unhappy because of the grade.

↓

10A—Problem Unhappy because of the grade, Ted's head was in his hands.

↓

10B Unhappy because of the grade, Ted put his head in his hands.

Remember: As you proofread, ask *Who?* or *What?* of the modifiers that open your sentences. For more help, refer to the Toolbox minilessons on subordinators (Unit 6), relative clauses (Unit 7), participle phrases (Unit 7), and misplaced modifiers (above).

SC with Dangling Modifiers

Directions Focus on dangling modifiers as you combine sentences to solve each of the problems below. Then check your work (odd-numbered exercises) in the Answer Key. Imitate at least five of these *corrected* sentences, using your own content.

1.1 The students were inspired by exams.
1.2 The students threw an impromptu party.

Problem 1 Inspired by exams, an impromptu party was thrown.

2.1 The fish came out of the water.
2.2 The fish tested the fisherman's skill.

Problem 2 Coming out of the water, the fisherman's skill was tested.

3.1 Thelma heard many unwanted sales pitches.
3.2 Thelma finally disconnected the phone.

Problem 3 After hearing many unwanted sales pitches, the phone was finally disconnected.

4.1 Mitch was dressed in a tuxedo.
4.2 The homeless man envied Mitch.

Problem 4 Dressed in a tuxedo, the homeless man envied Mitch.

5.1 Tess was driving down Main Street in a car.
5.2 A small dog snapped at the tires.

Problem 5 Driving down Main Street in a car, a small dog snapped at the tires.

6.1 The parent comforted the small child.
6.2 The child was overcome by emotion.

Problem 6 Overcome by emotion, the parent comforted the small child.

7.1 The teacher quizzed his students.
7.2 The teacher was afraid of looking unprepared.

Problem 7 Afraid of looking unprepared, the students were quizzed by the teacher.

8.1 Oliver worked on a factory assembly line.
8.2 Time passed slowly because of boredom.

Problem 8 Working on a factory assembly line, time passed slowly because of boredom.

9.1 I saved the bottle for a special occasion.
9.2 The bottle was unopened for many years.

Problem 9 Unopened for many years, I saved the bottle for a special occasion.

10.1 The surgeon was the "knife of the party."
10.2 The surgeon made cutting remarks about her guests.

Problem 10 The "knife of the party," cutting remarks were made by the surgeon about her guests.

FAULTY PARALLELISM

Parallel lines run side by side—like the rails on a railroad track. This same idea can be applied to sentences. With ***parallel*** (or ***balanced)*** construction, you use repeated phrases or sentence patterns. As long as you repeat the pattern, you don't "derail" your reader. Problems with parallelism occur when you're in a hurry—or when you haven't proofread carefully.

One kind of problem results from trying to use two different classes of phrases—say, a verb phrase and a noun phrase—as if they were parallel. Here's an example of such a nonparallel sentence.

Example 1

You can improve your skills.
You can do this by writing papers together.
You can do this through workshop discussions.

↓

1A—Problem *Writing papers together* and *workshop discussions* can improve your skills.

Sentence 1A joins a verb phrase (*Writing papers together*) with a nonparallel noun phrase (*workshop discussions*). To fix it, either make both italic items parallel verb phrases (as in 1B) or make both of them parallel noun phrases (as in 1C):

1B *Writing papers together* and *discussing them in workshops* can improve your skills.

or

1C You can improve your skills through *collaborative writing* and *workshop discussions*.

Try to spot what's wrong with the nonparallel sentence in example 2 and decide how it might be fixed.

Example 2

Workshop guidelines include respecting the work of others.
Workshop guidelines include a willingness to make changes.

↓

2A—Problem Workshop guidelines include *respecting the work of others* and *a willingness to make changes*.

As before, 2A has a verb phrase followed by a noun phrase. To fix it, we have two choices: parallel verb phrases (2B) or parallel noun phrases (2C):

2B Workshop guidelines include *respecting the work of others* and *being willing to make changes*.

or

2C Workshop guidelines include *respect for the work of others* and *a willingness to make changes*.

Here is another example of faulty parallelism caused by different parts of speech. The problem sentence, 3A, joins two adjectives (*defensive* and *insecure*) with a verb phrase (*argue their views*):

Example 3

Unfortunately, some writers are defensive.
Some writers are insecure.
Some writers argue their views.

↓

3A—Problem Unfortunately, some writers are *defensive*, *insecure*, and *argue their views*.

You can fix 3A by changing the series to parallel adjectives (as in 3B) or to parallel verb phrases (3C):

3B Unfortunately, some writers are *defensive*, *insecure*, and *argumentative*.

or

3C Unfortunately, some insecure writers *defend* and *argue* their views.

Sometimes faulty parallelism occurs even when phrases are in the same class—for instance, noun phrases or verb phrases—but are of different types. Here's an example; the problem sentence, 4A, has nonparallel noun phrases:

Example 4

Writers like comments that are positive.
Writers like suggestions that are specific.
Writers like criticism that is constructive.

↓

4A—Problem Writers like *positive comments*, *specific suggestions*, and *criticism that is constructive*.

To fix 4A, you have two choices, both of which use parallel noun phrases:

4B Writers like *positive comments*, *specific suggestions*, and *constructive criticism*.

or

4C Writers like *comments that are positive*, *suggestions that are specific*, and *criticism that is constructive*.

Because 4B is six words shorter than 4C, it is probably preferable.

Let's look at the same kind of parallelism problem with verb phrases. In example 5, the problem sentence (5A) uses two nonparallel verb phrases. The first verb phrase, an infinitive, begins with *to*; the second verb phrase, a participle, begins with *seeing*.

Example 5

But no writer likes to hear only critical remarks.
No writer likes to see a paper ripped apart.

↓

5A—Problem But no writer likes *to hear only critical remarks* or *seeing a paper ripped apart*.

To fix 5A, make both verb phrases the same type—parallel infinitive phrases (as in 5B) or parallel participle phrases (5C):

5B But no writer likes *to hear only critical remarks* or *to see a paper ripped apart*.

or

5C But no writer likes *hearing only critical remarks* or *seeing a paper ripped apart*.

Clearly, the secret to parallelism lies in *repeating* your phrasing as you construct or revise sentences.

To spot problems in parallelism, make sure to read your sentences aloud, taking time to *hear* their patterns. Serious interruptions in the "flow" of a sentence may be symptoms of faulty parallelism. You can practice this technique on a final example of nonparallelism:

Example 6

Writers vary in talent.
Writers vary in how much experience they have.
Writers vary in the topics they choose.
Yet all writers need feedback from readers.

6A—Problem Writers vary *in talent, how much experience*, and *the topics they choose*, yet they all need feedback from readers.

In 6A, a problem in parallelism results because three different types of phrases are being used together. To fix it, why not try one of the following?

6B Writers vary *in talent*, *in experience*, and *in topics chosen*, yet they all need feedback from readers.

or

6C Writers vary in *how much talent or experience they have* and *what topics they choose*, yet they all need feedback from readers.

or

6D Although their *talent*, *experience*, and *topics* may vary, writers all need feedback from readers.

Thus, the secret of good parallel structure is to set up a pattern, to stick with it, and to read your words aloud. For additional help on parallelism, refer to the Toolbox minilesson on coordinators (Unit 6) and review any grammar you're uncertain about (see Units 6 and 7).

 SC with Faulty Parallelism

Directions Focus on parallelism as you combine sentences to solve each of the problems below. Then check your work (odd-numbered exercises) in the Answer Key. Imitate at least five of the *corrected* sentences, using your own content.

1.1 The teacher was friendly.
1.2 The teacher was relaxed.
1.3 The teacher was intellectual.

Problem 1 The teacher was friendly, relaxed, and an intellectual.

2.1 I have worked as a fry cook.
2.2 I have worked as a sheet metal worker.
2.3 I have worked as a truck driver.

Problem 2 I have worked as a fry cook, a sheet metal worker, and driving trucks.

3.1 They argued their points logically.
3.2 They argued their points forcefully.
3.3 They argued their points persuasively.

Problem 3 They argued their points logically, forcefully, and with persuasion.

4.1 We prefer writing assignments.
4.2 The assignments challenge the mind.
4.3 The assignments do not cause boredom.

Problem 4 We prefer writing assignments to challenge the mind, not that are boring.

5.1 Sharon headed for the bus stop.
5.2 She waited in the rain there.
5.3 She shared a friend's umbrella.

Problem 5 Sharon headed for the bus stop, where she waited in the rain and a friend's umbrella was shared.

6.1 Jerry worked on the freight docks.
6.2 Jerry saved a few dollars each month.
6.3 Jerry depended on no one but himself.

Problem 6 Jerry worked on the freight docks, saved a few dollars each month, and was dependent on no one but himself.

7.1 Tonya wanted to visit her grandmother.
7.2 She has to study for a midterm exam.
7.3 She has to complete a major report.

Problem 7 Tonya wanted to visit her grandmother, but she has to study for a midterm exam and a major report needs completion.

8.1 Fred's protest was articulate.
8.2 Fred's protest was thoughtfully presented.
8.3 The city council listened carefully.

Problem 8 Because Fred's protest was articulate and a thoughtful presentation, the city council listened carefully.

9.1 Parallelism is important.
9.2 I write correct sentences the first time.
9.3 I do not worry about proofreading.

Problem 9 Although parallelism is important, I write correct sentences the first time, not to worry about proofreading.

10.1 Proofreading is a waste of time.
10.2 My skills in parallelism are advanced.
10.3 My skills in sentence construction are advanced.

Problem 10 Proofreading is a waste of time because my skills in parallelism and how to construct sentences are advanced.

PRONOUN PROBLEMS

Writers use pronouns to substitute for nouns (or other pronouns). In typical ***pronoun problems***—like the examples below—a pronoun doesn't agree with the noun (called an *antecedent)* that it refers to. Today, conventions for using pronouns, especially in everyday speech, are in transition. However, basic pronoun rules are still observed in situations that require carefully edited text, so it's important to study the problems and solutions here carefully.

Let's begin with examples of problems with ***pronoun agreement.***

Example 1

All office workers scurried to desks.
This was after a meeting that focused on working conditions.

1A—Problem All office workers scurried to his or her desk after a meeting that focused on working conditions.

In 1A, there's a lack of agreement between the plural noun phrase *all office workers* and the singular pronoun phrase *his or her.* To correct this sentence, you'd use *their,* a plural pronoun, to create agreement with *workers:*

1B All office workers scurried to their desks after a meeting that focused on working conditions.

Here's a similar pronoun problem, with a correction for comparison:

Example 2

Both were advocates for change.
Both had outlined plans.

↓

2A—Problem Both advocates for change had outlined his or her plan.

↓

2B Both advocates for change had outlined their plans.

Here's another example of an agreement problem between pronoun and antecedent:

Example 3

There was a strongly worded memo from the employer.
The memo was to each office worker.
It demanded cleaning up the worker's act.

↓

3A—Problem A strongly worded memo from the employer demanded that each office worker clean up their act.

Here, the problem is that *each office worker* is a singular noun phrase whereas *their* is a plural pronoun. According to the conventions of standard English, pronouns must agree (in number) with the words they refer to or replace. Here's a correction:

3B A strongly worded memo from the employer demanded that each office worker clean up his or her act.

Of course, if the office workers were all men, you'd choose 3C; if they were all women, you'd choose 3D:

> *3C* A strongly worded memo from the employer demanded that each office worker clean up his act.
>
> *or*
>
> *3D* A strongly worded memo from the employer demanded that each office worker clean up her act.

A similar problem arises with a noun like *person*, which also takes singular pronouns. Let's say your boss is talking to the office staff:

> "Any person in the office who stirs up trouble will have *(his or her? their?)* job eliminated."

Informally, your boss might choose the plural pronoun, *their*. Formally, however—in writing a memo, for instance—the boss should choose the singular form, *his or her*.

Problems in agreement often result when *indefinite pronouns* are used. These words are familiar to you (they were also listed above, under "Subject-Verb Agreement"); but what you may not realize is that all of these indefinite pronouns are *singular*.

-one pronouns	*-body pronouns*	*Other singular pronouns*
one	nobody	each
anyone	anybody	either
everyone	everybody	neither
someone	somebody	

Because such words can replace nouns, they serve as antecedents for other pronouns. Here's the problem: Should the follow-up pronouns be *singular* (and thus technically correct), or should they be *plural* (and thus follow common patterns of informal speech)?

Consider this sentence, a response to your boss:

"Everyone in the office wants *(his or her? their?)* paycheck."

Here, *everyone* has a plural meaning. So you might say *Everyone in the office wants their paycheck* when speaking informally. However, in writing about the matter—say, to a union attorney—you'd probably use more formal language:

Everyone in the office wants his or her paycheck.

Of course, you can get around the problem altogether by simply rewriting the sentence so that the required pronoun is plural:

All the office workers want their paychecks.

So much for pronoun agreement. Let's now consider another kind of pronoun problem: pronouns that lack an ***antecedent.*** Here's an example of problems with antecedents (it continues our office saga):

Example 4

I stand up to people in authority.
This is when they try to threaten me.
This is when their threat is without good reason.

4A—Problem When they try to threaten me without good reason, I stand up to them.

In 4A, to whom does *they* refer? When the cluster was combined, *people in authority* somehow got lost. Note the correct version:

4B When people in authority try to threaten me without good reason, I stand up to them.

In 4B, a pronoun has been replaced with a specific noun phrase (an antecedent); thus the sentence becomes clear. Vagueness can often be addressed by specifying an antecedent.

A third kind of pronoun problem results from ***shifts in pronoun viewpoint.*** For example, writers may shift from third-person pronouns *(he, his, him, she, her, it, its, they, their, them)* to second-person pronouns *(you, your)*. Here's an example of such a shift; note the corrected version:

Example 5

A person can be treated unfairly.
This lasts only so long.
Then action has to be taken.

↓

5A—Problem A person can be treated unfairly only so long before you have to take action. *(Shift from third person to second person)*

↓

5B A person can be treated unfairly only so long before he or she has to take action. *(Consistent third-person viewpoint)*

A shift in point of view often occurs between first-person pronouns *(I, my, mine, me, we, our, us)* and second-person pronouns *(you, your)*. Consider example 6.

Example 6

I was nervous.
I knew risks must be taken in life.

↓

6A—Problem I was nervous, but I knew you must take risks in life. *(Shift in viewpoint)*

↓

6B I was nervous, but I knew I must take risks in life. *(Consistent viewpoint)*

As you refer to the lists of *indefinite pronouns* in this unit, remember that all of these are third-person words.

 SC with Pronoun Problems

Directions Focus on pronoun problems as you combine sentences to solve each of the problems below. Then check your work (odd-numbered exercises) in the Answer Key. Imitate at least five of the *corrected* sentences, using your own content.

1.1 There are several proposals.
1.2 Each has merits.

Problem 1 Each of these proposals has *(its? their?)* merits.

2.1 Two bidders showed up.
2.2 Neither had a checkbook.

Problem 2 Although two bidders showed up, neither had *(his or her? their?)* checkbook.

3.1 A person votes.
3.2 This person must take the responsibility seriously.

Problem 3 A person who votes must take *(his or her? their?)* responsibility seriously.

4.1 One of the students has been questioned.
4.2 The student is suspected of plagiarism.

Problem 4 One of the students has been questioned because of *(his or her? their?)* suspected plagiarism.

5.1 Kim headed for the unemployment office.
5.2 The counselors could help her get a job.

Problem 5 Kim headed for the unemployment office because they could help her get a job.

6.1 Matt and his brother wondered something.
6.2 Were Matt's grades good enough for a scholarship?

Problem 6 Matt and his brother wondered whether his grades were good enough for a scholarship.

7.1 Daphne put the key into her coat pocket.
7.2 Daphne realized that the coat had vanished.

Problem 7 After putting the key into her coat pocket, Daphne realized that it had vanished.

8.1 Searchers worked for hours without success.
8.2 They refused to give up hope.

Problem 8 Although searchers worked for hours without success, you saw their refusal to give up hope.

9.1 We put finishing touches on our papers.
9.2 We just knew they would get high grades.

Problem 9 After we put finishing touches on our papers, you just knew they would get high grades.

10.1 Each person must write from his or her experience.
10.2 That experience provides a unique voice.

Problem 10 Each person must write from your own experience because that experience provides you a unique voice.

UNIT 9

Tools of Punctuation

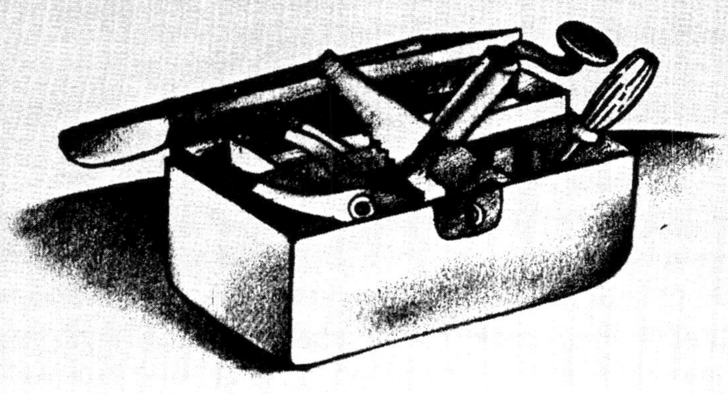

COMMAS

Are you often undecided about whether to put commas in or take them out? Welcome to the club! Commas can be a headache for any writer. On the other hand, knowing a few simple rules will help ensure that you don't bang your head needlessly against the wall.

Think of a ***comma (,)*** as a slight pause in the flow of written speech. By using or not using commas, you signal how a sentence should be read. Let's go through a few examples showing simple patterns for commas.

We'll start with the ***compound sentence:***

Example 1

A compound sentence has two halves.
These are joined by a comma.
These are joined by a coordinator.

A compound sentence has two halves, *and* these are joined by a comma and a coordinator.

In the compound sentence in example 1, you see two simple sentences joined by *and* plus a comma. Study this pattern, and you will hear a slight pause between its two halves. For more information on compound sentences, see the minilesson on coordinators in Unit 6.

Another basic comma pattern is called a ***series.*** You might use a series to write a list of grocery items (nouns) or explain steps in a process (verbs). You might want to describe a person's appearance (adjectives) or give a list of reasons (subordinate clauses). Whenever you have three or more items in a series, here is the punctuation pattern:

Example 2

Words can be put in a series like this.
Phrases can be put in a series like this.
Clauses can be put in a series like this.

Word, phrases, or clauses can be put in a series like this.

Notice, in example 2, that commas come after each item *except* the last one. What if you have just *two* items? In that case, *no comma is needed to separate the items!* (For more illustrations of the pattern in example 2, turn to the minilesson on coordinators in Unit 6.)

Punctuating ***adjectives before nouns*** is also easy once you understand the pattern involved. Let's say you have two modifiers before a noun, and you're wondering whether to separate them with a comma. Here's a simple, surefire test: If you can put *and* between the modifiers, use a comma. Here's an example of this rule in action:

Example 3

Modifiers can enrich sentences.
The modifiers are clear and vivid.
The sentences are boring and lifeless.

Clear, vivid modifiers can enrich *boring, lifeless* sentences.

For additional examples of this punctuation pattern, see the minilesson on adjectives in Unit 6.

So far, you've learned about compound sentences, items in a series, and modifiers (adjectives) before nouns. Let's turn now to punctuation patterns for ***sentence openers.*** Once you understand the patterns shown below, you can answer punctuation questions in your own writing and also help others. Example 4, illustrating a subordinate clause as a sentence opener, calls for a *when* construction:

Example 4

You make an introductory subordinate clause.
The clause is shown here.
You should set it off with a comma.

4A *When you make an introductory subordinate clause as shown here,* you should set it off with a comma.

This comma pattern consists of a subordinate clause (in italic) and an independent clause (a simple sentence).

The same punctuation would be used if, instead of an introductory clause, you used a shorter phrase:

> 4B *In making an introductory phrase*, you should set it off with a comma.

Such patterns are basic. When punctuating sentences like these, don't hesitate to put in the comma. For more on punctuating these patterns, see the minilessons on subordinators and prepositional phrases in Unit 6, and participle phrases in Unit 7.

Commas are also used to set off ***parenthetic, or nonessential, information.*** Let's take the sentence you just read as an example:

Example 5

> Commas are used to set off parenthetic information.
>
> Parenthetic information is nonessential.

> Commas are used to set off parenthetic, *or nonessential*, information.

The principle of nonessential information is quite important. In fact, you might consider it a key to many punctuation problems. When you can "take away" certain information, it's usually set off by a *pair* of commas (in the middle of a sentence) or a *single* comma (at the beginning or end of a sentence). Here are three illustrations:

> This sentence, *which illustrates a relative clause*, shows one way to punctuate nonessential information.
>
> *Clearly constructed and easy to follow*, this sentence illustrates how introductory phrases are punctuated.
>
> This sentence illustrates the appositive, *a word or group of words that renames a noun phrase*.

For more information on punctuating relative clauses, appositives, and participle phrases, see Unit 7.

Remember that you can answer many questions about commas by paying attention to good writing and by reading your own writing aloud, listening to punctuation. Don't hesitate to turn back to this lesson when you need to review comma basics.

SC with Commas

Directions Focus on commas as you combine sentences. Then check your work (odd-numbered exercises) in the Answer Key. Imitate at least five of these sentences, using your own content.

1.1 A compound sentence may sound difficult.
1.2 It is quite simple to punctuate correctly.

2.1 A compound sentence takes a coordinator.
2.2 It also needs a comma, dash, or semicolon.

3.1 Pairs of words do not require commas.
3.2 Pairs of phrases do not require commas.

4.1 But commas do separate words in a series.
4.2 But commas do separate phrases in a series.
4.3 But commas do separate clauses in a series.

5.1 Punctuation of adjectives follows a rule.
5.2 The rule is clear.
5.3 The rule is straightforward.

6.1 A sentence has an introductory clause.
6.2 This is illustrated here.
6.3 A comma sets off the introductory element.

Note Use a *when* construction in cluster 6.

7.1 You are unsure about punctuation.
7.2 It is helpful to read sentences aloud.
7.3 It is helpful to note pauses.

Note Use an *if* construction in cluster 7.

8.1 Studying commas in newspapers also helps.
8.2 Studying commas in magazines also helps.
8.3 Studying commas in books also helps.

9.1 Punctuation may seem mysterious.
9.2 Its basic rules are easy to master.
9.3 This is especially with close reading.
9.4 This is especially with common sense.

Note Use an *although* construction in cluster 9.

10.1 Punctuation provides the reader with cues.
10.2 Punctuation includes the comma.
10.3 The cues are subtle but explicit.
10.4 The cues are a series of signposts.

DASHES

Dashes (—) can appear in *pairs* (like commas and parentheses). However, a single dash can *stand alone* (like a comma or a colon). The dash is thus a very versatile mark of punctuation.

You can make a dash on your typewriter or word processor by pressing the hyphen key twice. When making a dash, incidentally, *don't* put a space before or after it. To do so signals that you're not sure about dashes.

Where and when do you include dashes? As you'll see in the examples below, dashes work as substitutes for commas, parentheses, and colons. The dash is stronger than a comma but not as formal as a colon. And compared with parentheses, dashes are showoffs; they draw attention to themselves.

As an illustration, consider how the pair of dashes here—interrupting the flow of the sentence—may create desirable emphasis, but how another dash adds little more—and may actually weaken the sentence.

The point is that too much of anything, even a good thing, can weaken your writing. In general, then, *use dashes only when other punctuation marks seem weak or inadequate*. With this caution in mind, let's consider some examples of paired dashes and single dashes.

Example 1

A jet rumbles onto the runway.
It is sleek and silvery.
It is ready for takeoff.
It pauses for tower clearance.

↓

1A A jet rumbles onto the runway—*sleek and silvery, ready for take-off*—and pauses for tower clearance.

In example 1, modifiers (in italic) are tucked between two verb phrases. The interruption created by the dashes is dramatic. The *top* level of punctuation is provided by the pair of dashes; the *second* level of punctuation is provided by a single comma. Compare sentence 1A with 1B:

1B A jet rumbles onto the runway, sleek and silvery, ready for take-off, and pauses for tower clearance.

Many readers find 1B more difficult to follow than 1A, because in 1B the two levels of punctuation are not immediately clear.

Keep the idea of punctuation "levels" in mind as you study another example of paired dashes:

Example 2

Its engines thunder down the concrete.
They wind up with a sudden roar.
They trail banners of black, stinking smoke.

↓

2A Its engines—*winding up with a sudden roar, then trailing banners of black, stinking smoke*—thunder down the concrete.

Example 2 has a pair of dashes between its subject *(engines)* and verb *(thunder)*. Let's see what sentence 2A looks like when commas replace the dashes. Which do you prefer, 2A or 2B?

2B Its engines, winding up with a sudden roar, then trailing banners of black, stinking smoke, thunder down the concrete.

Let's now consider the single dash—first at the end of the sentence (the typical placement), then at its beginning (an unusual placement). Here's an example with a pair of absolutes:

Example 3

Strapped into the plane are happy tourists.
Their faces are sunburned.
Their faces are exhausted.
Their wallets are empty.

Strapped into the plane are happy tourists—*their faces sunburned and exhausted, their wallets empty.*

And here's an example with three parallel appositives:

Example 4

Their memories are filled with images.
One image is endless rows of slot machines.
One image is crowds of other fun seekers.
One image is the Las Vegas sun above their pool.

Their memories are filled with images—*endless rows of slot machines, crowds of other fun seekers, and the Las Vegas sun above their pool.*

You can learn more about punctuating appositives and absolutes by reading about them in Unit 7. What's important to notice here is the dash—how it "sets up" the details that follow. In examples 3 and 4, a colon could be used to replace the dashes, but a comma seems weak in both contexts.

Finally, let's look at the dash used at the front end of a sentence. You won't use this technique often, but it does come in handy, particularly when you're working for sentence variety.

Example 5

The city promises sex.
The city promises sun.
The city promises slots.
The promises are not hidden.
These are the city's main attractions.

Sex, sun, and slots—these are the city's main attractions, its unhidden promises.

↓

The strategy in example 5 is to capture the reader's attention with key words and then to make an assertion. The up-front dash can work to open a paragraph—or, as shown here, to sum up.

Stay alert for opportunities to use the dash strategically. At the same time, of course, don't overdo your use of the dash.

 SC with Dashes

Directions Focus on dashes as you combine sentences. Then check your work (odd-numbered exercises) in the Answer Key. Imitate at least five of these sentences, using your own content.

1.1 Bruno worked all night on his assignment,
1.2 He then left it in his apartment.

2.1 Sarah whispered all the sentence options.
2.2 She then left the sentences uncombined.

3.1 The surfers studied the blue ocean.
3.2 It was clear and flat.
3.3 It was almost without any waves.

4.1 Dusk settled quietly on the city.
4.2 It smoothed the afternoon's rough edges.
4.3 It softly filled in the shadows.

5.1 We saw the light fixtures begin to move.
5.2 It was a slow, rhythmic back-and-forth sway.
5.3 We felt the building tremble beneath us.

6.1 My Thanksgiving dinner was all ready.
6.2 It was like a table set for a king.
6.3 There was no one with whom to share it.

7.1 A motorcycle has many advantages.
7.2 These include economy and maneuverability.
7.3 Safety is not among them.

8.1 The slender actor strode to center stage.
8.2 The actor was dressed in solid black.
8.3 The actor was surrounded by black.

9.1 Ingrid felt many emotions afterward.
9.2 These included denial.
9.3 These included anger.
9.4 These included grief.

10.1 Our company values honesty.
10.2 Our company values loyalty.
10.3 Our company values self-discipline.
10.4 These qualities are basic to success.

SEMICOLONS

***Semicolons* (;)** are used mainly to join sentences with closely linked ideas. The semicolon in the sentence you're now reading acts in some ways like a period; however, as you can see here, it also works like a kind of superglue, bonding two clauses together.

How is the semicolon like a period? To answer that question, let's compare 1A, 1B, and 1C below, all correctly punctuated.

Example 1

Human body cells have 46 chromosomes.
Genes are located on these chromosomes.
Genes govern hereditary traits.

↓

1A Human body cells have 46 chromosomes. Genes that govern hereditary traits are located on these chromosomes.

or

1B Human body cells have 46 chromosomes, and genes that govern hereditary traits are located on these chromosomes.

or

1C Human body cells have 46 chromosomes; genes that govern hereditary traits are located on these chromosomes.

Here, 1A uses a period; 1B uses a comma plus a coordinator *(and)*; and 1C uses a semicolon. Notice that the semicolon in 1C *separates* independent clauses just as the period does in 1A; but notice also that the semicolon in 1C *joins* the clauses with the same force as the comma plus *and* in 1B. Read 1A, 1B, and 1C aloud; listen to them.

The semicolon is clearly an "in-between" kind of punctuation mark—stronger than a comma, but not as abrupt as a period. It is "stronger" than a comma because it can link clauses, as 1C shows. If you used a comma in the same situation, you would have a *comma splice* (or a *run-on sentence*); see Unit 8.

Following is another example of the semicolon. Notice again how the semicolon both separates and joins the clauses.

Example 2

Chromosomes are divided into 23 matching pairs.
Each member of the pair contains genes.
The genes govern the same trait.

Chromosomes are divided into 23 matching pairs; each member of the pair contains genes that govern the same trait.

Notice, too, how a semicolon links short sentences, which would otherwise sound awkward:

Example 3

One gene will be dominant.
The other gene will be recessive.

One gene will be dominant; the other will be recessive.

As you can see from these examples, semicolons work effectively in sentences where the clauses have a *close* relationship; otherwise, however, semicolons seem stiff and awkward.

Now that you're familiar with the "superglue" aspect of semicolons, let's turn to another important pattern—one that uses the semicolon *plus* a transition word or phrase. The four basic types of transitions are described more fully under "Transitions" in Unit 7. Here's an overview of the categories, with some basic transitions:

Addition
also, furthermore, moreover, in addition, similarly, finally

Contrast
instead, rather, however, on the contrary, by contrast, on the other hand, even so

Reasons and results

therefore, consequently, thus, hence, as a result, in fact, of course

Renaming or reassertion

namely, specifically, that is, in other words, for example, for instance

Transitions like these can serve as sentence openers, linking one sentence to another; but they work in the same way when they team up with semicolons, as shown below. Example 4 calls for a *however* construction:

Example 4

A fact was noted earlier.
Human body cells contain 46 chromosomes.
Our sex cells contain only 23 chromosomes.
Our sex cells are eggs and sperm.

The fact that human body cells contain 46 chromosomes was noted earlier; *however,* our sex cells (eggs and sperm) contain only 26 chromosomes.

Notice the pattern in example 4: first a semicolon, then a transition word (or phrase), and finally a comma. Once you see this pattern, you can solve many problems with semicolons.

Study example 5, which calls for an *in other words* construction:

Example 5

Fertilization creates a new cell.
It has 46 chromosomes.
It is a totally unique blueprint.
The blueprint is coauthored.

Fertilization creates a new cell with 46 chromosomes; *in other words,* this cell is a totally unique, coauthored blueprint.

Finally, the semicolon can be used to separate items in a series, particularly when commas would be confusing. The semicolon is a "higher" punctuation mark than the comma, and therefore serves to categorize items with existing internal punctuation:

Example 6

But "authorship" today is shared by medical science.
It is shared, first, because of in vitro fertilization.
It is shared, second, because of embryo transplants.
It is shared, third, because of gene-splicing technology.

But "authorship" today is shared by medical science: first, because of in vitro fertilization; second, because of embryo implants; and third, because of gene-splicing technology.

Example 6 shows a special use of the semicolon to separate items in a series. For more on this pattern of series punctuation, see the section on colons below.

SC with Semicolons

Directions Focus on semicolons as you combine sentences. Then check your work (odd-numbered exercises) in the Answer Key. Imitate at least five of these sentences, using your own content.

1.1 Celebrities must lead two lives.
1.2 One life is public, the other private.

2.1 Being in the limelight has its costs.
2.2 One's life is never completely one's own.

3.1 Robert Redford is an artist and a businessman.
3.2 He also supports many environmental causes.

Note Use a *however* construction in cluster 3.

4.1 Madonna's self-promotion makes money.
4.2 She continues to challenge current standards.

Note Use *therefore* in cluster 4.

5.1 Michael Jordan has an all-American image.
5.2 He must carefully monitor his public comments.

Note Use *as a result* in cluster 5.

6.1 Gary Soto is an award-winning Hispanic writer.
6.2 He teaches Chicano Studies at UC-Berkeley.

Note Use *in addition* in cluster 6.

7.1 Shauna was granted amnesty for cooperating.
7.2 She was not charged with any offense.

Note Use *in other words* in cluster 7.

8.1 Alicia's paper was flawless and well reasoned.
8.2 It won the Promising Scholars Competition.

Note Use *consequently* in cluster 8.

9.1 Our menu called for the following courses.
9.2 The first was a green salad, with vegetables.
9.3 The second was an entree, grilled swordfish.
9.4 The third was dessert, a fresh fruit sorbet.

10.1 We loaded the pickup with woodcutting tools.
10.2 One item was a chain saw, just recently tuned.
10.3 One item was a box of wrenches and screwdrivers.
10.4 One item was a gas can filled with the wrong fuel.

COLONS

The ***colon (:)*** is much like a traffic cop: it directs your attention to something up ahead. Notice, for example, the colon in the sentence above as well as the colon here: both signal you to read on for more information. The colon separates more sharply than a comma and also seems more formal than a dash. Its main job is to point the reader forward to satisfy an expectation that has been raised.

Let's start with an easy example or two:

Example 1

Today's citizens ask educators a question.
The question is hard-nosed.
Why not make schools compete for customers?

Today's citizens ask educators a hard-nosed question: why not make schools compete for customers?

In the first part of the combined sentence above, the focus is on the word *question*; the second part explains what the specific question is.

Here's a second example, on the same topic. Notice that the word *assumption* is the focus for the first clause.

Example 2

The citizens' assumption is sometimes explicit.
The citizens' assumption is sometimes not explicit.
Competition is good.
It increases productivity.

2A The citizens' assumption is sometimes explicit, sometimes not: competition is good because it increases productivity.

As in example 1, the second part of sentence 2A—the part following the colon—explains a key word (in this case, *assumption*). In 2B this version is rewritten to highlight its two parts:

> *2B* *The citizens' assumption*—sometimes explicit, sometimes not—is that *competition is good because it increases productivity*.

Sentences 2A and 2B "say" the same thing, yet they have very different rhythms and effects. Read them both aloud.

So far, you've seen complete clauses following a colon. But a colon can also introduce a word, a phrase, or a series of phrases:

Example 3

These critics always come back to one concept.
These critics discuss the problems of education.
The concept is vouchers.

↓

These critics always come back to one concept when discussing the problems of education: vouchers.

Example 3 illustrates how the colon can nail your reader's attention to a single word. But, obviously, if too many of your sentences read like the combined sentence here, your reader will feel hammered.

The colon is an excellent way to introduce a list. In fact, this may be its most typical use in your writing. Study example 4:

Example 4

Vouchers have three main benefits.
This is according to their advocates.
The first benefit is to empower students.
The second benefit is to involve parents.
The third benefit is to reform the curriculum.

↓

4A According to their advocates, the three main benefits of vouchers are as follows: to empower students, to involve parents, and to reform the curriculum.

or

4B According to their advocates, vouchers have three main benefits: first, to empower students; second, to involve parents; and third, to reform the curriculum.

It's a general convention that a colon does *not* follow a verb like *are*. As shown in 4A, use a phrase like *as follows* or *the following* before the colon. Notice also a different matter: sentence 4A has phrases separated by commas, while 4B has phrases separated by semicolons. Both versions are correct. Semicolons are used in 4B to clearly delineate the subgroupings, which would otherwise be unclear. For more on this, see the minilesson on semicolons above.

If you look back at the text of this minilesson on colons, you'll see several places where colons are used to "set up" various examples. This style of writing is quite common in reports and term papers, and your instructor can help you understand its conventions more fully.

Finally, let's consider how the colon is used with quoted material:

Example 5

Yet critics of vouchers claim just the opposite.
"Vouchers will gut the public system."
"Vouchers will exacerbate racial tensions."

↓

Yet critics of vouchers claim just the opposite: that vouchers will "gut the public system" and "exacerbate racial tensions."

Of course, a complete direct quotation may also follow a colon. In that case, the exact words appear in quotation marks, and the first word is always capitalized. For more on this, see the section on quotation marks below.

Finally, here is a word about capitalization with colons. Except in the case of direct quotation, where a capital letter is required, you have your choice of using a capital letter or a lowercase letter after a colon. Here, we've used lowercase, but different publications use different styles. Given this situation, it's a good idea to check with your instructor to see which style is preferred at your school.

In summary, think of the colon as a traffic cop. And remember that it can help you achieve your basic goal: writing with clarity and power.

 SC with Colons

Directions Focus on colons as you combine sentences. Then check your work (odd-numbered exercises) in the Answer Key. Imitate at least five of these sentences, using your own content.

1.1 Her shoplifting had an unhappy result.
1.2 The result was a ride in a police car.

2.1 Advertisers have an annual bonanza.
2.2 The bonanza is Super Bowl Sunday.

3.1 Experience has taught me one lesson.
3.2 The lesson is never buy a sailboat.

4.1 We had a question for the committee members.
4.2 Why were facts ignored in their decision?

5.1 The teacher barked two sharp commands.
5.2 "Sit down!"
5.3 "Shut up!"

6.1 Clinton was moved by Kennedy's challenge.
6.2 "Ask not what your country can do for you."
6.3 "Ask what you can do for your country."

7.1 Carlos had two requests before his departure.
7.2 One was that friends enjoy his apartment.
7.3 One was that no one tell the landlord.

8.1 Michelle's anger was caused by two events.
8.2 One was Fred's late arrival for their date.
8.3 One was his refusal to take her dancing.

9.1 A textbook must appeal to three audiences.
9.2 One appeal is to editors, who produce it.
9.3 One appeal is to teachers, who adopt it.
9.4 One appeal is to students, who use it.

10.1 This term paper has three broad aims.
10.2 One aim is to review the history of AIDS.
10.3 One aim is to describe treatment programs.
10.4 One aim is to summarize research thrusts.

QUOTATION MARKS

You've probably heard the expression, "There's nothing new under the sun." It means that many ideas (including this one) have already been said or written by others. By skillfully weaving quoted material into your writing, you demonstrate your awareness of the work of others. Equally important, quotations can help you avoid the unnecessary work of "reinventing the wheel."

Quotation marks (" ") appear in pairs. One of their uses is to set off titles of stories, poems, and magazine (or journal) articles; another is to draw special attention to a word or phrase (like "reinventing the wheel" in the paragraph above).

But the main use for quotation marks, as their name suggests, is to set off either direct or indirect quotations. Here's an example:

Example 1

Our instructor said something.
"Your writing is due on Friday, without excuses!"

1A Our instructor said, "Your writing is due on Friday, without excuses!"

or

1B Our instructor said that the writing assignment was due on Friday, without excuses.

Notice the differences between the ***direct quotation*** in 1A and the ***indirect quotation*** in 1B. The direct quotation (1A) has a comma after *said* and puts the instructor's exact words in quotation marks. The indirect quotation (1B) uses a *that* connector and summarizes the gist of what the instructor said but does not use quotation marks. Notice, too, the tense of the direct quotation (*is*, present) compared with the tense of the indirect quote (*was*, past).

Now that you understand the difference between direct and indirect quotations, look at the following. Note that each direct quotation is indented as a new paragraph.

> "Friday? You've got to be kidding," I replied from the back of the room.
>
> "I'm not kidding," the instructor said.
>
> "But—"
>
> "That's the Friday *after* next," she interrupted. "We'll team up to make this paper your best work."

The same interchange could be summarized in a few sentences of indirect quotation:

> I protested from the back of the room about the Friday deadline. The instructor and I went back and forth for a moment. Then I learned that her Friday deadline was actually a week hence and that we'd be teaming up to do our best work in writing.

Once again, notice that no quotation marks appear in the indirect version. Instead, a *that* connector is used to summarize (or paraphrase) what was said.

So far, commas have been used to introduce direct quotations. However, when the writing context becomes more formal or academic—say with a memo, report, or term paper—the colon is frequently used. Following is an example.

Example 2

I was heading for the library to begin my paper.
I remembered an old saying.
"Never put off until tomorrow what you can begin today."

↓

2A Heading for the library to begin my paper, I remembered an old saying: "Never put off until tomorrow what you can begin today."

As you can see, a colon "sets up" a direct quotation in a way that a comma cannot. Consider another example:

Example 3

But the afternoon was warm and sunny.
Another old saying sprang to mind.
It was "Carpe diem," or "Seize the day."

↓

3A But because the afternoon was warm and sunny, another old saying sprang to mind: "Carpe diem," or "Seize the day."

Of course, a colon can also be used to introduce indirect quotations:

2B Heading for the library, I remembered an old saying: that one should not put off until tomorrow what might be begun today.

and

3B But because the afternoon was warm and sunny, another old saying sprang to mind: that one should seize the day.

Besides the quotation styles shown above, colons often introduce ***block quotations***—that is, quotations indented and set off from the running text. Throughout *Writer's Toolbox,* you can see many examples of "block" material introduced by colons. Just so you're clear on this point, here's an illustration. It is pointed out in Strunk and White's *The Elements of Style* (Macmillan, 1979):

> When quotations of an entire line, or more, of either verse or prose are to be distinguished typographically from text matter, . . . begin on a fresh line and indent. (p. 37)

It's important to note several points about this block quotation from another source.

- First, it's introduced by a colon.
- Second, it's indented as a "block."
- Third, *it has no quotation marks*, even though it's a direct quotation. For material in indented block format, quotation marks are unnecessary.
- Fourth, it includes three spaced periods, called an ***ellipsis,*** to indicate that words have been deleted. You use an ellipsis so that you can quote only those words which are pertinent to your purpose.
- Fifth, it gives a page number as a reference.

Your instructor can provide the specific guidelines at your school for citing and referencing sources you quote. If you're taking courses in different subjects—like biology, history, child development, and literature—you should check with individual instructors about their expectations for written work. Different academic fields and professions use different styles. It's one thing to be penalized for "seizing the day" and not doing written work at all; however, it's quite another to be marked down because you didn't know what was expected and didn't think to ask. Check with your instructors. The chances are that they'll be impressed by your savvy.

SC with Quotation Marks

Directions Focus on quotation marks as you combine sentences. Use both *direct* and *indirect* quotation styles. Then check your work (odd-numbered exercises) in the Answer Key. Imitate at least five of these sentences, using your own content.

1.1 After his library nap, Gil said this.
1.2 "I think I'll knock off for the day."

2.1 To her writing group, Mei said something.
2.2 "All of you have given me a lot of help."

3.1 Walt often repeated an old saying.
3.2 "A penny saved is a penny earned."

4.1 Grace analyzed a poem by William Stafford.
4.2 The poem was "Traveling through the Dark."

5.1 Marty yelled from the rooftop.
5.2 "Come on up! It's great up here!"

6.1 Elisa hesitated and finally asked this.
6.2 "Why wasn't I invited to attend?"

7.1 Before us was Martin Luther King's challenge.
7.2 "I have a dream."

8.1 Concluding the letter was memorable advice.
8.2 "Do the work, and success will follow."

9.1 On the foreign car was a bumper sticker.
9.2 "Keep Jobs at Home—Buy American!"

10.1 *Time* called Stephen Hawking "an equal of Einstein."
10.2 Hawking is a brilliant Cambridge physicist.
10.3 Hawking is a victim of motor neuron disease.

APOSTROPHES

Let's judge two student writers who have prepared almost identical texts (shown below). Who is the better writer?

Writer x

Its easy to make mistake's with the apostrophe. In fact, ones authority as a writer can be threatened by its' appearance or absence.

Writer y

It's easy to make mistakes with the apostrophe. In fact, one's authority as a writer can be threatened by its appearance or absence.

On the basis of these writing samples, most people would say that Y has a better command of basic writing skills. By contrast, X has made four apostrophe errors in 23 words. Which one would you be more inclined to hire in your office?

We'll review how the apostrophe works so that you're clear on its use. This knowledge will help you with proofreading.

To get started, we'll focus on the ***contraction***—a single word made up of two others. The apostrophe shows where one letter (or more) has been omitted. Here are some common contractions:

could + not = couldn't
do + not = don't
will + not = won't
I + am = I'm
I + will = I'll
we + are = we're
who + is = who's
you + are = you're
you + had = you'd
it + is (or has) = it's
they + are = they're
they + have = they've

When proofreading, you may sometimes glide over contractions. To remind you of them, here's a problem sentence (1A) followed by a corrected sentence (1B).

Example 1

We do not take time to proofread for apostrophes.
It is too much trouble.
We are always in a hurry.

1A—Problem We dont take time to proofread for apostrophes because its too much trouble and were always in a hurry. *(3 errors)*

1B We don't take time to proofread for apostrophes because it's too much trouble and we're always in a hurry.

The apostrophe is also used to show ***possession.*** Of course, it's also possible to show possession through words like *has*, *owns*, *belongs to*, or *possesses*; even the preposition *of* shows ownership or possession.

the convertible that Fran has = Fran's convertible
the dairy the school owns = the school's dairy
the CD that belongs to Jean = Jean's CD
the wisdom my dad possesses = my dad's wisdom
the goals of the program = the program's goals
the activities of today = today's activities

As these illustrations make clear, however, apostrophes are a kind of shorthand, enabling you to economize on words.

Let's consider an example that shows the economy apostrophes can provide. As a reader, do you prefer 2A or 2B?

Example 2

The marlin possessed tremendous strength.
It felt like a runaway locomotive.

2A The tremendous strength that the marlin possessed felt like a runaway locomotive.

or

2B The marlin's tremendous strength felt like a runaway locomotive.

Most readers find that 2B, with its possessive apostrophe, has more punch. Also, it is three words shorter than 2A.

Here's another example of economy through apostrophes; sentence 3A has 16 words while 3B has only 11:

Example 3

The fish had a sleek and powerful body.
It broke the glittering surface of the ocean.

↓

3A The fish had a sleek and powerful body that broke the glittering surface of the ocean.

or

3B The fish's sleek and powerful body broke the ocean's glittering surface.

Understanding that apostrophes show possession, you may be tempted to use them with possessive pronouns (as shown below):

Example 4

The fish splashed down.
The tail of the fish thrashed wildly.
This happened as the fish splashed down.

↓

4A—Problem It's tail thrashed wildly as it splashed down.

and

4B—Problem Its' tail thrashed wildly as it splashed down.

Remember, however, that *it's* is a contraction for *it is* or *it has*. Remember, too, that since words like *his*, *theirs*, *yours*, *ours*, and *its* are already possessive, it is unnecessary (and incorrect) to add an apostrophe. Here's the corrected version:

4C Its tail thrashed wildly as it splashed down.

So far we've added apostrophes to singular nouns—words like *marlin*, *fish*, and *ocean*. You can also add apostrophes to plural nouns (words ending in *-s* to show "more than one"). Simply add the apostrophe *after* the final *-s*, as shown below:

the workers' compensation
her parents' divorce
our friends' apartment
a machinists' strike
the airplanes' collision
his teammates' defeat

Sometimes you'll encounter proper nouns that already end in *-s* (words like *Charles*, *Jones*, *Paris*, or *Parisians*). If such a name is singular, add *-'s*. If it is plural, add an apostrophe after the final *-s*.

Charles's first publication
Mr. Jones's assignment
Paris's boulevards
Parisians' favorite restaurants

Knowing about apostrophes will help you polish your prose. And every time you use an apostrophe correctly, you'll make a personal statement to the reader of your text: "Hey, I care enough to sweat the details!"

 SC with Apostrophes

Directions Focus on apostrophes as you combine sentences to solve each of the problems below. (There are *two errors* in each problem sentence.) Then check your work (odd-numbered exercises) in the Answer Key. Imitate at least five of the *corrected* sentences, using your own content.

1.1 You are aware of something.
1.2 A power surge destroyed the computer.
1.3 The computer belonged to Mort.

Problem 1 Your aware that a power surge destroyed Morts computer.

2.1 We are sure of something.
2.2 Your desk has a cluttered surface.
2.3 It makes work almost impossible.

Problem 2 Were sure that your desks cluttered surface makes work almost impossible.

3.1 We will not back down on the effort.
3.2 Our community has made an effort.
3.3 The effort is to eliminate illegal drugs.

Problem 3 We wont back down on our communitys effort to eliminate illegal drugs.

4.1 Something is quite unclear.
4.2 Can the company survive a tragic death?
4.3 Its founder had a tragic death.

Problem 4 Its unclear whether the company can survive its founders tragic death.

5.1 The musicians had a white limousine.
5.2 It pulled up to the stage door.
5.3 The stage door was for the concert hall.

Problem 5 The musicians white limousine pulled up to the concert halls stage door.

6.1 There is street violence today.
6.2 It may result from the impact of television.
6.3 The impact is on impressionable children.

Problem 6 Todays street violence may result from televisions impact on impressionable children.

7.1 The couple made a decision to get married.
7.2 This came in spite of objections.
7.3 Both families had objections.

Problem 7 The couples decision to get married came in spite of their families objections.

8.1 The senators made a controversial decision.
8.2 This was to fund restoration of a mansion.
8.3 The governor lived in the mansion.

Problem 8 The senators controversial decision was to fund restoration of the governors mansion.

9.1 The fire severely damaged the retail store.
9.2 The fire had heat and smoke.
9.3 The store belonged to the Smiths.

Problem 9 The fires heat and smoke severely damaged the Smiths retail store.

10.1 Something is clear to me.
10.2 Our instructor has a positive attitude.
10.3 It helps many students to work hard.

Problem 10 Its clear to me that our instructors positive attitude helps many students to work hard.

UNIT 10

Using the Toolbox

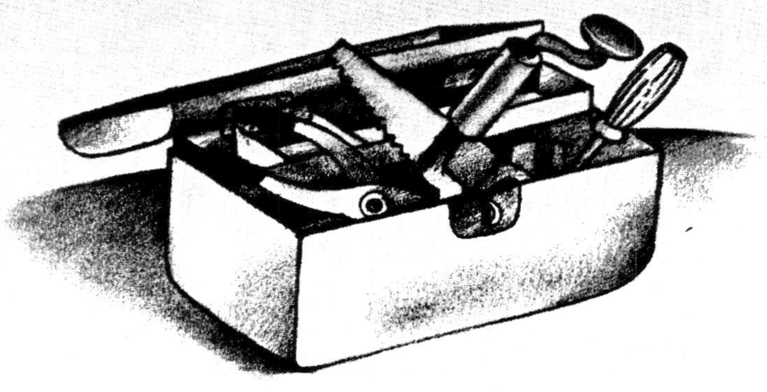

SC FOR INDEPENDENT PRACTICE

Directions Use the writing tips to combine sentences in stylistically different ways. Refer to the minilessons in Units 6 through 9 as you work through these exercises. Afterward, check your work in the Answer Key (odd-numbered exercises) or against answers provided in class by your instructor.

At the Beach

Interesting stories sometimes unfold from chance encounters. Or is it chance? You decide.

1.1 His soul drank long.
1.2 His soul drank deep.
1.3 His soul tasted the sweetness of ease.
1.4 His ease was unhurried.

Writing Tip Try the participle *drinking* as your opener for cluster 1. See "Participle Phrases" in Unit 7.

2.1 Light lay on the water's surface.
2.2 The light was molten.
2.3 It glittered in silence.
2.4 The silence was golden.

Writing Tip In cluster 2, put adjectives (*molten* and *golden*) in front of nouns. See "Adjectives" in Unit 6.

3.1 A young woman strolled the wet sand.
3.2 Her figure was sharply outlined by the sunset.

Writing Tip To make an absolute, delete *was* in sentence 3.2. See "Absolutes" in Unit 7.

4.1 He smiled to himself.
4.2 She paused for a moment.
4.3 She brushed back her hair.
4.4 She glanced in his direction.

Writing Tip For cluster 4, try opening the sentence with *as*. Then try changing one of the verbs *(brushed* or *glanced)* into a participle.

5.1 He took a deep breath.
5.2 He flexed the muscles in his shoulders.
5.3 He flashed a smile at her.
5.4 The smile was dazzling.

Writing Tip Use series punctuation in cluster 5. See "Commas" in Unit 9.

6.1 She began moving toward him.
6.2 She was tall against the glare.
6.3 She was lean against the glare.
6.4 Long hair streamed over her shoulders.

Writing Tip Try attaching *tall* and *lean* as modifiers after sentence 6.1. See "Adjectives" in Unit 6.

7.1 He adjusted his sunglasses.
7.2 His adjustment was careful.
7.3 He felt his mouth go dry.

Writing Tip Add an *-ly* ending to *careful* in 7.2. See "Adverbs" in Unit 6.

8.1 What happened next was a surprise.
8.2 He would never forget the surprise.

Writing Tip Try *that* as a connector in cluster 8. See "Relative Clauses" in Unit 7.

Invitation Extend this narrative with your own imaginative writing. You may wish to use dialogue in your story.

Black Feminism

While achieving success in today's competitive world is no easy task, African American women have strong role models.

1.1 African American women have felt double discrimination.
1.2 The first is for their skin color.
1.3 The second is for their gender.
1.4 Their historical achievements have been many.

Writing Tip Try *although* as a sentence opener in cluster 1. See "Subordinators" in Unit 6.

2.1 Particularly famous was Sojourner Truth.
2.2 She was born a slave in 1797.
2.3 She went on to become a preacher.
2.4 She went on to become an ardent abolitionist.

Writing Tip Try *who* as a connector for cluster 2. See "Relative Clauses" in Unit 7.

3.1 Truth lectured against slavery.
3.2 Truth spoke out for women's rights.
3.3 Such causes were controversial then.
3.4 Such causes were even dangerous then.

Writing Tip For cluster 3, try a *not only . . . but also* construction. See "Coordinators" in Unit 6.

4.1 In 1851 she addressed a women's convention in Ohio.
4.2 She stole the show with her eloquence.
4.3 Her eloquence was passionate.
4.4 Her eloquence was unschooled.

Writing Tip To review punctuation for paired adjectives, see "Adjectives" in Unit 6.

5.1 Another famous black woman was Maggie Lena Walker.
5.2 She was a native of Richmond, Virginia.
5.3 She was born in 1867.
5.4 This was just after the Civil War.

Writing Tip Try an appositive—a renaming phrase like this—with sentence 5.2. See "Appositives" in Unit 7.

6.1 Walker founded the St. Luke Bank in 1903.
6.2 Walker became a bank president.
6.3 She was the nation's first woman to do so.

Writing Tip Try a dash for special emphasis in cluster 6. See "Dashes" in Unit 9.

7.1 Yet another milestone was passed by a woman.
7.2 The woman was African American.
7.3 She was an orphan at six.
7.4 She was a widow at twenty-two.
7.5 She supported herself doing laundry.

Writing Tip Try *who* as a connector for sentences 7.3 to 7.5.

8.1 Sarah McWilliams Walker invented a formula.
8.2 The formula was for hair straightening.
8.3 She peddled her product door to door.
8.4 She ended up a self-made millionaire.
8.5 This was another "first" for American women.

Writing Tip Try a dash and an appositive with sentence 8.5.

Invitation Using your imagination, write a letter from one of the women above to today's women of color.

Rock Replay

Have you noticed how key words reveal a writer's intentions? Pay attention to words that signal a critical attitude in what follows.

1.1 The TV announcer reminisces.
1.2 She recounts rock music's past.
1.3 The past was glorious.
1.4 It was an era when Elvis was king.

Writing Tip Try an appositive as you combine sentence 1.4.

2.1 Videotape begins to roll.
2.2 Hysteria fills the screen.
2.3 The hysteria is from a live concert.
2.4 The concert was in the 1960s.

Writing Tip Use a comma plus *and* for cluster 2. See "Coordinators" in Unit 6.

3.1 A singer steps into the red spotlight.
3.2 The singer is young.
3.3 The singer is swarthy.
3.4 His shirt is unbuttoned.
3.5 This is to bare his chest.

Writing Tip Try making an absolute in sentence 3.4 by deleting *is*. See "Absolutes" in Unit 7.

4.1 Sounds balloon around him.
4.2 The sounds are guitars.
4.3 The sounds are drums.
4.4 The sounds are screaming girls.

Writing Tip Use series punctuation as you combine cluster 4. See "Commas" in Unit 9.

5.1 He winks to his lead guitarist.
5.2 He rakes long fingers through his hair.
5.3 He then dances with gyrations.
5.4 The gyrations are spastic.

Writing Tip For cluster 5, try *winking* as a sentence opener. See "Participle Phrases" in Unit 7.

6.1 His body is loose and writhing.
6.2 His legs are like rubber.

Writing Tip Try making an absolute by deleting *are* in sentence 6.2.

7.1 His head is thrown back.
7.2 He twists toward the audience.
7.3 He lifts a fist skyward.
7.4 He wails into the microphone.
7.5 The microphone is at his lips.

Writing Tip Try *with* as a sentence opener for cluster 7 and use series punctuation.

8.1 His voice becomes a garble.
8.2 The garble is frenzied.
8.3 Fans go berserk over the music.
8.4 The fans are wild-eyed.

Writing Tip Try combining cluster 8 with the connector *as*.

Invitation Maintaining the same tone as "Rock Replay," describe the music that you enjoy in contrast with music from years gone by.

Snorkeling Sunday

It's fun to kick back on a Sunday afternoon and try something different. Take snorkeling, for example.

1.1 Brilliant sunshine warmed our backs.
1.2 We carried our gear toward the water's edge.
1.3 The ocean murmured invitingly.
1.4 The ocean lapped at our ankles.

Writing Tip Try *with* as a sentence opener and *where* as a later connector in cluster 1.

2.1 Its color was a stunning blue.
2.2 The blue was a mirror for the sky.
2.3 The sky was nearly cloudless.

Writing Tip Try an appositive as you combine sentence 2.2. See "Appositives" in Unit 7.

3.1 We put on our face masks.
3.2 We put on our swim fins.
3.3 We put on our flotation vests.
3.4 We waded into foaming water.
3.5 It swirled warm around our knees.
3.6 It swirled white around out knees.

Writing Tip For sentence variety in cluster 3, try *after* plus *putting* as a sentence opener. See "Participle Phrases" in Unit 7.

4.1 Then we secured our face masks.
4.2 We put the snorkel tubes into our mouths.
4.3 We plopped face-down into the sea.
4.4 It was a world of silence and color.

Writing Tip Try another appositive as you combine sentence 4.4.

5.1 Breathing seemed surprisingly natural.
5.2 Breathing was through the snorkel.
5.3 The fins gave us mobility.
5.4 The vests gave us security.

Writing Tip Put the phrase in sentence 5.2 close to the word *breathing*. See "Prepositional Phrases" in Unit 6.

6.1 The only sound was our own breathing.
6.2 It was steady and relaxed.
6.3 We glided above all kinds of fish.
6.4 We glided above all colors of fish.
6.5 Our gliding was like shadows.

Writing Tip Try putting the adjectives in sentence 6.2 after the word *breathing*. See "Adjectives" in Unit 6.

7.1 These ranged from tiny neons.
7.2 These ranged from delicate angelfish.
7.3 These ranged to brilliant parrot fish.
7.4 These ranged to Moorish idols.

Writing Tip Try combining all the sentences in cluster 7 without using any commas.

8.1 We even glimpsed a sea snake.
8.2 The sea snake was timid.
8.3 His shyness was our good fortune.
8.4 The sea snake's venom is potent.
8.5 Its potency is tremendous.

Writing Tip In cluster 8, try *whose* as a connector; add an *-ly* ending to *tremendous*.

Invitation Write about a "just-for-fun" activity that sticks in your mind because it was interesting and different.

Bioscope Feedback

Americans like fast food, quick photocopies, and lube jobs done in a jiffy. What's the logical extension? Instant meditation!

1.1 For centuries people have used yoga.
1.2 For centuries people have used self-hypnosis.
1.3 For centuries people have used meditation.
1.4 Their aim has been to "turn on" mental energy.

Writing Tip Use commas for items in a series in cluster 1. See "Commas" in Unit 9.

2.1 Zen masters achieve trancelike states.
2.2 The states are serenely relaxed.
2.3 The states provide psychic clarity.
2.4 The clarity is profound.

Writing Tip Focus on the modifiers in sentences 2.2 and 2.4. See "Adjectives" in Unit 6.

3.1 Today's possible "shortcut" uses feedback.
3.2 The "shortcut" is to nirvana.
3.3 The feedback is through a bioscope.
3.4 The bioscope is a device.
3.5 The device monitors brain waves.

Writing Tip Try an appositive—a renaming phrase—with sentences 3.4 and 3.5. See "Appositives" in Unit 7.

4.1 Sensory electrodes are taped to the skull.
4.2 The bioscope provides a graph.
4.3 The graph is constantly changing.
4.4 The graph shows the brain's activity.
4.5 The activity is electrical.

Writing Tip Try *that* as a connector with sentence 4.4.

5.1 Bioscope enthusiasts look for alpha waves.
5.2 These offer feelings of tranquility.
5.3 The feelings are associated with meditation.
5.4 The meditation is successful.

Writing Tip Try *because* as a connector in cluster 5. See "Subordinators" in Unit 6.

6.1 Such waves are rewarded with an audible beep.
6.2 The beep is from the bioscope.
6.3 Such waves result from clearing one's mind.
6.4 Such waves result from achieving alertness.
6.5 The alertness is passive.

Writing Tip Use *which* with sentences 6.3 and 6.4.

7.1 This is according to bioscope advocates.
7.2 Such feedback helps produce alpha waves.
7.3 It is from visual sources.
7.4 It is from auditory sources.
7.5 It confirms interior feelings.
7.6 The feelings are subtle.

Writing Tip Embed prepositional phrases from sentences 7.3 and 7.4 after *feedback*. See "Prepositional Phrases" in Unit 6.

8.1 Bioscope feedback may become a common tool.
8.2 The tool is for stress management.
8.3 This is in the future.
8.4 Some observers remain skeptical.
8.5 Some observers urge caution.

Writing Tip Try *while* or *although* as a sentence opener for cluster 8.

Invitation Explain why you would—or wouldn't—try bioscope feedback if the opportunity presented itself.

The Woodcarver

Do you ever "lose yourself" in creative pursuits like art or music? How is it that human beings can create something out of nothing?

1.1 The woodcarver sits in the shadows.
1.2 Her shoulders are hunched.
1.3 Her mouth is a line of concentration.
1.4 The line is thin-lipped.

Writing Tip To make absolutes, delete *are* in sentence 1.2 and *is* in sentence 1.3. See "Absolutes" in Unit 7.

2.1 Curls of wood chips surround her.
2.2 The wood chips are white.
2.3 The wood chips are sweet-smelling.
2.4 They litter the earth.
2.5 The earth is hard-packed.

Writing Tip For cluster 2, try *curls* and *surrounding* as alternative sentence openers.

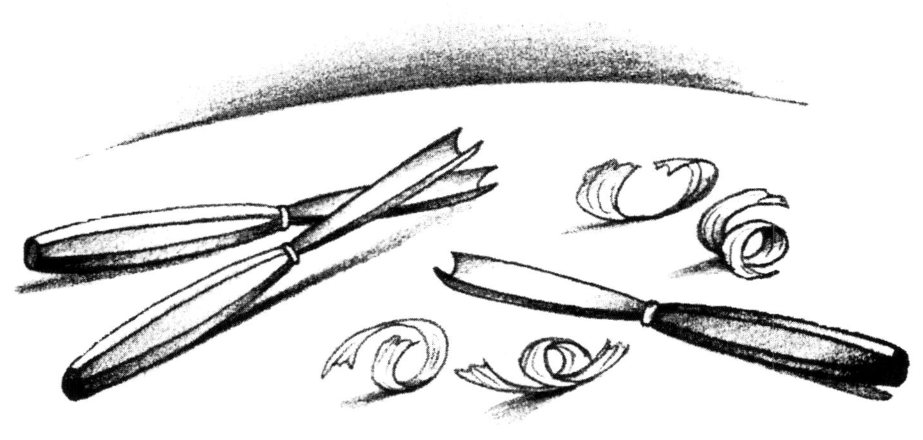

3.1 An eyebrow slowly emerges.
3.2 A cheekbone slowly emerges.
3.3 Her knife peels away the wood skin.
3.4 The wood skin drifts to one side.

Writing Tip Check the verb *(emerges)* as you combine sentences 3.1 and 3.2. See "Verbs" in Unit 6.

4.1 Beneath the eyes is a straight nose.
4.2 The eyes are staring.
4.3 The nose flares slightly above a mouth.
4.4 The mouth is grimly patient.

Writing Tip Try *that* as a connector in cluster 4. See "Relative Clauses" in Unit 7.

5.1 The carving's texture is rough.
5.2 Its lines express emotion.
5.3 The lines are bold and clean.
5.4 The emotion is deeply felt.

Writing Tip Try *but* as a connector in cluster 5. See "Coordinators" in Unit 6.

6.1 Finally the carver lifts her work.
6.2 She brushes away the shavings.
6.3 She examines it with an artist's care.

Writing Tip For variety, try a participle phrase in cluster 6. See "Participle Phrases" in Unit 7.

7.1 Her own mouth relaxes into a half-smile.
7.2 She compares carved lips with those in memory.
7.3 The carved lips are frozen in wood.
7.4 The memory is from her childhood.

Writing Tip In cluster 7, using commas, put *frozen in wood* after *carved lips*.

8.1 The carving is not her father.
8.2 Her father's spirit speaks through it.
8.3 Her father's spirit guides her hand.

Writing Tip Try a semicolon plus *however* for cluster 8. See "Transitions" in Unit 7 and "Semicolons" in Unit 9.

Invitation Perhaps you're not a woodcarver, but you can draw a word portrait of an important person from your past. Choose a person and describe him or her as fully as you can.

Pep Assembly

Think back to the "good old days" in high school. Can you recreate a particular scene and your relationship to that scene?

1.1 It was a hot afternoon.
1.2 The afternoon was in September.
1.3 The bleachers were a riot of color.
1.4 The bleachers were above the gym floor.

Writing Tip For cluster 1, try moving *above the gym floor* close to *bleachers*. See "Prepositional Phrases" in Unit 6.

2.1 The band pounded out a fight song.
2.2 The fight song was loud and brassy.
2.3 The fight song was for the school.

Writing Tip Experiment with the positioning of *loud* and *brassy* in cluster 2. See "Adjectives" in Unit 6.

3.1 The cheerleaders were down on the gym floor.
3.2 The cheerleaders moved in unison.
3.3 They looked like marionettes.
3.4 The marionettes were excited.

Writing Tip Try opening with the prepositional phrase from sentence 3.1.

4.1 Their faces were bright.
4.2 Their faces were perky.
4.3 Their smiles looked pasted on.
4.4 Their smiles were rehearsed.

Writing Tip Try using *but*, *although*, and *however* as you combine cluster 4.

5.1 The noise was like a wave.
5.2 The noise began to build.
5.3 The noise was shouts.
5.4 The noise was whistles.
5.5 The noise was stamping feet.
5.6 The coach stepped forward to the microphone.

Writing Tip In cluster 5, try using *like a wave* to open the sentence.

6.1 He was a large man.
6.2 The man had a red face.
6.3 He was sweating profusely.

Writing Tip Try using *red-faced* as a modifier in cluster 6.

7.1 He smoothed a belly.
7.2 The belly sagged over his belt.
7.3 He grinned at the students.
7.4 He lifted a fist.
7.5 His fist was clenched.

Writing Tip In cluster 7, use commas for items in a series. See "Commas" in Unit 9.

8.1 The coach made a victory salute.
8.2 The coach cleared his throat.
8.3 The coach leaned toward the mike.
8.4 This was to thank the cheerleaders.
8.5 The cheerleaders were frenzied.

Writing Tip Try *making* and *clearing* as openers in cluster 8. See "Participle Phrases" in Unit 7.

Invitation Continue this narrative by describing what happens next. Or use this narrative as a model for writing about a high school event you remember well.

Nazi Movement

Before World War II, Adolf Hitler presided over a huge military buildup in Germany. What caused his rise to power?

1.1 Bigotry takes many forms.
1.2 Prejudice takes many forms.
1.3 Racial hatred takes many forms.
1.4 One of the most bizarre is Nazism.

Writing Tip For cluster 1, put commas after items in a series; change the verb form to *take;* try a semicolon plus *however* for emphasis.

2.1 This belief system arose in Germany.
2.2 The belief system was a political movement.
2.3 The political movement was right-wing.
2.4 Its rise followed World War I.

Writing Tip For cluster 2, try an appositive—a renaming phrase like this—plus a pair of dashes. See "Appositives" in Unit 7.

3.1 The Nazi party was founded by Adolf Hitler.
3.2 The Nazi party whipped up nationalism.
3.3 The Nazi party promoted a dream of greatness.
3.4 The dream was based on military power.
3.5 The dream was based on state control.

Writing Tip For variety in cluster 3, try *founded* as a sentence opener. See "Participle Phrases" in Unit 7.

4.1 Such ideas threatened individual freedom.
4.2 They appealed to many Germans for two reasons.
4.3 One was psychological.
4.4 The other was economic.

Writing Tip Try *while* or *although* to open the sentence; use a dash after sentence 4.2; delete *was* in sentences 4.3 and 4.4.

5.1 Germany had experienced war losses.
5.2 The losses were devastating.
5.3 The losses were nearly 2 million deaths.
5.4 The losses were 4 million injuries.
5.5 It had been humiliated by the Treaty of Versailles.
5.6 Its humiliation was profound.

Writing Tip In cluster 5, try another appositive—beginning with *nearly*—and another pair of dashes; change *profound* to an adverb by adding *-ly*.

6.1 Equally painful were Germany's economic problems.
6.2 The problems included hyperinflation.
6.3 The problems included unemployment.
6.4 The unemployment was widespread.

Writing Tip Try *which* as a connector in cluster 6. See "Relative Clauses" in Unit 7.

7.1 German pain needed only to be channeled.
7.2 German anger needed only to be channeled.
7.3 Hitler accomplished this task with speed.
7.4 His speed was frightening.

Writing Tip Try a comma plus *and* for sentence 7.3. See "Coordinators" in Unit 6.

8.1 Hitler blamed Germany's problems on the Jews.
8.2 Hitler created a historic scapegoat.
8.3 This scapegoat was a target for anger.
8.4 This scapegoat was a target for frustration.
8.5 The target was unfair.

Writing Tip For variety, try *by* plus *blaming* as a sentence opener; use a colon after sentence 8.2 plus an appositive to conclude.

Invitation Today's Germany has experienced a strong resurgence of Nazi support, particularly among young people. Why is this?

 Sexist Satire

You've heard the old sexist cliché, "Gentlemen prefer blondes." With satire, you can use humor and irony to your advantage.

1.1 Blondes prefer bums.
1.2 The blondes are discriminating.
1.3 The bums drink whiskey.
1.4 The bums are surly.

Writing Tip Try reducing sentence 1.3 to a modifying phrase (*whiskey-drinking*).

2.1 A blonde likes a man.
2.2 The man carouses.
2.3 The man bathes infrequently.
2.4 The man is prone to brutal violence.
2.5 The brutality is unpredictable.

Writing Tip In cluster 2, try adding an *-ly* ending to *unpredictable*. See "Adverbs" in Unit 6.

3.1 This macho quality demands dedication.
3.2 This macho quality demands self-discipline.
3.3 The quality distinguishes bums from boys.
3.4 The boys masquerade as real men.

Writing Tip Try *which* and *who* as connectors for sentences 3.3 and 3.4. See "Relative Clauses" in Unit 7.

4.1 First-class bums are made.
4.2 First-class bums are not born.
4.3 They must train in front of TV sets.
4.4 There they drink beer.
4.5 There they watch football.
4.6 Wives, mothers, and girlfriends wait on them.

Writing Tip Try *because* as a sentence opener for cluster 4. See "Subordinators" in Unit 6.

5.1 Similarly, bums prefer blondes.
5.2 The bums are degenerate.
5.3 The blondes eat garlic and onion rings.
5.4 The blondes heap on blue cheese dressing.
5.5 The blondes don't talk back.

Writing Tip Put commas after items in a series in cluster 5. See "Commas" in Unit 9.

6.1 Bums deplore table manners.
6.2 They applaud belching.
6.3 They applaud foul language.
6.4 They regard these as "cute" and "sexy."

Writing Tip Try contrast connectors like *but*, *although*, and *however* in cluster 6.

7.1 Bums like style in their women.
7.2 Bums like gusto in their women.
7.3 They look for yellow fingers.
7.4 The fingers are stained with nicotine.
7.5 They look for heavy red lipstick.
7.6 They look for thick slabs of makeup.
7.7 The makeup is gooey.

Writing Tip Try a semicolon plus *therefore* in cluster 7. See "Transitions" in Unit 7.

8.1 Bums have standards.
8.2 The standards are exacting.
8.3 The standards are not easily met.
8.4 Brunettes must sometimes be substituted.
8.5 The substitution is for blondes.
8.6 The blondes don't measure up.

Writing Tip Try *since* or *because* as a sentence opener; try *that* and *who* with sentences 8.3 and 8.6.

Invitation Try your hand at satirizing a particularly silly or obnoxious idea. Here are some possibilities: (1) "A woman's place is in the home." (2) "Big boys don't cry." (3) "The only thing women care about is security." (4) "The only thing men care about is sex."

 Slave Keepers

As a child, you may have been fascinated just watching ants. As an adult, you may find their sinister behavior equally interesting.

1.1 Amazon ants are slave keepers.
1.2 Their patterns of behavior are scripted.
1.3 The scripting is selective.

Writing Tip In cluster 1, try *whose* as a connector and add *-ly* to *selective*.

2.1 They assemble outside their nest.
2.2 They then march toward a colony.
2.3 The colony is inhabited by black ants.
2.4 They raid the colony.

Writing Tip In cluster 2, try *after* as a sentence opener and *that* as a connector.

3.1 A fierce battle takes place.
3.2 It is around the nest of the victims.
3.3 The victims are unlucky.
3.4 The victims are no match for the Amazons.

Writing Tip Try *who* as a connector in cluster 3. See "Relative Clauses" in Unit 7.

4.1 Black ants gnaw at their attackers' legs.
4.2 Their self-defense is short-lived.
4.3 The short life is hopeless.

Writing Tip For cluster 4, try a contrast connector such as *but, although*, or *however*; add *-ly* to *hopeless*.

5.1 The Amazons use their jaws.
5.2 Their jaws are sharp and sickle-shaped.
5.3 The Amazons pierce their opponents' heads.
5.4 The Amazons pierce their opponents' bodies.

Writing Tip For variety in cluster 5, try opening with a participle phrase. See "Participle Phrases" in Unit 7.

6.1 The Amazons then raid the nest.
6.2 The Amazons seize the pupae.
6.3 The pupae are unprotected.
6.4 The Amazons carry off the offspring.
6.5 The offspring are kidnapped.

Writing Tip Use series punctuation as you combine cluster 6. See "Commas" in Unit 9.

7.1 The pupae develop into black ants.
7.2 They spend their lives working.
7.3 They spend their lives finding food.
7.4 The work and food are for their captors.
7.5 Their captors are the warlike Amazons.

Writing Tip Try an appositive—a renaming phrase like this—as you combine sentence 7.5. See "Appositives" in Unit 7.

8.1 And yet nature works in curious ways.
8.2 The ways are even poetic.

Writing Tip Use a pair of commas with a parenthetic expression in cluster 8.

9.1 Amazons depend on their slaves.
9.2 Their dependence is total.
9.3 Their own jaws are useless for digging.
9.4 Their own jaws are useless for finding food.
9.5 Their own jaws are useless for feeding themselves.

Writing Tip Add *-ly* to *total* in cluster 9. See "Adverbs" in Unit 6.

10.1 The Amazons have specialized in fighting.
10.2 The specialization is genetic.
10.3 They are now enslaved by their slaves.
10.4 They soon perish without them.

Writing Tip Try *because* as a sentence opener in cluster 10. See "Subordinators" in Unit 6.

Invitation What moral—or lesson—might be drawn from the story of Amazon ants? Develop this in a follow-up paragraph.

Voucher Schooling

Is competition healthy? Should schools and teachers compete for funding? Some critics say yes, but what do you think?

1.1 Today's critics are asking a question.
1.2 The critics are conservative.
1.3 The question is provocative.
1.4 The question is about the nation's schools.
1.5 Why not make schools compete for customers?

Writing Tip Try a colon after sentence 1.4. See "Colons" in Unit 9.

2.1 These reformers argue this.
2.2 Competition improves efficiency in business.
2.3 It can make teaching more productive.
2.4 It can make learning more productive.
2.5 It can make teaching and learning less costly.

Writing Tip Substitute *that* for *this* in sentence 2.1. See "Noun Substitutes" in Unit 7.

3.1 Their philosophical premise is this.
3.2 Survival depends on one's ability to compete.
3.3 Only the most competitive survive.
3.4 Only the most adaptive survive.

Writing Tip Use two *that* connectors as you combine cluster 3.

4.1 What they propose is a voucher system.
4.2 The system will stimulate competition.
4.3 The competition will be among districts.
4.4 The competition will be among schools.
4.5 The competition will be among teachers.

Writing Tip In cluster 4, use commas to punctuate items in a series.

5.1 This is according to some plans.
5.2 The vouchers will be given directly to parents.
5.3 The vouchers will pay for educational services.
5.4 These services can be delivered by any school.
5.5 The school can be public, private, or home-based.

Writing Tip For sentence variety, try a semicolon to create two shorter clauses in cluster 5.

6.1 Parents and students will shop for schools.
6.2 They will examine teachers.
6.3 They will examine buildings.
6.4 They will examine courses of study.
6.5 They will examine teaching approaches.
6.6 They will then weigh their alternatives.

Writing Tip For cluster 6, consider using two levels of series punctuation (semicolons and commas). See "Semicolons" in Unit 9.

7.1 They will consider policies for testing.
7.2 They will consider policies for grading.
7.3 They will consider policies for discipline.
7.4 They will also note the school's goals.
7.5 They will also note its reputation.
7.6 The reputation is in athletics and academics.

Writing Tip Try a *not only . . . but also* construction in cluster 7. See "Coordinators" in Unit 6.

8.1 Advocates of vouchers contend this.
8.2 Such a system will engage parents.
8.3 It will engage students.
8.4 It will help make them critical consumers.
8.5 It will not make them passive bystanders.

Writing Tip In cluster 8, make a noun clause beginning with a *that* connector. Consider an emphatic dash as you combine sentence 8.5.

9.1 They acknowledge this.
9.2 Some schools will lose money.
9.3 Some schools will lose students.
9.4 Teachers will be forced to retire.
9.5 The teachers cannot "hold an audience."
9.6 Certain schools will close their doors.

Writing Tip For cluster 9, make a series of noun clauses, each beginning with *that*. See "Noun Substitutes" in Unit 7.

10.1 The critics believe this.
10.2 Such dislocations are painful.
10.3 They are actually healthy in the long run.
10.4 They may revitalize an educational system.
10.5 The system has lost touch with reality.

Writing Tip Try *although* as a connector with sentence 10.2 and *because* as a connector with sentence 10.4.

Invitation You've heard what advocates of vouchers say. In follow-up writing, either support the positions above or challenge them. Write from an "I" viewpoint, using personal experience and personal values to make your case.

Ethnic Beliefs

Are you afflicted with triskaidekaphobia (fear of the number 13)? Do you knock on wood for good luck? If so, you're not alone!

1.1 Many people watch out for black cats.
1.2 Many people don't walk under ladders.
1.3 Many people avoid travel on Friday the thirteenth.
1.4 They fear the consequences.
1.5 The consequences are potentially negative.

Writing Tip Try *because* or *who* as a connector in cluster 1.

2.1 Such beliefs go back hundreds of years.
2.2 They are entwined with culture.
2.3 They are passed down orally.
2.4 The passage is from generation to generation.

Writing Tip Try *which* as a connector in cluster 2. See "Relative Clauses" in Unit 7.

3.1 In Jamaica a nose twitch means this.
3.2 Someone is spreading evil gossip about you.
3.3 An Armenian knows the same thing.
3.4 The left ear begins to tingle.

Writing Tip Try a semicolon plus *however* in cluster 3. See "Transitions" in Unit 7 and "Semicolons" in Unit 9.

4.1 This is definitely a bad omen.
4.2 You should not spill wine on clothing.
4.3 You are visiting a pub in England.
4.4 You should journey to nearby Ireland.
4.5 A spilled drink is considered lucky.

Writing Tip Try opening with *because* in cluster 4. See "Subordinators" in Unit 6.

5.1 Some African Americans watch black cats.
5.2 The black cats cross their path.
5.3 A cat veering right brings good luck.
5.4 A cat veering left brings the opposite.

Writing Tip Try *whereas* as a connector for sentences 5.3 and 5.4.

6.1 Black cats are seen yet another way in Japan.
6.2 They are widely regarded as protection against devils.
6.3 They are an unambiguously positive sign.

Writing Tip Try an appositive as you combine sentence 6.3.

7.1 You tie old shoes to a newlywed couple's car.
7.2 You tie tin cans to a newlywed couple's car.
7.3 You are part of a Scottish-Irish tradition.
7.4 The tradition is "shooing away" evil spirits.
7.5 This is for those who are beginning a journey.

Writing Tip For cluster 7, try *when* as a sentence opener and use a dash later. See "Dashes" in Unit 9.

8.1 Jewish weddings communicate another message.
8.2 The bridegroom breaks a glass after the ceremony.
8.3 This is to symbolize the destruction of the temple in Jerusalem.
8.4 This is to remind the congregation of a fact.
8.5 Sadness may be felt even in moments of great joy.

Writing Tip For cluster 8, use *when* as a connector again, but not to open the sentence.

9.1 Some Arabs carry a rabbit's ankle bone.
9.2 This is protection against all kinds of evils.
9.3 African Americans developed a related tradition.
9.4 It was carrying a rabbit's foot for good luck.
9.5 Their folktales often feature a cunning hare.
9.6 The hare outwits would-be predators.

Writing Tip For cluster 9, try *although* as a sentence opener and *because* as a later connector. See "Subordinators" in Unit 6.

10.1 Finally, you should take care of all worldly affairs.
10.2 You visit the Pima Indians in North America.
10.3 You hear an owl hooting outside your window.
10.4 Owls carry dead souls to another world.
10.5 Your journey seems imminent.

Writing Tip Try *when* and *because* as connectors in cluster 10.

Invitation What beliefs are part of your culture? Discuss these with your workshop partners and then write about one belief that you see as particularly interesting when you stop to think about it.

Answer Key

Note This Answer Key enables you to check your work on the *odd-numbered* sentence-combining (SC) exercises in Units 2, 3, and 5 through 10. Your instructor has answers for even-numbered exercises. (There are no entries in the Answer Key for Unit 1, Introduction, since it has no SC exercises; or for Unit 4, Shaping and Revising, since it has "open" SC exercises for which answers will vary.)

Note that *your answers may differ from those in the Answer Key and still be correct*.

UNIT 2

SC: Happiness (page 28)

1. Happiness is a mystery like religion, and it should never be rationalized. (G. K. Chesterton)
3. Remember that happiness is a way of travel—not a destination. (Roy M. Goodman)
5. To be without some of the things you want is an indispensable part of happiness. (Bertrand Russell)
7. There is only one way to happiness, and that is to cease worrying about things which are beyond the power of our will. (Epictetus)
9. When one door of happiness closes, another opens; but often we look so long at the closed door that we do not see the one which has been opened for us. (Helen Keller)

SC: Work (page 30)

1. Miracles sometimes occur, but one has to work terribly hard for them. (Chaim Weizmann)
3. Work and love—these are the basics. Without them is neurosis. (Theodor Reik)
5. Because it is less structured than work, leisure time leaves workaholics at a loss for what to do. (Marilyn Machlowitz)
7. Work is the inevitable condition of human life, the true source of human welfare. (Leo Tolstoy)
9. No fine work can be done without concentration and self-sacrifice and toil and doubt. (Max Beerbohm)

SC: Money (page 33)

1. Money isn't everything—but it's a long way ahead of what comes next. (Edmund Stockdale)
3. Money is like muck—not good unless it be spread. (Francis Bacon)
5. When it is a question of money, everybody is of the same religion. (Voltaire)
7. Making money is fun, but it's pointless if you don't use the power it brings. (John Bentley)
9. The conspicuously wealthy turn up urging the character-building value of privation for the poor. (John Kenneth Galbraith)

SC: Politics (page 35)

1. Politics is war without bloodshed, and war is politics with blood. (Mao Tse-Tung)
3. Politics is the gizzard of society, full of gut and gravel. (Henry David Thoreau)
5. The great nations have always acted like gangsters, and the small

nations like prostitutes. (Stanley Kubrick)

7. Politics and the fate of mankind are shaped by men without ideals and without greatness. (Albert Camus)
9. The world is a dangerous place to live—not because of the people who are evil but because of the people who don't do anything about it. (Albert Einstein)

SC: Writing (page 38)

1. The limits of my language are the limits of my mind. All I know is what I have words for. (Ludwig Wittgenstein)
3. An original writer is not one who imitates nobody, but one whom nobody can imitate. (François Auguste-René de Chateaubriand)
5. A woman must have money and a room of her own if she is to write fiction. (Virginia Woolf)
7. Your manuscript is both original and good; but the parts that are good are not original, and the parts that are original are not good. (Samuel Johnson)
9. Writing is no trouble: you jot down ideas as they occur to you. The jotting is simplicity itself—it is the occurring which is difficult. (Stephen Leacock)

SC: Life (page 41)

1. Life is a handful of short stories, pretending to be a novel. (Anonymous)
3. Life can only be understood backwards; but it must be lived forwards. (Sören Kierkegaard)
5. The trouble with the rat race is that even if you win, you're still a rat. (Lily Tomlin)
7. A single event can awaken within us a stranger totally unknown to us. To live is to be slowly born. (Antoine de Saint-Exupéry)
9. Life is made up of sobs, sniffles, and smiles, with sniffles predominating. (O. Henry)

SC for Extra Practice (page 42)

1. Education is not the filling of a pail, but the lighting of a fire. (William Butler Yeats)
3. Entrepreneurship is the last refuge of the trouble-making individual. (James K. Glassman)
5. For three days after death, hair and fingernails continue to grow but phone calls taper off. (Johnny Carson)
7. Slang is language which takes off its coat, spits on its hands—and goes to work. (Carl Sandburg)
9. Science is built of facts the way a house is built of bricks; but an accumulation of facts is no more science than a pile of bricks is a house. (Jules-Henri Poincaré)

UNIT 3

School Dance (page 55)

1. Standing on the shadowy sidelines, I watched the dance scene at school.
3. The room was sweaty and dark—an intense drama of jostling flesh.
5. Tight-lipped boys pawed the dusty floor, scratching out mysterious patterns.

7. Like an echo from the distant past, the music was pulsing and heavy, almost hypnotic.

Eric's Locker (page 57)

1. Eric's locker is a very unpleasant place—a kind of disaster area.
3. An oily bike chain, covered with grime, hangs from the coat hook.
5. Decayed fruit has collected on the top shelf, and an open can of soda has a gray culture growing at its rim.
7. At the bottom of the locker is a box, where a small green turtle lives.

Body Defenses (page 60)

1. A remarkable series of efficient defenses safeguards our bodies.
3. Suppose, for example, that some germ-laden dust gets into your eye.
5. Not only do these tears help wash away the dust, but they also serve another important purpose.
7. Lysozyme dramatizes how the body "overprotects" itself, both for self-defense and for survival.

TV Stereotypes (page 63)

1. TV kids come in two adorable categories—children who wear glasses and those who don't.
3. But neither group has unwashed hair, ill-fitting jeans, or torn sneakers that older children have worn out.
5. TV kids always seem to have new toys and nice clothes that their loving parents provide.
7. Their summers are for airplane travel and long vacations, not for sweltering boredom.

Free Ride (page 66)

1. Imagine a straight road, almost deserted, through an oppressively hot landscape.
3. The country is mostly parched, unforgiving ranchland; it is dotted with a few run-down farms that have seen better days.
5. The drive is monotonous and mind-numbing; however, picking up a stranger whose motives may be questionable makes me uneasy.
7. The young man stands lean and wiry in sweltering blue denim, with a satchel and bedroll at his feet.

Major Move (page 68)

1. With the curtains down, afternoon light flooded the apartment from the tall west windows overlooking the street.
3. Inside them were personal effects she valued deeply, even though she wasn't sure why she kept them.
5. Then she heard a car's horn honking from the curb out front, its sound abrupt and impatient.
7. Challenges, opportunities, and new friends were elsewhere, and she would make the best of her decision.

Greenhouse Effect (page 71)

1. Combustion releases energy essential for modern life; however, it also releases carbon dioxide (CO_2).

3. Although the effects of CO_2 buildup are still unknown, many scientists predict a "greenhouse effect" that would result in global warming.
5. By affecting weather patterns, such warming could have devastating effects in the polar regions, where massive ice caps are located.
7. According to some geologists, seas would rise 20 feet in 200 years—an unprecedented disaster for many nations.

Human Branding (page 74)

1. Fraternity brothers gather around as one of their members takes off his shirt and agrees to be branded with a coat hanger twisted into a Greek letter.
3. With the coat hanger glowing red-hot, the room grows tense and quiet.
5. In just a few moments, the young man's shoulder bears a permanent stigma that expresses love for his fraternity.
7. Now part of the group, the young man is no longer an outsider.

Getting Organized (page 76)

1. It is approaching midnight as a young writer turns words and phrases, thinking about possibilities for organization.
3. Notes that await assembly into a logical, well-built structure litter the work table.
5. Familiar, unanswered questions reverberate like echoes.
7. It feels good to relax for a moment and not stare at the notes that represent hours of library research.

The Pawnbroker (page 79)

1. Moving behind his counter, the pawnbroker surveys his estate with a cat's quiet cunning.
3. His face is like a loosely fitting rubber mask, and his voice is a raspy whisper from years of smoking.
5. His disheveled appearance and rude manner belie a razor-quick mind.
7. Years of business have honed his negotiating skills and taught him hard-won lessons.

Upward Mobility (page 82)

1. Young, freshly combed trainees ease into the elevator, and the door closes with a faintly mocking hiss.
3. Although they have minor physical differences, their similarities in appearance are striking.
5. Each wears a fashionably conservative jacket matched to trim, cuffless slacks.
7. All have the same stamped-out, well-rounded look—as if produced from a mold that shapes workers for corporate life.

White Christmas (page 84)

1. Raw white light glared from a globe high on the ceiling.
3. On a shelf that held bent, stained utensils was a soot-blackened frying pan.
5. Although the fire gave off little heat, two people bundled in winter coats huddled close to it.

7. The man's face, chapped and scowling, had watery blue eyes and a red-veined nose.
9. The man touched his wife, who sat unmoving, with gloved hands folded in her lap.

UNIT 5

SC for Practice with Editing (page 128)

1. We have provided a full report and hope that it answers your questions. *(13 words)*
3. Presently the lab is shut down because it has not complied with safety standards. *(14 words)*
5. Technological change is accelerating in today's world. *(7 words)*
7. Undeniably, we must meet the deadline to keep our jobs. *(10 words)*
9. This paper's aim is to interpret facts that others have verified. *(11 words)*

SC for Practice with Proofreading (page 137)

1. There are three proofreading problems that we're going to spot here.
3. Serious errors stop the readers cold, creating strong feelings of irritation.
5. Other details, such as missing apostrophes and commas, can interrupt a reader's concentration.
7. Exercises can build one's level of awareness; however, there are some writers who are unwilling to proofread.
9. If you're having trouble proofreading, a pacer can slow down your reading and focus your attention.

Still Life (page 142)

1. The night had been cruel, and now a grieving man sat in a sunlit doorway. *(15 words)*
3. He wore bib overalls—faded and shapeless from washing—and a blue denim shirt. *(14 words)*
5. Silent tears stained his face, weathered by a lifetime of field work. *(12 words)*
7. His loved one was gone, and he had never felt so completely alone. *(13 words)*

Health Care (page 145)

1. Traditional medicine sees the body as a tremendously complicated machine. *(10 words)*
3. After the problem is diagnosed, the doctor removes, repairs, or replaces the defective part—or prescribes chemicals to treat the problem's symptoms. *(22 words)*
5. Holistic medicine, which challenges traditional ideas about health, takes a radically different viewpoint. *(13 words)*
7. Because maladies such as arteriosclerosis, lung cancer, and chemical dependencies are often caused by the way we live, they can often be cured by changes in lifestyle. *(27 words)*

Think about Writing (page 148)

1. Think of writing as a "one-way" conversation with an invisible, but real, audience. *(14 words)*

3. Clearly, paragraphs must be organized well and sequenced carefully so that readers can follow your discussion and participate in it. *(20 words)*
5. Or think of writing as mountain climbing, with you serving as a guide for readers and leading the way to the summit. *(22 words)*
7. Guiding readers through slippery, potentially dangerous territory, you try to keep the lines clear and ensure they don't get tangled. *(20 words)*

Laser Light (page 151)

1. The laser beam, a special kind of intense light, differs from ordinary light. *(13 words)*
3. Photons in ordinary light spread out, diffusing their energy, whereas laser-beam photons are focused, which concentrates their power. *(19 words)*
5. These narrow beams may be continuous or pulsing, visible or invisible. *(11 words)*
7. But infrared lasers—invisible to human eyes—can cut metal or pierce armor, making them enormously potent as military weapons. *(20 words)*
9. Lasers now carry TV signals and telephone communications, but this same technology could also be space-based in the future to serve as a destructive tool. *(26 words)*

Hopi Way (page 154)

1. The Hopi are a remarkable culture living on a mountainous reservation in the Arizona desert. *(15 words)*
3. Like other Native Americans in North America, the Hopi have a strong sense of "extended" family; this means a love for other Hopi, for their heritage, and for ceremonies. *(29 words)*
5. The family teaches the "Hopi way," a system of values and behavior running deeply through the culture. *(17 words)*
7. The society is matriarchal, not patriarchal; the mother's family represents lineage and authority. *(13 words)*

Hopi Values (page 157)

1. As children, the Hopi learn self-discipline, restraint, and concern for others in the extended family. *(16 words)*
3. To the Hopi, all work has worth; it is not to be dreaded or done for rewards. *(17 words)*
5. Because they view "things" as dynamic processes, their prayer is an exercise of will, not a supplication to a higher being. *(21 words)*
7. Each Hopi is thus responsible for directing thoughts toward constructive ends and away from destructive aims. *(16 words)*

Inversions (page 159)

1. Inversions occur when fog hangs in mountain valleys, trapped by frigid air at higher elevations.
3. Trees and bushes become coated with frost that gathers in heavy layers.
5. The fog, mixing with smoke and

other pollutants, becomes choking and oppressive.

7. When it lasts for several days or weeks, it can become a serious health threat, especially for those with respiration problems.

Slavery Today (page 162)

1. Most Americans value human worth and individual dignity, but few realize how such values are abused in third world countries.
3. This figure—astonishing, but apparently reliable—exceeds the combined work force of Canada, the United States, and Mexico.
5. In impoverished countries, slave traders abduct children, trick young women, and cut deals with desperate parents who sell family members into captivity.
7. Because they are often forced into prostitution, these women and children experience unthinkable abuse.

The Nerd (page 164)

1. The nerd is a nonconformist who wears baggy clothes and white socks; he often has his fly unzipped.
3. He walks into walls, loses his glasses, falls asleep in class, and always carries badly tattered textbooks and several pens that don't work.
5. Because his appearance and behavior are different, the nerd's life is one of ridicule and aching loneliness.
7. They put gum in his books, add taco sauce to his milk, and write passionate love notes, to which his name is attached.

Ski with Me (page 167)

1. Come with me to the mountain: there the early morning air is calm and clear and cold, and fresh snow lies in untracked drifts.
3. You'll look out over the valley below, where fir trees stand like sentinels, each wearing a white mantle, and aspen huddle in quiet groves, slender and bare-limbed.
5. And then you'll push off like a bird, letting gravity take you on a swooping, breathless flight down the mountain's face.
7. Clouds of snow, bright and swirling, will follow your birdlike path, their crystals glittering in the sun.

Stereotyped Thinking (page 169)

1. Stereotyping, a way of thinking about groups of people, emphasizes similarities in groups but ignores differences among group members.
3. Stereotyping also stresses differences between groups and ignores a group's similarities to other people.
5. While a stereotype for redheads or Scots does little harm and typically leads only to jokes and good-natured kidding, such thinking also has its dangers.
7. By exaggerating our differences, we ignore what we share as human beings and inevitably become narrow-minded and prejudiced.

Racial Stereotypes (page 172)

1. An extreme form of destructive prejudice is racism, which can lead to physical and psychological violence.
3. Whites who think that blacks are all alike show racist leanings; so do blacks who think that Koreans are all alike.
5. Knowing no ethnic boundaries, racism requires only a target that can be ridiculed, discriminated against, or attacked.
7. Attacks are expressed in labels like *chink*, *nigger*, *honky*, *wop*, *spic*, *kike*, and *gook*.

UNIT 6

SC with Nouns (page 182)

1. Matt was a fat cat who sat on his hat and flattened it.
3. After Sue heard from you, she felt somewhat blue, so she ordered a brew or two and decided to start anew.
5. The nicely dressed dentist who testified in a lawsuit swore to tell the whole tooth and nothing but the tooth.
7. Our ranch offers a stable environment for horses that includes groom and board—and even features a Bridle Suite.
9. The surgeon, the knife of the party, made a cutting remark: "I removed the comedian's appundix because he had an infectious sense of humor."

SC with Verbs (page 187)

1. Alex crossed the finish line and raised a fist in victory salute.
3. Turning to head downstairs, Seijo faced a gang of armed thugs.
5. Elden and Henry were asked to retake the exam.
7. Jake and Fred do not know how to handle compliments.
9. The proposal introduced the problem, reviewed previous research, and outlined a new methodology.

SC with Adjectives (page 192)

1. Theo found a forgotten slice of greasy pizza in his backpack.
3. The frustrated class turned to Sabrina for helpful answers.
5. The path led to a stunning, unobstructed view of the shimmering lake.
7. Kwan Ho strode toward the speaker's platform, confident and thoroughly prepared.
9. Mark sold his handcrafted, turquoise-studded bracelet for tuition.

SC with Adverbs (page 197)

1. Hector carefully reviewed the lesson on adverbs.
3. After their argument, they left the cafe quietly and unobtrusively.
5. Customarily, the security man checked in sleepily at midnight.
7. Unexpectedly—and ironically—the storm's fury moved inland.
9. The richly detailed analysis of results arrived, belatedly.

SC with Coordinators (page 201)

1. Wan Su and Sung Ho were among the first to be honored.

3. Benito recently bought a stereo, new tires, and a battery for his car.
5. The restaurant's food was delicious and satisfying, but much too expensive.
7. Either you may work on coordination or you may do 100 sit-ups and 50 push-ups.
9. Not only was the concert sold out, but also all the rooms in town and for miles around were booked.

SC with Subordinators (page 206)

1. After the morning paper had arrived, Julian was ready to begin his routine.
3. Although friendships take years to build, they can be wrecked with a few careless remarks.
5. Until Maxine gets some kind of job and cuts her monthly expenses, her parents are reluctant to buy her a Porsche.
7. Before the weather began to turn cold, we took one last camping trip into the hills, where we hope to build a cabin someday.
9. Because senior citizens are a powerful voting bloc, most politicians are reluctant to cut entitlements, although everybody wants to reduce the deficit.

SC with Prepositional Phrases (page 211)

1. Andy felt confident and prepared before the exam.
3. In his "heart of hearts," Sol understood what he had to do.
5. With a toothpick in his mouth, Leroy stood at the edge of the crowd.
7. Everyone attended the poetry reading at a neighborhood cafe, except for Mark and Michelle.
9. A compost pile for grass clippings and leaves helps relieve pressure on landfills in our nation's suburban communities.

UNIT 7

SC with Relative Clauses (page 217)

1. George asked for help from his instructor, who set up an appointment after class.
3. Phil took a coffeepot that had been salvaged from the trash to the office.
5. On the same lot, we looked at two cars, both of which seemed to be in good shape.
7. The young couple who had camped in our living room finally found an apartment, which is located just down the street.
9. The park's superintendent, who was subsequently fired for misconduct, hired six workers—all of whom were relatives or family members.

SC with Appositives (page 222)

1. We hope to open a computer dating service, not a commuter dating service.
3. Two new students, Toshio Goya and Marita Rivera, joined our writing group.
5. A hard-working and talented artist, Mike recently won a major regional prize, one that carried a cash award.
7. Relaxed and self-assured, Anthony waited for his job inter-

view, a culmination of years of work.

9. For dessert we had expected cannoli, cream-filled pastries—not cannelloni, a type of pasta.

SC with Participle Phrases (page 227)

1. Standing on the deck of the boat, Marcus raised one hand to shade his eyes.
3. Relieved that his friends were safe, Sam gave each of them a bear hug.
5. The batter stepped up to the plate, pulling nervously at his cap and squinting into the afternoon sun.
7. Offended by the loud music, we headed for another part of the beach, not wanting to cause a scene.
9. A crowd swept past the security guards—fanning out through the store, searching for December 26 bargains.

SC with Transitions (page 231)

1. Sasha is only 5 feet, 6 inches tall; nevertheless, he wants to play professional basketball.
3. Konomu recently emigrated from rural Japan; therefore, he has struggled to understand American customs.
5. Our writing teacher gets cooperation; previously, she held a black belt in karate.
7. The auto had sustained serious body damage; however, the car dealer concealed that fact from us.
9. Our entree consisted of rich French food; in addition, we had heavy chocolate cake with whipped cream.

SC with Noun Substitutes (page 236)

1. The fact that Ralph asked to borrow my term paper surprised me.
3. It seemed rather rude for Danny to ignore his instructor's apology.
5. Willy clearly understood whose paragraphs were judged superior.
7. In our paper we argued that cartoons for children contain much violence and that advertising for children preys on young minds.
9. The proposal's opponents wondered why their concerns had not been addressed and what provisions would be made for public safety.

SC with Absolutes (page 241)

1. Mark stood on the library steps, his hand lifted to shade his eyes.
3. A small dog huddled in a roadside ditch, its wet body trembling with fear and cold.
5. Nate sized up the situation in a glance—his eyes darting toward the inflatable raft, his left hand scooping up a yellow life vest.
7. The team members rushed from the locker room, their fists raised in salute and their voices united in a cheer.
9. A young salesman stood at the door—his face scrubbed and earnest, a nervous smile creasing his mouth.

UNIT 8

SC with Fragments (page 247)

1. Not wanting to be noticed by his parents, Michael ducked his head at the corner. (You could also reverse the order: *Michael ducked his head at the corner, not wanting to be noticed by his parents.*)
3. Let's suppose you forget to proofread, which is often the case among students of writing.
5. After final exams we celebrated together and ordered a big plate of Chinese appetizers that everyone soon devoured.
7. Like potholes in a road, fragments provide a major nuisance for readers, one that usually makes them angry.
9. It was a festive Thanksgiving—a meal that brought loved ones together, including the ones who didn't deserve love.

SC with Run-Ons (page 253)

1. The sun rose on the eastern horizon, making clouds the color of apricot.
3. Kim chee, a popular Korean side dish, consists of spicy marinated cabbage.
5. Old friends, whom we had not heard from in years, arrived on Sunday afternoon, looking for a bed and a meal.
7. The brown envelope from the IRS caused a wave of panic in Mark, who doubted that it was a refund check.
9. Driving to work is one thing, driving to the ocean another; one's attitude, or feeling of anticipation, is so different.

SC with Subject-Verb Agreement (page 259)

1. George's friendly manner and upbeat attitude make him a good choice.
3. Racism, which affects the lives of all our children, needs to be addressed in a positive way.
5. Each of the magazines that have high distribution figures appeals to sleazy interests.
7. There were feelings of anger and sadness that evening.
9. Neither of the men—whose campaign posters were everywhere—was elected to office.

SC with Misplaced Modifiers (page 265)

1. The used car, which had a 1,000-mile warranty, came with a pair of fuzzy dice.
3. A zookeeper holding a large capture net approached the escaped monkey.
5. Not wanting to see the place again, Melanie left school with her dog.
7. During their psychology exam, students considered the problem of snoring.
9. Jason picked a tattoo shaped like a dumbbell from the computer.

SC with Dangling Modifiers (page 272)

1. Inspired by exams, the students threw an impromptu party.
3. After hearing many unwanted sales pitches, Thelma finally disconnected the phone.
5. While Tess drove down Main Street in a car, a small dog snapped at the tires.

7. Afraid of looking unprepared, the teacher quizzed his students.
9. Unopened for many years, the bottle was saved for a special occasion.

SC with Faulty Parallelism (page 279)

1. The teacher was friendly, relaxed, and intellectual.
3. They argued their points logically, forcefully, and persuasively.
5. Sharon headed for the bus stop, where she waited in the rain and shared a friend's umbrella.
7. Tonya wanted to visit her grandmother, but she has to study for a midterm exam and complete a major report.
9. Although parallelism is important, I write correct sentences the first time and don't worry about proofreading.

SC with Pronoun Problems (page 286)

1. Each of these proposals has its merits.
3. A person who votes must take his or her responsibility seriously.
5. Kim headed for the unemployment office because the counselors could help her get a job.
7. After putting the key into her coat pocket, Daphne realized that the coat had vanished.
9. After we put finishing touches on our papers, we just knew they would get high grades.

UNIT 9

SC with Commas (page 292)

1. A compound sentence may sound difficult, but it is quite simple to punctuate correctly.
3. Pairs of words and phrases do not require commas.
5. Punctuation of adjectives follows a clear, straightforward rule.
7. If you are unsure about punctuation, it is helpful to read sentences aloud and note pauses.
9. Although punctuation may seem mysterious, its basic rules are easy to master, especially with close reading and common sense.

SC with Dashes (page 296)

1. Bruno worked all night on his assignment—then left it in his apartment.
3. The surfers studied the blue ocean—clear and flat, almost without any waves.
5. We saw the light fixtures begin to move—a slow, rhythmic back-and-forth sway—and felt the building tremble beneath us.
7. A motorcycle has many advantages—including economy and maneuverability—but safety is not among them.
9. Ingrid felt many emotions afterward—denial, anger, grief.

SC with Semicolons (page 301)

1. Celebrities must lead two lives; one life is public, the other private.
3. Robert Redford is an artist and a businessman; however, he also supports many environmental causes.
5. Michael Jordan has an all-American image; as a result, he must carefully monitor his public comments.

7. Shauna was granted amnesty for cooperating; in other words, she was not charged with any offense.
9. Our menu called for the following courses: a green salad, with vegetables; an entree, grilled swordfish; and a dessert, fresh fruit sorbet.

SC with Colons (page 306)

1. Her shoplifting had an unhappy result: a ride in a police car.
3. Experience has taught me one lesson: never buy a sailboat.
5. The teacher barked two sharp commands: "Sit down, and shut up!"
7. Carlos had two requests before his departure: that friends enjoy his apartment and that no one tell the landlord.
9. A textbook must appeal to three audiences: editors, who produce it; teachers, who adopt it; and students, who use it.

SC with Quotation Marks (page 311)

1. *Direct:* After his library nap, Gil said, "I think I'll knock off for the day." *Indirect:* After his library nap, Gil said that he thought he'd knock off for the day.
3. *Direct:* Walt often repeated an old saying: "A penny saved is a penny earned." *Indirect:* Walt often repeated an old saying that a penny saved is a penny earned.
5. *Direct:* From the rooftop Marty yelled, "Come on up! It's great up here!" *Indirect:* From the rooftop Marty yelled for us to come up because it was great up there.
7. *Direct:* Before us was Martin Luther King's challenge: "I have a dream." *Indirect:* Martin Luther King's challenge—that he had a dream—was before us.
9. *Direct:* On the foreign car was a bumper sticker: "Keep Jobs at Home—Buy American!" *Indirect:* On the foreign car was a bumper sticker that urged readers to keep jobs at home by buying American products.

SC with Apostrophes (page 316)

1. You're aware that a power surge destroyed Mort's computer.
3. We won't back down on our community's effort to eliminate illegal drugs.
5. The musicians' white limousine pulled up to the concert hall's stage door.
7. The couple's decision to get married came in spite of their families' objections.
9. The fire's heat and smoke severely damaged the Smiths' retail store.

UNIT 10

At the Beach (page 319)

1. Drinking long and deep, his soul tasted the sweetness of unhurried ease.
3. A young woman strolled the wet sand, her figure sharply outlined by the sunset.
5. He took a deep breath, flexed the muscles in his shoulders, and flashed a dazzling smile at her.
7. He adjusted his sunglasses carefully, feeling his mouth go dry.

Black Feminism (page 321)

1. Although black women have felt double discrimination—for their skin color and gender—their historical achievements have been many.
3. Truth not only lectured against slavery but also spoke out for women's rights when such causes were controversial and even dangerous.
5. Another famous black woman was Maggie Lena Walker—a native of Richmond, Virginia—who was born in 1867, just after the Civil War.
7. Yet another milestone was passed by an African American woman who was an orphan at six, was a widow at twenty-two, and supported herself doing laundry.

Rock Replay (page 323)

1. The TV announcer reminisces, recounting rock music's glorious past—an era when Elvis was king.
3. A young, swarthy singer steps into the red spotlight, his shirt unbuttoned to bare his chest.
5. Winking to his guitarist, he rakes long fingers through his hair and then dances with spastic gyrations.
7. With head thrown back, he twists toward the audience, lifts a fist skyward, and wails into the microphone at his lips.

Snorkeling Sunday (page 325)

1. With brilliant sunshine warming our backs, we carried our gear toward the water's edge, where the ocean murmured invitingly and lapped at our ankles.
3. After putting on our face masks, swim fins, and flotation vests, we waded into foaming water that swirled warm and white around our knees.
5. Breathing through the snorkel seemed surprisingly natural; the fins gave us mobility, and the vests gave us security.
7. These ranged from tiny neons and delicate angelfish to brilliant parrotfish and Moorish idols.

Bioscope Feedback (page 328)

1. For centuries, people have used yoga, self-hypnosis, and meditation to "turn on" mental energy.
3. Today's possible "shortcut" to nirvana uses feedback through a bioscope—a device that monitors brain waves.
5. Bioscope enthusiasts look for alpha waves because these offer feelings of tranquility associated with successful meditation.
7. According to bioscope enthusiasts, such feedback from visual and auditory sources helps produce alpha waves and confirms subtle interior feelings.

The Woodcarver (page 330)

1. The woodcarver sits in the shadows, her shoulders hunched, her mouth a thin-lipped line of concentration.
3. An eyebrow and cheekbone slowly emerge as her knife peels away the wood skin that drifts to one side.
5. The carving's texture is rough,

but its bold, clean lines express deeply felt emotion.

7. Her own mouth relaxes into a half-smile as she compares carved lips, frozen in wood, with those in childhood memory.

Pep Assembly (page 332)

1. It was a hot September afternoon, and the bleachers above the gym floor were a riot of color.
3. Down on the gym floor, the cheerleaders moved in unison, looking like excited marionettes.
5. Like a wave, the noise of shouts, whistles, and stamping feet began to build as the coach stepped forward to the microphone.
7. He smoothed a belly that sagged over his belt, grinned at the students, and lifted a clenched fist.

Nazi Movement (page 334)

1. Bigotry, prejudice, and racial hatred take many forms; however, one of the most bizarre is Nazism.
3. Founded by Adolf Hitler, the Nazi party whipped up nationalism and promoted a dream of greatness based on military power and state control.
5. Germany had experienced devastating war losses—nearly 2 million deaths and 4 million injuries—and had been profoundly humiliated by the Treaty of Versailles.
7. German pain and anger needed only to be channeled, and Hitler accomplished this task with frightening speed.

Sexist Satire (page 337)

1. Discriminating blondes prefer surly, whiskey-drinking bums.
3. This macho quality, which distinguishes bums from boys who masquerade as real men, demands dedication and self-discipline.
5. Similarly, degenerate bums prefer blondes who eat garlic and onion rings, heap on blue cheese dressing, and don't talk back.
7. Bums like style and gusto in their women; therefore, they look for yellow fingers stained with nicotine, heavy red lipstick, and thick slabs of gooey makeup.

Slave Keepers (page 339)

1. Amazon ants are slave keepers whose patterns of behavior are selectively scripted.
3. A fierce battle takes place around the nest of the unlucky victims, who are no match for the Amazons.
5. Using their sharp, sickle-shaped jaws, the Amazons pierce their opponents' heads and bodies.
7. The pupae develop into black ants that spend their lives working and finding food for their captors, the warlike Amazons.
9. Amazons depend totally on their slaves, because their own jaws are useless for digging, finding food, or feeding themselves.

Voucher Schooling (page 342)

1. Today's conservative critics are asking a provocative question about the nation's schools: why not make schools compete for customers?

3. Their philosophical premise is that survival depends on one's ability to compete and that only the most competitive and adaptive survive.
5. According to some plans, the vouchers will be given directly to parents to pay for educational services; these can be delivered by any school—public, private, or home-based.
7. Not only will they consider policies for testing, grading, and discipline, but they will also note the school's goals and its reputation in athletics and academics.
9. They acknowledge that some schools will lose money and students, that teachers who cannot "hold an audience" will be forced to retire, and that certain schools will close their doors.

Ethnic Beliefs (page 344)

1. Many people who watch out for black cats, don't walk under ladders, and avoid travel on Friday the thirteenth fear the potentially negative consequences.
3. In Jamaica a nose twitch means that someone is spreading evil gossip about you; however, an Armenian knows the same thing when the left ear begins to tingle.
5. Some African Americans watch black cats that cross their path; whereas a cat veering right brings good luck, a cat veering left brings the opposite.
7. When you tie old shoes and tin cans to a newlywed couple's car, you are part of a Scottish-Irish tradition—"shooing away" evil spirits for those who are beginning a journey.
9. Although some Arabs carry a rabbit's ankle bone as protection against all kinds of evils, African Americans developed a related tradition—carrying a rabbit's foot for good luck—because their folktales often feature a cunning hare that outwits would-be predators.

INDEX